INVASION AND TRANSFORMATION

MESOAMERICAN WORLDS
From the Olmecs to the Danzantes

After Monte Albán: Transformation and Negotiation in Oaxaca, Mexico, Jeffrey P. Blomster, editor

The Apotheosis of Janaab' Pakal: Science, History, and Religion at Classic Maya Palenque, Gerardo Aldana

Commoner Ritual and Ideology in Ancient Mesoamerica, Nancy Gonlin and Jon C. Lohse, editors

Eating Landscape: Aztec and European Occupation of Tlalocan, Philip P. Arnold

Empires of Time: Calendars, Clocks, and Cultures, Revised Edition, Anthony Aveni

Encounter with the Plumed Serpent: Drama and Power in the Heart of Mesoamerica, Maarten Jansen and Gabina Aurora Pérez Jiménez

In the Realm of Nachan Kan: Postclassic Maya Archaeology at Laguna de On, Belize, Marilyn A. Masson

Invasion and Transformation: Interdisciplinary Perspectives on the Conquest of Mexico, Rebecca P. Brienen and Margaret A. Jackson, editors

Life and Death in the Templo Mayor, Eduardo Matos Moctezuma

The Madrid Codex: New Approaches to Understanding an Ancient Maya Manuscript, Gabrielle Vail and Anthony Aveni, editors

Mesoamerican Ritual Economy: Archaeological and Ethnological Perspectives, E. Christian Wells and Karla L. Davis-Salazar, editors

Mesoamerica's Classic Heritage: Teotihuacan to the Aztecs, Davíd Carrasco, Lindsay Jones, and Scott Sessions, editors

Mockeries and Metamorphoses of an Aztec God: Tezcatlipoca, "Lord of the Smoking Mirror," Guilhem Olivier, translated by Michel Besson

Rabinal Achi: A Fifteenth-Century Maya Dynastic Drama, Alain Breton, editor; translated by Teresa Lavender Fagan and Robert Schneider

Representing Aztec Ritual: Performance, Text, and Image in the Work of Sahagún, Eloise Quiñones Keber, editor

Ruins of the Past: The Use and Perception of Abandoned Structures in the Maya Lowlands, Travis W. Stanton and Aline Magnoni, editors

Skywatching in the Ancient World: New Perspectives in Cultural Astronomy—Studies in Honor of Anthony F. Aveni, Clive Ruggles and Gary Urton, editors

The Social Experience of Childhood in Mesoamerica, Traci Ardren and Scott R. Hutson, editors

Stone Houses and Earth Lords: Maya Religion in the Cave Context, Keith M. Prufer and James E. Brady, editors

Tamoanchan, Tlalocan: Places of Mist, Alfredo López Austin

Thunder Doesn't Live Here Anymore: Self-Deprecation and the Theory of Otherness Among the Teenek Indians of Mexico, Anath Ariel de Vidas; translated by Teresa Lavender Fagan

Topiltzin Quetzalcoatl: The Once and Future Lord of the Toltecs, H. B. Nicholson

The World Below: Body and Cosmos in Otomi Indian Ritual, Jacques Galinier

INVASION AND TRANSFORMATION

Interdisciplinary Perspectives on the Conquest of Mexico

edited by

REBECCA P. BRIENEN AND MARGARET A. JACKSON

University Press of Colorado

Published by the University Press of Colorado
245 Century Circle, Suite 202
Louisville, Colorado 80027

First paperback edition 2020
Printed in the United States of America

The University Press of Colorado is a proud member of the Association of University Presses.

The University Press of Colorado is a cooperative publishing enterprise supported, in part, by Adams State University, Colorado State University, Fort Lewis College, Metropolitan State University of Denver, Regis University, University of Colorado, University of Northern Colorado, University of Wyoming, Utah State University, and Western Colorado University.

∞ This paper meets the requirements of the ANSI/NISO Z39.48–1992 (Permanence of Paper)

ISBN: 978-0-87081-886-8 (hardcover)
ISBN: 978-1-64642-154-1 (paperback)
ISBN: 978-1-60732-001-2 (ebook)

Library of Congress Cataloging-in-Publication Data

Invasion and transformation : interdisciplinary perspectives on the conquest of Mexico / edited by Rebecca P. Brienen and Margaret A. Jackson.
p. cm. — (Mesoamerican worlds)
Papers originally presented at an international symposium, 'Invasion and Transformation: Interdisciplinary Perspectives on Images of the Conquest of Mexico', which took place in 2003 at the University of Miami, Coral Gables, Fla.
Includes bibliographical references and index.
ISBN 978-0-87081-886-8 (hardcover : alk. paper) —ISBN 978-1-64642-154-1 (pbk. : alk. paper) — ISBN 978-1-60732-001-2 (ebook)
1. Aztecs—History. 2. Aztecs—First contact with Europeans. 3. Aztecs—Social life and customs. 4. Mexico—History—Conquest, 1519–1540 5. Cortis, Hernan, 1485–1547. 6. Montezuma II, Emperor of Mexico, ca. 1480–1520. 7. Marina, ca. 1505–ca. 1530. I. Brienen, Rebecca Parker. II. Jackson, Margaret A. (Margaret Ann)
F1219.73.I68 2007
972'.02—dc22

2007037332

Support for this publication was generously provided by the Jay I. Kislak Foundation.

Contents

Illustrations

Black-and-White Illustrations

Color Plates

Acknowledgments

This volume of essays has its origin in an international symposium, "Invasion and Transformation: Interdisciplinary Perspectives on Images of the Conquest of Mexico," which took place in 2003 at the University of Miami, Coral Gables, Florida. The symposium was held in conjunction with an exhibition, *Visions of Empire: Picturing the Conquest in Colonial Mexico,* at the university's Lowe Art Museum. An exceptional series of seventeenth-century paintings showing scenes from the Conquest of Mexico was the centerpiece of the exhibition. Formerly in the collection of the Jay I. Kislak Foundation, Miami Lakes, Florida, the series was recently donated by the foundation to the Library of Congress, Washington, D.C.

We are grateful to our speakers from the 2003 conference for their stimulating papers, which form the basis for the chapters in this collection. In addition, we warmly acknowledge the contributions by our colleagues Dr. Martha

Few and Dr. Traci Ardren, with whom we organized the symposium and exhibition and whose continued encouragement has made this project possible. We would also like to express thanks for the support provided by President Donna Shalala of the University of Miami, Senior Associate Dean Perri Lee Roberts, the Center for Latin American Studies, and the Departments of Anthropology, Art and Art History, and History. Special thanks to Mr. and Mrs. Jay I. Kislak and the Kislak Foundation whose generosity made the exhibition, the conference, and the production of this book possible. Arthur Dunkelman, curator of the Kislak Collection, and his staff should be singled out for praise; we have benefited from their good humor, encouragement, and expertise throughout this entire project. Finally, we express our appreciation for the support and patience demonstrated by Darrin Pratt, director of the University Press of Colorado. We thank everyone who contributed time, advice, and intellectual effort to make it all come together.

REBECCA P. BRIENEN
MARGARET A. JACKSON

INVASION AND TRANSFORMATION

Introduction

In the fall of 2001, the Jay I. Kislak Foundation invited a small group of scholars to view a series of eight seventeenth-century paintings depicting events from the Conquest of Mexico.[1] As the paintings were removed from their crates, they revealed a vivid and highly detailed visual history of the Conquest distilled into eight key moments, including the meeting of Cortés and Moteuczoma, the *Noche triste,* and finally the siege of Tenochtitlan. Although they reproduced an official Spanish version of the Conquest, the content and narrative style of the images immediately evoked a lively discussion and provocative observations, making it clear that these remarkable works of art could serve brilliantly as a catalyst for a variety of cross-disciplinary exchanges and debates surrounding the history of the Conquest and the subsequent colonization of Mexico. In the spring of 2003, *Visions of Empire: Picturing the Conquest in Colonial Mexico* opened at the Lowe Art Museum at the University of Miami. In conjunction with this exhibition, which publicly displayed the Kislak paintings for the first time to a North American audience, the university hosted an international symposium, "Invasion and Transformation: Interdisciplinary Perspectives on Images of the Conquest of Mexico." Prominent scholars from the United States and Mexico—representing the disciplines of anthropology, archaeology, art history, foreign languages and literatures, history, and religion—made presentations in which the Kislak paintings formed a common point of reference.

By an extraordinary coincidence, the symposium took place the same weekend U.S. president George W. Bush ordered U.S. armed forces to enter Iraq to remove Saddam Hussein from power; the painted images of tense encounters, destruction, and full-scale battles between the Spanish and the Mexica resonated strongly with reports about the contemporary invasion. The parallels between past and present events also heightened awareness of the themes that bound the papers together. Collectively, the speakers brought attention to the fact that wartime events are not simply recorded: they are written down, visualized, negotiated, and embellished by the victors as well as the vanquished.[2]

The present volume includes essays based on the original symposium papers, color reproductions of the Kislak paintings, and detailed descriptions of these works of art, which we are pleased to present to a wider audience. Some of the authors have closely studied the Kislak paintings, addressing the style, content, and intended function of the works for their contemporaries. Other contributors have used the paintings only tangentially, focusing their attention on colonial period religion, theater, science, and literature. In viewing the Conquest and its complex legacy from multiple perspectives, these chapters make important new contributions to the scholarship on this important event and increase awareness of its long-term effects.[3]

At the most basic level, the title of this volume, *Invasion and Transformation*, refers to the military invasion of the Aztec Empire by Spanish forces and the transformations in political, social, cultural, and religious life that occurred in Mexico both during the Conquest and in the colonial period that followed. As we have employed it, however, the concept of invasion goes far beyond a simple definition of armed advance to include, among other things, the introduction of new diseases into the Americas, the forced conversion of the indigenous population to Christianity, and the immigration of Europeans into the young colony of New Spain. The fact that these changes and invasions brought about by the Conquest were negotiated through a process of *mestizaje* by the indigenous population is evident in art and architecture, literature, music, language, religion, social customs, clothing, and many other related areas. Of course, the Spaniards, including Hernán Cortés and others of Spanish ancestry in Mexico, also addressed and interpreted these traumatic events of the past in their own ways, and this volume includes their voices as well.

Given the variety of methodological approaches and disciplines represented by the authors in this volume, there were bound to be occasional areas of disagreement. The spelling of the Aztec emperor's name was one such contested area. For English speakers, "Montezuma," which approximates the Spanish pronunciation of the Nahuatl name, is the most common spelling in popular use. In trying to establish the correct spelling and pronunciation, one is faced with the fact that colonial sources use a variety of orthographic conventions that do not agree. As Susan Gillespie explains, the etymology of the name (usually translated as "Angry Lord") comes from the roots *teuctli* (lord) and *zoma* (to frown in anger); mo- is a possessive prefix.[4] The spelling of his name in sixteenth-century Nahuatl-language or Nahuatl-influenced documents varies little. In the *Codex Mendoza* it is Moteçςuma. Sahagún's *Florentine Codex* and *Primeros Memoriales* record his name as Motecuçoma. The *Codex Telleriano-Remensis* spells it Moteuhcçoma. Other documents have the same or similar spellings. Today, we use the small "z" for the "ç" (cedilla), which was the medieval form of z.

Other orthographic variations can be traced to the vowels "o" and "u," which were used by different Nahuatl speakers in the Basin of Mexico for the same morphemes (e.g., Culhuacan and Colhuacan, Chapultepec and Chapoltepec).[5] According to Frances Karttunen (1983:xxiii), "cu" was used to express the "kw" sound (like "qu" does in English), and it could appear at the beginning or the end of a syllable. When it came at the beginning, as in *cualli* (kwalli), the "u" followed the "c." But when the sound appeared at the end of a syllable, as in *teuctli* (tekwtli), the "c" and "u" were supposed to be inverted. As Karttunen has nonetheless noted, not everyone followed this practice (see, for example, Sahagún's spelling), so one finds *teuctli* spelled as *tecutli* (or *tecuhtli*), giving the incorrect impression that the word has an extra syllable, which is then mispronounced tay-koo-tlee. Some writers left out the "u" altogether, simplifying the sound from "kw" to just "k" (as in the *Codex Mendoza*). Based on the current research on Nahuatl pronunciation, and to avoid the confusion of multiple spellings, "Moteuczoma" has been adopted as the favored spelling throughout the volume, except in direct quotations from primary source material.

In addition, although Cortés would have been called Hernando (or Fernando) by his contemporaries, he is generally referred to as Hernán in today's literature. We have chosen to follow this practice in this volume.[6]

Throughout this volume, the reader is repeatedly made aware of the ways people remember and reconfigure historical events, rituals, and even art forms from the past to address the needs and interests of the present. From a discussion of how the legendary meeting between Moteuczoma and Cortés influenced a sixteenth-century Nahua play about the birth of Jesus to an investigation of indigenous death rituals and their influence on Christian burials during the colonial period, the chapters in this volume shed new light on the complexity of cultural responses to the Conquest.

REMEMBERING THE LEGENDS

Although the Conquest of Mexico employed a cast of millions, three central characters have attained mythic status: Hernán Cortés, the emperor Moteuczoma II, and the native translator Malinche (also called Malintzín). The name of each of these figures calls up vivid stereotypes—the ruthless soldier, the fearful emperor, the traitorous harlot, to name but a few. The third canvas in the Kislak series (plate 3) depicts the meeting of these three extraordinary people, who stand in the middle of an elaborate ceremony on the shores of Lake Texcoco. In this painting, one of the most compelling in the series, cross-cultural miscommunication, as well as brewing tensions between the Old World and the New, are embodied by the two men. Clad in gleaming armor but with his arms outstretched in a clear gesture of embrace, Cortés approaches the elegant but scantily clad emperor. Moteuczoma does not allow the Spaniard to touch him, however; access to the royal body, it seems, was only for the privileged few. Although Malinche is also present, the narrative focus is clearly on the two men. A comet, faintly visible in the sky above the smoking volcano in the background, portends disaster, including the death of Moteuczoma, the fall of the Aztec Empire, and the destruction of Tenochtitlan.

Why did Moteuczoma, Cortés, and, to a somewhat lesser extent, Malinche achieve such prominence in our understanding of the events of the Conquest? As Louise Burkhart argues in Chapter 1, "The Cortés-Moteuczoma encounter stands synechdochically for the larger cultural encounter" between the Spanish and the Mexica. As such, it is not surprising that references, sometimes veiled, to this pivotal event are made throughout colonial literature. In her chapter she analyzes a Nahua colonial drama of Herod's encounter with the three Magi, which she argues makes a critique of Cortés and Moteuczoma while at the same time offering more appropriate models of kingly behavior. She highlights the complex ways Nahuas sought to position themselves in relation to the events of the past in light of the colonial reality.

The transformation of the Conquest's principal players into figures of iconic importance during the colonial period is addressed by several authors in this volume. They approach the phenomenon by examining written as well as visual materials. In Chapter 2, Susan Gillespie addresses the historical characterization of Moteuczoma as a "fearful, fawning failure of a ruler." By turning her attention to colonial accounts of the Conquest from the sixteenth century, she enriches our perspective by examining both how and why indigenous writers assigned blame to Moteuczoma for the defeat of the empire. Gillespie pays special attention to the role of omens in this literature, which she notes are very much focused on Moteuczoma's body and person. She demonstrates that these omens should not be understood at the fatalistic response of a subjected group; rather, they are the active production of a people who needed to accommodate, explain, and resist their new political and social realities.

Viviana Díaz Balsera, in Chapter 3, focuses our attention on Cortés through a critical examination of his letters, which she argues hold "a crucial place in the founding discourses about the New World." In her chapter she demonstrates how Cortés's own version of the events contributed to the anthropomorphization of the Conquest as a struggle between two heroic men whose attributes, negative and positive, mirrored the character of their respective nations. According to Díaz Balsera, Cortés's skillful rhetoric allowed him to present himself as a master strategist, a faithful vassal, and a military hero to his most important reader—the king of Spain and the Holy Roman emperor, Charles V.

By focusing on images of Malinche, an important indigenous woman who worked as a translator for Cortés, Constance Cortez, in Chapter 4, introduces the last of the three key figures in the history of the Conquest. In recent years Malinche, characterized variously as a "whore, victim, avenger, stoic observer, [and] survivor," has come to share some of the blame with Moteuczoma for the defeat of the empire. Cortez explores the roots of these contradictory descriptions by comparing and contrasting images of Malinche produced in New Spain in the sixteenth and seventeenth centuries. By tracing Malinche's transformation from a dynamic participant in the early colonial period to a passive, European-looking bystander in the Kislak paintings, Cortez raises important questions about race and gender as presented in these works of art.

TRANSFORMING HISTORY

As a group, the Kislak paintings distill the highly complicated events of the Conquest into a series of carefully selected scenes, all of which are based on Spanish accounts. A number of authors in this collection, including Matthew Restall and Michael Schreffler, have carefully studied the content and style of the Kislak paintings. For Restall these works are examples of mythistory, which he defines as "a vision of the historical past heavily infused with misconceptions and partisan interpretations so deeply rooted as to constitute legends or myths." In his analysis, presented in Chapter 5, he brings attention to a number of mythic elements in these works, from their presentation of Cortés and his men as professional soldiers to the portrayal of the Mexica as representatives of a barbarian empire. He also notes that the implied superiority of the Spanish—as represented by Cortés and his captains—is what ultimately brings about their victory, both in the histories and in the Kislak paintings.

In a complementary manner, Schreffler argues in Chapter 6 that representations of the Conquest of Mexico, including the Kislak series, must be situated within the discourse of Spanish imperial power in the late seventeenth century. He brings attention to the laudatory treatment of the Conquest in these works of art and the manner in which they highlight "the ritual formation of loyal subjects." As such, he challenges earlier scholarship on images of the Conquest produced in New Spain, which have tended to explain the subject's popularity as evidence of Creole nationalism. Schreffler's close reading of the paintings highlights the ways they stimulated memories of the past while simultaneously presenting the improved version of the present.

Diana Magaloni-Kerpel shifts attention back to the Nahua in Chapter 7 in her discussion of how the Conquest of Mexico is represented visually and verbally in Friar Bernardino Sahagún's *Florentine Codex*. Magaloni-Kerpel and Gillespie differ in their approaches, as well as their interpretations, of the eight omens in Sahagún's work. Whereas Gillespie's analysis aligns the omens closely to the person of Moteuczoma, the destruction of the empire, and the realities of the post-Conquest environment, Magaloni-Kerpel uses the omens to draw direct parallels with the sacred texts of the Nahua "red and black" tradition. In bringing attention to the Nahua notion of cyclical time, Magaloni-Kerpel suggests that Book 12 of the *Florentine Codex* functions as a "sacred text that tells the story of the foundation of a new cycle of time and a new people: the era of the Nahua Christians of New Spain." Native texts and paintings functioned as agents of speech and memory in the pre-Conquest period; Magaloni-Kerpel's analysis suggests the manner in which text and image continued to play an important role in connecting events of the past to the present.

EFFECTS OF INVASION

The invasion is remembered, but the transformation is what remains. Unlike the heroic and mythologized renditions of history seen in the Kislak paintings and gloriously recounted in colonial histories, disease, death, and violence were more common realities for large portions of the middle and lower classes in post-Conquest Mexico. The imposition of foreign economic structures, religious institutions, deadly viruses, and an uncertain political future led to social responses previously unimagined. The kinds of radical social alterations detailed by Martha Few and Ximena Chávez Balderas point very literally to the consequences of invasion and transformation.

As Few argues in Chapter 8, even in the face of horrific illness, biases about race and ethnicity profoundly influenced scientific practice in New Spain. Few addresses *cocolitzli*, one of the terrible diseases that devastated Mexico in the wake of the invasion. She focuses attention on several autopsy reports on *cocolitzli*, written by Spanish colonial physicians brought in to study what many considered an "Indian" disease. As Few argues, "The process of the construction of racial difference in this context, legitimized by the language and practice of colonial medicine, interacted with broader ideologies of colonial authority and power in New Spain."

As a consequence of the vicious cycle of disease and death and in response to the introduction of Catholicism, subtle transformations occurred in funerary practices, which Ximena Chávez Balderas details in Chapter 9. Although the Spanish sources suggest that the indigenous population readily adopted Christian rituals, Chávez Balderas's research proposes a more nuanced interpretation by addressing the changes in religious ideology and spatial function in an urban context. Like many of the authors in this volume, she brings attention to the fact that during the colonial period, "new institutions, forms, and meanings emerged that demonstrate the unmistakable influence of the customs and habits of the native population."

FULL CIRCLE

In the final chapter, we examine the Conquest through the lens of the Kislak paintings. This chapter introduces the reader to these extraordinary works of art by means of a detailed discussion of each painting's content and how it relates to the traditional history of the Conquest. Because these works present a highly conservative and pro-Spanish version of history, they serve as a foil to the new interpretations of the Conquest offered by the contributors to this volume.

NOTES

1. In this Introduction we have drawn upon a number of sources, including the essays and descriptions of the Kislak paintings found in Jackson and Brienen (2003).

2. See Schwartz (2000).

3. We would like to acknowledge symposium participants David Carrasco, Tom Cummins, and Oscar Vazquez, who chose not to participate in this volume but whose contributions have proven invaluable.

4. Personal communication, November 24, 2004. Gillespie cites Kartunnen (1983).

5. Ibid.

6. Thanks to Matthew Restall for raising this point. See Pagden (1986).

PART I

REMEMBERING THE LEGENDS

Moteuczoma, Cortés, and Malinche

1

Meeting the Enemy

Moteuczoma and Cortés, Herod and the Magi

Louise M. Burkhart

Colonial Nahuas used their forms of expressive culture—plays, rituals, art, historiography, and others—to encode responses to the Spanish Conquest and its aftermath. These symbolic responses were often subtle and veiled, as Spanish cultural artifacts were recast into native forms that bore secondary levels of meaning in addition to the overt, surface meanings continuous with their European sources. Taking as a point of departure the Kislak Conquest of Mexico painting of the initial meeting between Hernán Cortés and Moteuczoma, in this chapter I explore the significance of this particular moment in the narrative of Conquest for both Spaniards and Nahuas (plate 3). I suggest that its iconic status as a point of juncture between two clashing cultures was such that it was symbolically replayed in other formats. Specifically, the Nahua author (or authors) of a colonial drama about the meeting between King Herod and the three Magi saw a connection between that narrative from the Gospel of Matthew and the pivotal meeting between Spanish and Aztec leaders in his (or their) own people's recent history. The drama implies a critique of both Cortés and Moteuczoma and offers the three Magi as more positive, alternative models of ancestral Nahua leaders.

Each of the eight paintings of the Conquest of Mexico from the Kislak Collection depicts a key moment extracted from the Spanish chronicles of Cortés's enterprise against the Aztecs (plates 1–8). Among the eight, only one is not a scene of violence. Painting 3 depicts the initial meeting, on November 8, 1519, between Cortés and the Aztec emperor Moteuczoma along the causeway leading from Ixtapalapan into Tenochtitlan. The Spaniards' weapons are depicted but, for once, are not aimed at native people. The military invasion pauses for a moment, as representatives of two worlds engage in greetings and dialogue on what, were it not for the thicket of Spanish spears to the right of the painting, might seem like equal terms. The Mexica, although exotic in their fanciful feather array, are represented as "worthy foes" for the Europeans, Moteuczoma as dignified and kingly (Brienen 2003:36). This meeting is so commonly included in both verbal and pictorial treatments of the Spanish Conquest that it was clearly a standard part of Conquest lore, among Nahuas as well as Europeans.

The Cortés-Moteuczoma encounter stands synechdochically for the larger cultural encounter and for the doomed splendor of the Mexica Empire, about to yield to a new world order. In the Gospel account of the three Magi (Matthew 2:1–12), Herod is, like Moteuczoma in the Conquest narratives, a proud king who faces foreigners whose arrival from the East heralds a new age, in this case the three wise men who come in search of the newborn Christ. I will compare the Moteuczoma-Cortés encounter with the Herod-Magi encounter as represented in a colonial Nahuatl Epiphany drama. This play is one of three anonymously authored and undated early colonial Nahuatl dramas surviving in an eighteenth-century copy housed today in the Clements Library at the University of Michigan. It has been published by Paso y Troncoso (1900) and Horcasitas (1974:253–327) under the title *La Adoración de los Reyes.* With the English title *The Three Kings,* it is included in a new compilation of colonial Nahuatl plays prepared by Barry D. Sell and me (Sell and Burkhart 2004:118–145).[1]

I begin by examining some aspects of the event depicted in Painting 3, as recorded in textual accounts, considering why and how this meeting became enshrined in the narrative of the Conquest. This is intended not to thoroughly survey and critique Conquest accounts and their revisionist excrescences (a task addressed more directly in other chapters in this volume) but simply to establish the iconic nature of this meeting in local legendary history as a key point in the Conquest narrative and a potential model for scenes of parley. I then discuss the Epiphany drama, noting similarities to the Moteuczoma-Cortés encounter as well as other accounts of Moteuczoma's behavior.

PARLEY SCENE ONE: MOTEUCZOMA MEETS CORTÉS

Narrators on both sides so quickly draped the events of the Conquest in legend that it is very difficult to know what actually happened. The Nahuas sought to justify their defeat by casting Moteuczoma as an arrogant but ineffectual ruler addled by inexplicable omens, trembling in his fancy sandals and abusing his soothsayers while the Spaniards and their allies advanced toward Tenochtitlan—what Susan Gillespie refers to as "blaming Moteuczoma" (Chapter 2, this volume; see also Magaloni-Kerpel, Chapter 7, this volume; Restall 2003; Townsend 2003). Spaniards had immediately to glorify and legitimate what Cortés had done. Jaime Cuadriello (1999:71–80) discusses the meeting's construction as an allegory for the foundation of the colonial state. Especially for Creoles, the causeway encounter took on the trappings of a triumphal entry: the two leaders recognize one another's imperial credentials, Moteuczoma capitulates, and Cortés is invested with authority over Mexico, such that this event—more than the final fall of the city and capture of Cuauhtemoc—marked the birth of the colony (Cuadriello 1999:74). It also symbolized the triumphal entry of Christianity, the opening of Mexico to the faith (Cuadriello 1999:74).

If the meeting had not happened, memories on both sides may have had to invent it. But it seems at least probable that Moteuczoma and Cortés did indeed meet one another during the latter's advance into the Mexica capital. Sixteenth-century written accounts of the meeting emphasize the accompanying pageantry, the exchange of necklaces, and the exchange of greetings. Apparently, Cortés and other Spaniards behaved rudely, by Mexica standards. Cortés himself, in his letter to the Spanish king the following October, says he tried immediately to embrace Moteuczoma but was held back by two of the lords who accompanied the emperor (Pagden 1986:84). Bernal Díaz del Castillo, one of Cortés's soldiers, recalled in the 1550s that Cortés extended his hand, which Moteuczoma took reluctantly, and that he later tried to embrace the emperor but was prevented by the lords, "for they considered it an indignity" (Díaz del Castillo 1956:193). Friar Diego Durán's 1581 account, which derives from a native source, lacks this detail; it states that Cortés went to embrace Moteuczoma and treated him with great reverence, as the Mexica ruler did him in return, and that later Cortés took off his hat to show respect (undoubtedly making a great impression on people who did not use hats) (Durán 1994:530).

The principal native-language history of the Conquest was written decades after the fact, in 1555, and was incorporated as Book 12 of the *Florentine Codex*, the Franciscan friar Bernardino de Sahagún's monumental ethnographic-style treatise. James Lockhart has noted that the earlier part of this narrative, including the Moteuczoma-Cortés meeting, is a late reconstruction in the "blame Moteuczoma" mode, while the later part, beginning with the slaughter of Mexica nobles during the Toxcatl festival, derives directly from oral accounts of eyewitnesses (1993:18–19). Hence, this cannot be construed as an "authentic native account" of the meeting. Even so, its description of how the Spaniards touched Moteuczoma and stared at him, dismounting from their horses to get a better look, may well bear a trace of actual memory (Lockhart 1993:118). It was forbidden to stare at the emperor. According to the *Florentine Codex* book on the kings and lords, when a ruler walked about, "none might cross in front of him, none might come forth before him, none might look up at him, none might come face to face with him" (Sahagún 1950–1982:Bk. 8, 29). Díaz del Castillo noted that Moteuczoma's own attendants, except his four nephews, kept their gaze averted from him as a sign of respect (Díaz del Castillo 1956:193). In addition to looking Moteuczoma right in the face, Cortés in the Sahaguntine account has the gall to address him by his personal name—his first words to the Mexican monarch are "Is it not you? Is it not you then? Moteucçoma?" (Lockhart 1993:116). For the Mexica, this was aggressive and insulting behavior (Sell 2004:12).

Cortés's failure to observe Mexica rules of etiquette is a detail that seems unlikely to have been fabricated as the story became mythologized, for it does not obviously support his clever-hero persona. Hence the reports, although inconsistent, may well reflect some actual faux pas, a memory of social discomfort amid the high-level diplomacy. Later, as the legends developed, this motif supported emerging constructions of Cortés's audacity, of Moteuczoma's despotism, and of what Gillespie (Chapter 2, this volume) describes as the "desacralization" of Moteuczoma's body.

We will never know what exact words were exchanged—awkwardly, through two interpreters—at this presumed meeting. Many sources include at least some reference to this dialogue; the most detailed versions are those of Cortés's second letter to Charles V and Book 12 of the *Florentine Codex.* Hugh Thomas (1993:284) asserts that Moteuczoma's alleged speech, recounted in disparate and unrelated sources, cannot be a total fabrication. Whatever the ruler's actual words and however distorted they were by the interpreters, the emperor expressed not only "elaborate courtesy" but also "[s]ome surprising element of submission" in response, Thomas surmises, to the "visual propaganda" of the Spaniards' military array and news of the massacre they had carried out in Cholula (1993:284). Even this may be saying too much: Moteuczoma's "submission" may have initially been Cortés's invention.

Moteuczoma in Cortés's version (Pagden 1986:85–86), citing the writings of the ancestors, stated that he and his forebears were descended from foreigners who came to this land and intermarried with the locals. They then refused to follow their chief when he went away, but they had always known that "those who descended from him would come and conquer this land and take us as their vassals." Hence, since Cortés came from where the sun rises and spoke of his great lord there, he should "be assured that we shall obey you and hold you as our lord in place of that great sovereign of whom you speak [Charles]; and in this there shall be no offense or betrayal whatsoever. And in all the land that lies in my domain, you may command as you will, for you shall be obeyed; and all that we own is for you to dispose of as you choose."

This version, in which Moteuczoma seems to abdicate his throne, is hardly credible in that it precedes Cortés's self-aggrandizing and self-legitimizing claim that he took the emperor prisoner almost immediately afterward and this speech conveniently justifies that claimed action. Camilla Townsend has argued that Cortés did not imprison or otherwise control Moteuczoma until several months later, but his deception of the king had to be maintained, by himself and others, to legitimate Spanish actions (2003). The supposed speech of abdication, then, was a necessary fiction right from the beginning. Added to the mix later was the fiction that Cortés's arrival was seen as a return of the god Quetzalcoatl, which developed quickly enough to spice Durán's 1581 version of the emperor's speech in which it is Quetzalcoatl's kingdom and vassals that Moteuczoma so willingly handed over to the Spanish captain (1994:530).

The Nahuatl version of Moteuczoma's speech given in the *Florentine Codex*, although written in formal Nahuatl, is better seen as a Nahuatlized version of the Cortés-based tradition and a reflection of prevailing anti-Moteuczoma sentiments than an accurate transcription passed through Nahua tradition. Even so, in Nahuatl the abdication is more subtly stated and could be read, as Lockhart observes, as "hardly more than the ordinary rhetoric of polite greeting among Nahua lords and rulers" (Lockhart 1993:18). The text, as translated by Lockhart, is as follows:

> O our lord, be doubly welcomed on your arrival in this land; you have come to satisfy your curiosity about your altepetl [city] of Mexico, you have come to sit on your seat of authority, which I have kept a while for you, where I have been in charge for you, for your agents the rulers Itzcoatzin, the elder Moteucçoma, Axayacatl, Tiçocic and Ahuitzotl [Moteuczoma's predecessors]—have gone, who for a very short time came to be in charge for you, to govern the altepetl of Mexico. It is after them that your poor vassal [myself] came. Will they come back to the place of their absence? If only one of them could see and behold what has now happened in my time, what I now see after our lords are gone! For I am not just dreaming, not just sleepwalking, not just seeing it in my sleep. I am not just dreaming that I have seen you, have looked upon your face. For a time I have been concerned, looking toward the mysterious place from which you have come, among clouds and mist. It is so that the rulers on departing said that you would come in order to acquaint yourself with your altepetl and sit upon your seat of authority. And now it has

> come true, you have come. Be doubly welcomed, enter the land, go to enjoy your palace; rest your body. May our lords be arrived in the land. (Lockhart 1993:116)

Like Cortés's version, this speech expresses the notion that Moteuczoma and his predecessors were ruling temporarily in the place of a higher authority who had now returned. Had the author(s) of this version been working independent of the Cortés-based tradition, while imagining Moteuczoma to be greeting a new ruler or an emissary acting on behalf of a new ruler, the speech might have more pronounced formulaic similarities to the model oration, recorded elsewhere in the Sahaguntine treatise, to be made to a newly installed ruler (Sahagún 1950–1982:Bk. 6, ch. 10). Moteuczoma's speech bears only a slight resemblance to that one.

Gillespie summarized Moteuczoma's character, as represented in Conquest accounts, as "an oxymoronic mixture of arrogance, tyranny, and decisive, terrible punishments in dealing with his own people alongside cowardice, meekness, and indecision when dealing with the Spaniards" (Chapter 2, this volume). Turning now to the comparison between the Cortés-Moteuczoma encounter and the Epiphany story dramatized in the Nahuatl script, I first note the similarity between the character ascribed to Moteuczoma and that attributed to King Herod. Like the Aztec emperor, Herod shows obsequious politeness toward outsiders and cruelty to his own people and, like Moteuczoma with his omens, is trapped by the fulfillment of prophecies over which he has no control. Yet the Magi, although they too came from the East, were nothing like Cortés.

PARLEY SCENE TWO: HEROD MEETS THE THREE KINGS

The Nahuatl drama *The Three Kings,* although it survives only in an eighteenth-century copy, features the high rhetoric of traditional formal oratory composed in the sixteenth and early seventeenth centuries. Indeed, this old-fashioned and formal linguistic register is the drama's most striking feature and argues for a relatively early date for its original composition. It actually quotes the Sahaguntine speech to the new ruler to which I referred before, suggesting that the text emerged from the Franciscan or Jesuit intellectual circles of the late sixteenth and early to mid-seventeenth centuries. It may be of native authorship or a product of collaboration between a priest and an educated Nahua. An author or authors with access to Sahagún's collection of formal oratory likely had access to his Conquest history as well and could also have been familiar with other accounts of those events.

Consider the similarities between the two scenarios. Herod, a proud and angry man (Moteuczoma's name means "angry lord"), rules over the Jews, whose ancestral writings prophesy the coming of a new king, the descendant of an old royal lineage. Strangers come from the East—and in the play this directional origin is repeated over and over. They are following a star, suggestive of the celestial omens that allegedly preceded Cortés's arrival and indicate that the prophecy has been fulfilled. The legitimacy of Herod's rulership is thus undermined, overshadowed by the power and authority of Jesus Christ, just as Moteuczoma's rule gave way to that of Christian Spaniards. The entry of the Magi into Jerusalem is mirrored in the triumphal entry of Christianity into Tenochtitlan, manifested in Cortés's march up the causeway.

But it is not that simple. Nahuatl dramas can support dual or even multiple readings (Burkhart 1996, 2000). In this case, the drama turns the tables on the ethnicity of the principal characters in such a way that Herod comes off seeming like a rude and duplicitous Spaniard and the three Magi like noble and courteous pre-Conquest lords, or like the proto-Christians colonial native and mestizo elites liked to imagine their ancestors had been. So Herod is, in a sense, Cortés as well as Moteuczoma. The three Magi, I suggest, represent what Moteuczoma—in the eyes of later, Christian Nahuas—should have been: a lord of impeccable nobility who could accept Christianity while dealing peaceably but firmly with Cortés instead of a failed king who did neither. They represent good ancestral leaders, Moteuczoma a rejected ancestor. This layer of meaning within the Epiphany drama indicates that the repercussions of the encounter between Moteuczoma and Cortés were being worked out symbolically for generations after the original events, not only in histories of the Conquest but also through the manipulation of narrative and dramatic forms adapted from Old World models.

In developing this interpretation I am drawing on previous work, by myself and others, that explores how colonial Nahua elites accepted the legitimacy of Christianity while also asserting continuity with a still respected ancestral past, downplayed the significance of the military Conquest, and questioned the legitimacy of Spanish colonial exploitation (for example, Burkhart 1992, 1996; Klor de Alva 1992; Lockhart 1991, 1992; Wood 1991, 2003). I also find evocative a statement by Motolinia, author of the earliest Franciscan chronicle that describes Nahua adoption of Christian customs. The friar said, "They also take great delight in the festival of the Kings, which seems their very own, on which the provinces of the gentiles went out to search for and adore the Lord and Savior of the world" (Motolinia 1996:236). He goes on to describe dramatizations in which the star is carried from afar on ropes and Mary is in the church with Jesus in the manger, before which the actors make offerings. "Every day," he concluded, "they have more and more devotion to this festival" (1996:236). It seemed like their very own festival because it commemorated the acceptance of Jesus by pagan lords—on their own initiative, rooted in prophecy, no military or spiritual conquest required.[2] Christianity could make its triumphal entry without Cortés to bear its standard.

The play begins when the Magi have reached the outskirts of Jerusalem, where the star they have followed disappears from view. The Magi are referred to in stage directions and in spoken parts using both the Nahuatl word for rulers, *tlahtohqueh,* and the Spanish *reyes*; this is one sign of their ambivalent character, although it also suggests their high status in two worlds. They ride on horses, another Spanish trapping first encountered with Cortés's arrival but later adopted by elite Nahuas. They send a servant to Herod (who is referred to as a *tlahtoani* but not as a *rey*) to request an audience with him. This servant, interestingly, is represented as a worshipper of multiple deities, while the Magi themselves speak of only one god. Thus, the elites are described as proto-Christians or at least monotheists, while idolatry is confined to the lower ranks of their society. This servant meets first with Herod's steward, who then conveys the message to his master, doffing his hat as a sign of respect—to indigenous audiences the hat would be an indicator of Spanish ethnicity, seemingly contradicting the avoidance of the term *rey*. Herod tells the messenger to thank his masters for the honor they are paying him, concluding, "Let them come here, let them enter their royal home, let me be deserving of their wondrous faces, let me learn what their problem is. I await them" (Sell and Burkhart 2004:123). This seems polite enough, but the playwright has the messenger exaggerate Herod's courtesy when he reports back to the Magi, misquoting him as follows: "He says, 'Let them enter, let them come, let them rest inside their house, for everything is their possession, for everything will belong to them, whatever is my property, my possession.'" This is a polite invitation, conveyed through a lower-status intermediary and altered in the transition, perhaps to accord with the messenger's own cultural presumptions, which could be construed as an offer to give away the kingdom. This is what likely happened on the causeway that day.

When Herod greets the Magi in person he inquires after their health, expressing his hope that God gives them health; he then invites them into the city: "Ascend to your home, your altepetl [city]. Enter. You are to eat, since it is at your home that you have arrived" (Sell and Burkhart 2004:125). His statement is consistent with his direct speech to the messenger, conveying a "mi casa es su casa" level of politeness that stops short of offering all he possesses. Apart from the naming of the Judeo-Christian deity, this is, again, conceivably what Moteuczoma said to Cortés. When the visitors enter the city, Herod has his nobles adorn them with flowers. This was a traditional Nahua practice and something that, according to the Sahaguntine account, Moteuczoma's nobles did to Cortés (or, in the friar's Spanish gloss, to the other captains) at that first encounter (Lockhart 1993:114). There is ambivalence here about both the religion of the visitors and the ethnic status of the locals; yet, as if the play were a palimpsest, that Conquest episode seems to bleed through its lines.

Herod is at first very gracious, but when he learns that the kings have come, following a star, in search of the King of the Jews whose birth has been revealed to them by a vision, he goes into an embarrassingly unseemly rage. How dare anyone challenge his right to rule, for Caesar Augustus himself granted him his office? He sends for the Jewish priests and sages to explain to him what the three kings are talking about. The Gospel according to Matthew (2:3–4) relates, "When Herod the king had heard these things, he was troubled and all Jerusalem with him. And when he had gathered the chief priests and scribes of the people together, he demanded of them where Christ should be born." In the drama, Herod challenges the priests as to why they did not see the new star, accusing them of laziness for being asleep in the night and of an anachronistic failure to recite matins, the midnight office of Catholic, not Jewish, devotions. The priests tell of the prophecy that God will someday send his child to earth and express reluctance to tamper with such serious business. Herod then demands to know where this ruler is to be born. The priests look in their sacred book and report on Isaiah's prophecy (11:1–2) that the child is to come from the lineage of David. Herod retorts that he already knows that and again demands to know where. The priests by now fear for their lives. One of them finds and reads the passage in the book of Micah (5:2) that names Bethlehem as the prophesied location. Throughout this interchange Herod repeatedly hurls insults at the priests, threatening to destroy, singe, or flay them; ultimately, he chases them from the stage, calling them pigs and children of the Devil.

Some of the insults Herod hurls at the priests are Spanish words. These leap out from their Nahuatl surroundings and support my suggestion that Herod's identity can be read as Spanish. In addition to using the Spanish word *diablo* for devil, rather than the Nahuatl word *tlacatecolotl*, which was commonly used for that figure, Herod twice calls the priests Judiazos, meaning, roughly, "big rotten Jews," and threatens to turn them into *chicharrones*, that is, "pork rinds" (Sell and Burkhart 2004:129).[3] These usages are rather odd in an early colonial text. They could be a later addition to the script, for it may well have been revised between its initial composition and the redaction of the surviving version. However, they may also indicate a deliberate attempt by an earlier playwright to imitate Spanish cursing habits, which Nahuas surely noted from the beginning.

The unsavory view of Herod that thus develops is exacerbated by the excessive use of his personal name, a practice considered aggressively rude by Nahuas but perfectly acceptable to Spaniards (Sell 2004:12)—as noted earlier in reference to Cortés's first greeting of Moteuczoma. In the drama, Herod's name occurs seventeen times in the characters' speeches, including nine instances of direct address by the priests or the Magi. And in one case, defending his right to rule, he says his own name: "Am I not Herod?" (Sell and Burkhart 2004:127). By contrast, the personal names of the three kings—Casper, Melchior, and Balthasar—are given in the stage directions but never stated aloud by any character in the play. This is a sharp contrast in terms of respect and undermines Herod's legitimacy. If he is not a rude and aggressive Spaniard, he is certainly talking like one, and neither his own priests nor his foreign guests address him with proper respect.

Even though Herod speaks like an arrogant Spaniard, his angry scene echoes Moteuczoma's supposed consultation with, and abuse of, his soothsayers. According to Durán's version (1994:491–494), before the Spaniards had appeared on the coast, some elderly people reported troubling dreams: they saw the great temple of the god Huitzilopochtli aflame and his statue cast down; they saw the emperor's palace destroyed by a deluge and the chieftains and lords abandoning the city. Moteuczoma responded by throwing these dreamers into prison and letting them starve. Henceforward, none of the priests or diviners dared to tell him of their strange dreams and visions for fear of like punishment, prompting repeated angry interchanges with Moteuczoma. Just like Herod in the play, he accused his priests of lies and deceit and of not attending to their duties during the night. When some diviners he has imprisoned disappeared from jail, apparently by magic, he had their wives and children killed. A proud ruler, helpless in the face of divinely ordained events, he refused to accept what the prophecies said and lashed out in anger at his own priests and soothsayers.

Later in Durán's account (1994:503–506), after the Spaniards had landed and news of them was brought to Tenochtitlan, Moteuczoma consulted with his painters and keepers of manuscripts to try to determine who the strangers were. None could help him until an elderly Xochimilcan named Quilaztli told of a prophecy, recorded in a painting passed down to him by his ancestors, about white, bearded men who would come "in a great wooden hill" and possess the country. This episode does not portray Moteuczoma abusing his experts, but he parallels Herod's behavior in seeking explanations in the ancient manuscripts and finding the needed answer after being frustrated in initial attempts.

In the drama, after chasing away his priests, Herod turns to the three kings; stage directions instruct the actor to display much humility. He says, "Pardon me, you very honorable lords and rulers. I got a bit angry at my noblemen in front of you because they did not explain to me that it [the birth] would happen in such a wondrous manner" (Sell and Burkhart 2004:13r). Thus, he tries to make amends for his loss of self-control by again behaving in a properly courteous manner toward his elite guests. However, his politeness is obviously feigned, and he does not possess the composure commensurate with his political position. He tells the kings to go to Bethlehem and then report back to him so that he too can go to worship and declare fealty to the new deity and ruler.

ESCAPING HEROD, ELIDING CONQUEST

The kings take leave of Herod. On their departure, according to the stage directions, "in front of the church they discover the star under the arch" (Sell and Burkhart 2004:133). Herod's palace was probably intended to be a stage set on a platform in the open churchyard, with the church itself representing the stable in Bethlehem. The Magi send their servant in first, and he reports on what he sees inside: a child, a maiden, an elderly man, two animals, and "wondrous little children with wings," as this pagan idolater calls the attendant angels (Sell and Burkhart 2004:135). They are surrounded by light, and flowers of different colors are bursting forth like roseate spoonbills—in referencing these Nahua symbols of sacredness, this pagan makes himself sound very Nahua. The kings dismount, enter the church, and humbly approach the altar. The playwright probably intended that Mary, Joseph, and the Christ child be represented by the statues customarily placed in the church for the occasion, in the manner described by Motolinia, for they have no speaking parts in this play.

One by one the Magi address the infant Christ and present their gifts. While traditional formulas of polite address and formal speech have been used throughout the play, it is here that discursive forms associated with pre-Conquest elite culture are most directly incorporated, for the speeches of Casper and Melchior very closely parallel sections of the speech for the installation of a new ruler transcribed in Sahagún's book of oratory—much more closely, as noted earlier, than does Moteuczoma's alleged speech to Cortés (Sahagún 1950–1982:Bk. 6, 47, 48–49). Here, as an example, is the relevant portion of Casper's speech:

> O personage, O our lord, O precious jade, O quetzal plume, O fine turquoise, O bracelet! You have seated yourself here. Your precious father, God, has placed you here, O Lord of the Near, O Lord of the Nigh, O He by Whom All Live. It is true that your progenitors, your great-grandfathers, the prophets, the patriarchs have gone, have gone to lie down and the personage, the ruler, David and the personage, the ruler, Abraham, who go along further back.[4] They left behind, they set aside the carrying frame, the instrument of carrying, the instrument of bearing, which is very heavy, which cannot be lifted, which is unbearable.[5] Is it possible that they still come to know, that they still come to see what is behind them, in back of them? Is it possible that they come to frequent their water, their hill, which lies now as in the beginning, which now is becoming like his desolate place? Is it possible that they still frequent the forest or grassland, where the instrument of carrying, the instrument of bearing lies scattered?[6] And truly the tail, the wing[7] no longer has a mother, no longer has a father. And truly it no longer has eyes, it no longer has ears. It is as if it stands mute. It does not speak, it does not talk. It is as if it stands beheaded. No longer is there anyone who is its head, who goes in front of it. (Sell and Burkhart 2004:13717r–17v)

Then the speech shifts from the traditional oration to the immediate Christian context, as Casper acknowledges that he has passed from darkness into light, pledges his soul and his life to the divine child, and offers his gift of incense.

Placing such words into these characters' mouths and shifting directly from the old metaphors into a declaration of Christian conversion makes the speakers sound like pre-Conquest elites pledging fealty to Christ as their new legitimate ruler. The ambiguity in the kings' identity is, here at the end of the play, resolved in favor of the indigenous side. The scene can be read as representing the Nahuas' noble ancestors accepting Christianity, of their own free will and in accordance with their own prophecies, in direct fealty to Christ himself rather than to any Spaniard acting in his name.

After all three kings have presented their speeches and their gifts, an angel comes and warns them that Herod is very angry and has no intention of worshipping the child but instead wants to sentence him to death. They should not return to Jerusalem but should take another road, lest they fall into Herod's hands. Then the angel tells Joseph to flee with the child to Egypt, for Herod is coming to kill all the little children. In the angel's speeches, Herod is identified not as a ruler or a king but only as a *tlahueliloc*, a wicked person or scoundrel (Sell and Burkhart 2004:145); the term derives from *tlahuelli*, "indignation, anger or fury of one who is wrathful and full of savage cruelty" (Molina 1970:144v). It is as though Herod, through his behavior, has relinquished any true claim to rulership, much as those who came to blame Moteuczoma for the Conquest stripped him of his legitimacy, leaving an angry, cruel, and paranoid villain.

The old-style speeches the Magi deliver are composed in a register the ethnographer-priests sought to document and emulate, as in the collection made by Sahagún that is quoted in the play. The playwright, in quoting this speech, was undoubtedly aware of the respect Sahagún and other observers had for this mode of talking and for many aspects of the old moral and ethical order it encoded. The speeches serve here as a synecdoche for what was most worthy in native culture. By setting them into a Christian narrative, the playwright suggests the successful fusion of Nahua culture and Christian religion that he, as a literate, colonial, and Christian Nahua, hopes to sustain. A return to Moteuczoma's reign is not to be desired, nor is the adoption of Spanish ways; the play's negative and contradictory ethnic references render these alternatives unappealing. Rather, one may follow the example of the Magi toward an appropriate accommodation with the new.

In the Epiphany story, the Magi cannot prevent the slaughter of the innocents, just as the native leaders, betrayed by the wrath and duplicity of both Cortés and Moteuczoma, could not prevent the massacres and battles that followed that initial encounter. But these Nahua Magi, modeling the proper speech and demeanor of elite Nahuas as well as proto-Christian piety, make a seamless transition from the old order to the new and safely escape from Herod's wrath. Similarly, most Nahuas sought to retain continuity with their much-respected past while accommodating themselves, with grace and courage, to the exigencies of their colonized condition.

The iconic moment of parley imaginatively represented in *The Meeting of Cortés and Moteuczoma* held multiple meanings for descendants of both sides of the conflict. For the painter, the exotically feathered Mexica evoked the fantasy world of a pagan empire capitulating, as was necessary and appropriate, to the political and religious authority of Spain. Nahuas viewing such scenes might reflect on what they had heard about Cortés's arrogance or Moteuczoma's ineffectual rages or his willingness to give away the kingdom. That face-to-face moment of peace, though, also points to a path past the violence of the other paintings, to the possibility of a more expansive dialogue between native and foreigner, which, although always shadowed by the violence inherent in colonial domination, did occur in colonial Mexico and left a rich textual legacy, of which the Epiphany play is one piece.

NOTES

1. Another Nahuatl Epiphany play survives, which will be published in Volume 4 of *Nahuatl Theater* (Sell and Burkhart n.d.). It is dated 1717 and comes from Metepec; the manuscript is in the Biblioteca Nacional de Antropología e Historia in Mexico City. An earlier manuscript of this second drama, currently missing, was published by Francisco del Paso y Troncoso (1902) and adapted into his idiosyncratic orthography. Fernando Horcasitas, using Paso y Troncoso's version, included this play in his *El teatro náhuatl* (1974:281–327). The contrast between angry Herod and dignified Magi is drawn less vividly in this other drama. It has a considerably larger cast and tells a more extended story, including the original sighting of the star and the slaughter of the innocents.

2. The fact that European artists sometimes portrayed a Native American magus (Tom Cummins, personal communication, March 23, 2003) indicates a sense that America should be included among the pagan nations represented by these rulers.

3. Nahuatl speakers today code-switch into Spanish when uttering curses and insults (Hill and Hill 1986), but I have no evidence that this practice began early enough to be reflected in this play.

4. Here Old Testament figures are substituted for pre-Conquest Mexica rulers.

5. These are metaphors for government.

6. These passages describe the ruler-less city or, in this new Christian context, the world awaiting salvation.

7. That is, the common people, now bereft of leadership.

2

Blaming Moteuczoma

Anthropomorphizing the Aztec Conquest

Susan D. Gillespie

The Aztec Conquest has long been depicted as a struggle between two towering historical figures—Cortés and Moteuczoma. The "noble, valiant Cortés" was contrasted with a "timorous, cowardly" Moteuczoma in the earliest Hispanic narratives of the Conquest written only a few decades after the 1521 fall of the Aztec capital city, Tenochtitlan (Clendinnen 1991:65; e.g., see López de Gómara 1964:179). William Prescott's *History of the Conquest of Mexico* (1843) further personified the clash between the Old and New Worlds in terms of the contrariety of these two leaders, the European and the Indian, such that the former, by dint of cultural superiority, was bound to emerge victorious. This attitude not only continues to permeate current perspectives on the Conquest (Clendinnen 1991:65; Lockhart 1993:17; see, e.g., Collis 1954; Thomas 1993), but it has been generalized to all of Latin America in the form of the "*conquistador*-myth: the notion that Spaniards displaced incumbent elites in the early modern New World because they were in some sense better, or better equipped, technically, morally or intellectually" (Fernández-Armesto 1992:288). But in the case of Mexico, there is another side to the story: Cortés cannot truly monopolize the credit for victory because Moteuczoma is equally awarded the blame for the Aztec defeat. This is a curious phenomenon, well-known to Conquest historians, but it has not received proper attention (Fernández-Armesto 1992:288).

On the European side—the side best represented in subsequent historiography—the Spanish victory was attributed to Hernando Cortés's political skill, courage, and luck and, no less important, the hand of God (Elliott 1967:55; see also Díaz Balsera, Chapter 3, this volume). Such characterizations appear in the hagiographic accounts, such as those by Francisco López de Gómara (1964), Cortés's secretary, and the Franciscan writers, including Friars Sahagún, Motolinia, and Mendieta (Cline 1988:99). They also concurred with the dominant approach in nineteenth-century European political history that emphasized the actions of major political figures as driving historical change (e.g., von Ranke 1981:17). The legacy of these earlier attitudes continues to shape understandings of the Conquest today, despite contemporary concerns for a more balanced view of past events. Thus, we now also take into consideration the impact of non-personal factors in explaining the outcome, such as the superior technology of the Spaniards, the political instability and weaknesses of the Aztec Empire, and, especially, the devastation and disruption wrought by European diseases (Fernández-Armesto 1992:303).

Nevertheless, even as Cortés's role in the Spanish victory is now somewhat downplayed, the blame for the Aztec loss still falls heavily on Moteuczoma. Much has been written about Moteuczoma's personal failings, as though the protracted struggle for European hegemony in the Americas was solely his to lose. Indeed, it has been suggested that if someone less superstitious and conceited than Moteuczoma had been in charge—an aggressive warrior like the Tlaxcaltec general Xicotencatl or Moteuczoma's young successor, Cuauhtemoc—the Conquest would not have been possible (Martínez 1986:398).

Because of the long-standing focus on these two men in the battle for control of Mexico, specific actions that impacted their changing relationship were frequently chosen to illustrate the course of the Conquest, and they continue to resonate with audiences today. These events constitute only a small sample of the actual occurrences, and they were not necessarily critical to the eventual outcome. However, they were transformed into icons of the victory of Christendom over the Aztecs and, by extension, of America itself. They form a mini-narrative that encapsulates the lengthy multifaceted processes of encounter, intrigue, battle, defeat, and subjugation.

The seventeenth-century Kislak paintings are prime examples of what one might call the "Hispanic corpus" (Spanish- and Creole-produced) of iconic depictions that entwine the actions of Cortés and Moteuczoma. These include the reception of Moteuczoma's delegates in Veracruz (plate 2), followed by the fateful meeting of Cortés and Moteuczoma on the edge of the city of Tenochtitlan (plate 3). Cortés moved into the city and soon afterward imprisoned Moteuczoma, bringing the two in close juxtaposition. A series of events that is *not* depicted then led to their separation, artistically represented by the death of Moteuczoma while in Spanish custody (plate 4), followed immediately by the flight of Cortés from the city (plate 5). A final iconic event that connotes their relationship is the presentation to Cortés of Cuauhtemoc, Moteuczoma's successor and surrogate, the final painting in the series (plate 8). Through this abbreviated sequence of events, their relationship of opposition has been reversed: Cortés, the intrepid invader, has defeated the supreme emperor within his own capital. The Spanish outsider, who came into the Aztec realm by sea, became the insider, while Cuauhtemoc attempted to flee that realm by water but was captured. He was executed several years later by Cortés in the region that is now Campeche, during the latter's journey to Honduras (Scholes and Roys 1968:112).

Another perspective of the Conquest has also survived in the form of pictorial and written accounts produced by indigenous elites or representing their views, dating from the mid- to late sixteenth century into the early seventeenth century. As one might expect, this "indigenized corpus" highlights certain events not found or prominently depicted in the Hispanicized corpus. Perhaps most significant is the massacre carried out by Pedro de Alvarado during the Toxcatl ceremony in Tenochtitlan's main ceremonial precinct (*Codex Aubin* 1963:81; *Codex Ríos* 1996:fol. 89r; Durán 1994:pl. 59; *Histoire Mexicaine* 1998:21; *El Lienzo de Tlaxcala* 1979:pl. 14; Sahagún 1950–1982 (*Florentine Codex*) [hereafter FC]: Bk. 12, figs. 66–70). This occurred in May 1520 and was a critical turning point for the Aztecs in their relationship with the Spanish intruders (Cline 1989:7; Lockhart 1993:16–17). The massacre precipitated the hatred and war that led to the Spaniards' ouster from the city on the *Noche triste*, June 30 (according to Fr. Sahagún 1989a:98). Its counterpart in the Hispanicized corpus may be the Battle of Otumba, a heroic turning point for the Spaniards still greatly suffering from their humiliating retreat from the city, which is not part of the indigenized corpus. Another important event illustrated in some indigenous-authored documents but not in the Hispanicized portrayals is the execution of Cuauhtemoc (e.g., *Codex Ríos* 1996:fol. 90r; Tira de Tepechpan 1978:pl. 15).

Despite these discrepancies, some of the same iconic events in the Kislak paintings were depicted in the sixteenth century by native artists of New Spain. These include the first meeting of Moteuczoma and Cortés (Durán 1994:pl. 58; FC Bk. 12:fig. 44; *El Lienzo de Tlaxcala* 1979:pl. 11), the stoning death of Moteuczoma (*El Lienzo de Tlaxcala* 1979:pl. 15), the flight of the *Noche triste* (FC Bk. 12:figs.

89–93; *El Lienzo de Tlaxcala* 1979:pls. 18–19), and the presentation of the captured Cuauhtemoc to Cortés (*El Lienzo de Tlaxcala* 1979:pl. 48); it is an exaggeration to state that Cuauhtemoc formally surrendered (Cortés 1986:264–265).

More significant, it is in the post-Conquest indigenous written historical traditions that we see the blame for their defeat fall most heavily on Moteuczoma. On the one hand, the weaknesses attributed to Moteuczoma in the Conquest accounts were partly a by-product of Spanish representations, derived especially from Cortés's political strategy to save his own neck (Clendinnen 1991:75). His Second Letter (Cortés 1986) has Moteuczoma virtually giving away his kingdom to Cortés, who illegitimately represented himself as ambassador of the Spanish monarch, at their first meeting. Cortés soon made Moteuczoma his prisoner, impeding the emperor's capacity to oust the Spanish intruders. Moteuczoma's apparent willingness to kowtow to the Europeans seemed inexplicable other than by reference to failings of his character, and he was disparaged by his own people. In his Third Letter, Cortés (1986:188) reported that as the Spaniards were preparing to attack Tenochtitlan, the enemy warriors taunted him, saying, "Do you think there is not another Mutezuma to do whatever you wish?" Cortés's actions and his reasons for them, as laid out in his letters to the king of Spain, became embedded within the Hispanic rationale for the events of the Conquest. They greatly contributed to the notion that the most powerful man on the North American continent was rendered virtually impotent upon his first encounter with the Spanish conquistador.

On the other hand, the native accounts are far more critical in their assessments of Moteuczoma's reaction to the Spanish *entrada*. More important, they provide detailed reasons why a widely feared military leader had been reduced to an indecisive coward long before the Europeans even set foot on Mexican soil. In these narratives Moteuczoma, the *huey tlatoani* ("great speaker") of the Mexica city of Tenochtitlan, looms large as the locus for the conjunction of human and cosmic factors that made defeat inevitable, just as Cortés was magnified and almost venerated in some sixteenth-century Hispanic accounts of victory (e.g., Aguilar 1993; Díaz del Castillo 1994; López de Gómara 1964). It was the indigenous characterization of a "quaking, indecisive, quiescent, effete" Moteuczoma (Lockhart 1993:17) that was brought to scholarly attention by William Prescott in the nineteenth century.[1] We thus to need to examine the reasons for representing Moteuczoma as a fearful, fawning failure of a ruler.

BLAMING MOTEUCZOMA

God was given ultimate credit for the Spanish victory, with Cortés acting as His agent on earth (Cline 1989:6, 9). By the same token, Moteuczoma's fate was also attributed to divine intervention, but as a punishment for his shortcomings. Both indigenous authors and Spaniards relying on native informants depicted Moteuczoma as uncertain, passive, paralyzed with fear, and ultimately hopeless. He simply stood back and let the alien invaders do what they would because he believed his fate was in the hands of his gods, who had turned against him. Their divine intervention in Aztec destiny was relayed by cosmic omens or portents said to have begun approximately ten years before Cortés arrived on the scene and interpreted as foretelling the impending destruction of Moteuczoma's reign. In some accounts Moteuczoma is said to have been singled out by these ominous signs sent directly by the gods because of his tyranny and oppression. Adding further to his distress, according to some accounts, was his belief that the Spaniards might be gods.

The most elaborate descriptions of the fear and paralysis that gripped Moteuczoma because of these strange auguries appear in the *General History* written by Franciscan friar Bernardino de Sahagún in its last edition, the version known as the *Florentine Codex* (FC; Sahagún 1950–1982). Written in parallel Nahuatl and Spanish texts, this twelve-book encyclopedia was completed in the years 1578–1580. The twelfth book is dedicated entirely to the Conquest (see Lockhart 1993). Sahagún continued to edit Book 12, and a final revision was finished in 1585, which survives as a Spanish copy (Sahagún 1989b). The 1585 Revision of Book 12 varies considerably from the earlier *Florentine Codex,* and it represents Sahagún's view of the Conquest more so than that of his indigenous (mostly Tlatelolcan) informants (Cline 1988, 1989:3–4). A second major source of information on Moteuczoma's state of mind is the Tenochtitlan-biased *Historia* of Friar Diego Durán (1967, 1995) completed in ca. 1581, along with closely related accounts (Acosta 2002; Alvarado Tezozomoc 1980; *Codex Ramirez* 1980). Some of the information found in Sahagún's and Durán's histories is repeated in other late-sixteenth and early-seventeenth-century records, but these two document groupings provide the greatest detail and have garnered the most attention from historians.

For example, Sahagún's Book 12 was the major source used in the popular rendering of native accounts of the Conquest—Miguel León-Portilla's (1962) *The Broken Spears*, especially in the chapter he entitled "Moteuczoma's Terror and Apathy." An excerpt from FC Book 12 succinctly encapsulates Moteuczoma's supposed state of mind as the Spaniards moved ever closer to Tenochtitlan:

> Moctezuma loudly expressed his distress. He felt distress, he was terrified, he was astounded . . . He would flee; he wished to flee; he needed to flee; he would take himself hence. He would hide himself . . . But this he could not do. He could not hide. He could not take refuge. No longer had he the strength; no longer was there any use; no longer had he energy. . . . [Moteuczoma] only

> awaited [the Spaniards]; he made himself resolute; . . . he submitted himself entirely to whatsoever he was to see, at which he was to marvel. (FC Bk. 12:ch. 9, 25–26)

The elaborate repetitive and poetic language of Sahagún's elite Nahuatl informants dramatically highlights Moteuczoma's sheer terror and his ultimate inability even to run away from his enemies.

However, he was not completely passive or indecisive, at least early on. Moteuczoma is said to have reacted to the onset of the omens by demanding explanations and responses to them from his soothsayers and magicians, whose job it was to regularly negotiate with the supernatural realm. He also sent his magicians to try to stop the Spaniards, but, of course, they failed. Only when Moteuczoma realized that he was dealing with divine forces against which he had insufficient power to deter them is he said to have given up these ineffective efforts (especially in the FC; see Colston 1985:254). To the Euro-American mind he epitomizes the irrational superstitions of the native peoples of the Americas, forming a sharp contrast with modern Western rationality and practicality that today we mistakenly credit to late medieval Spaniards and in that sense seeming to provide some justification for the conquest of civilized rationality over primitive superstition (Clendinnen 1991:66).

In the various historical accounts, however, this superstitious and irrational attitude is *not* extended to all the Aztecs—although the nameless masses were also said to have exhibited dread, weeping, and despair—but was most strongly attributed to Moteuczoma among native leaders. In contrast, Moteuczoma's cousin Cuauhtemoc is credited with rallying his people to fight the Spaniards until the bitter end, when—his city in ruins, his people starving or dead—he was quickly captured while leaving the city. Cuauhtemoc's name—"Descending Eagle"—came to signify his fate, symbolizing the setting sun (Caso 1958:33). Nevertheless, for his valor, Cuauhtemoc remains a hero to the Mexican people and "an emblematic figure of Mexican nationalism," honored with statues, schools, towns, and streets in his name (León-Portilla 2001:289). No such honor has been given to Moteuczoma, the solitary personified repository of blame for the Aztec defeat.

Significantly, the record of Moteuczoma's actions and reactions in these accounts produced generations afterward contrasts greatly with the conquistadors' retellings of their interactions with high-ranking ambassadors and noble officials sent by Moteuczoma—not magicians and soothsayers. The latter documents paint a picture of a powerful man very actively engaged, cunning and ruthless in trying to stop the Spaniards' advance. In his Second Letter, Cortés (1986) cited multiple examples of Moteuczoma's power and dominion, the fear and obedience shown him by even the highest lords, as well as Moteuczoma's numerous attempts to deceive the Spaniards, to ambush them (the official reason given for the Cholula and Toxcatl massacres), to block their way, bribe them, cajole them, and in every way possible prevent them from coming to Tenochtitlan (1986:58, 69, 73, 77, 81). Even after being taken into their custody, Moteuczoma was accused of sending men to kill Spaniards and of plotting with Pánfilo de Narváez when he arrived on the Gulf Coast in 1520 to arrest Cortés (1986:91, 123).

Moreover, no confirming evidence exists for Moteuczoma's "terror and apathy" contemporary to the events of the *entrada* and Conquest. Durán's and Sahagún's descriptions of Moteuczoma's state of mind do not describe public behaviors that could have formed the basis of an accurate recounting of events decades later. The lengthy speeches attributed to Moteuczoma and his closest advisers cannot be taken at face value given that there was no one writing them down and no indication that those who heard his words lived to repeat them verbatim to later chroniclers (Clendinnen 1991:69; Todorov 1985:56). Sahagún's propensity to insert moralizing speeches into his narrative to fulfill his own agenda has also been recognized (this was not an atypical occurrence during that era). In Sahagún's case, his insertions were designed to absolve the Spaniards of culpability for the more heinous acts of cruelty—the Toxcatl massacre and the subsequent death of Moteuczoma—instead blaming the Aztecs (Cline 1988:100, 1989:7–8).

Historian James Lockhart (1993:17–18) further observed that the elaborate descriptions in the first part of the FC of an agonized Moteuczoma, the supernatural events said to have caused his distress, and his magicians' failed attempts to stop the invaders (constituting the "first phase" of the Conquest) are very much at odds with the remaining chapters in Sahagún's account. They are also strikingly unlike other early accounts based on native oral traditions that relate events in a straightforward and rational manner, especially the battles and intrigues following the expulsion of the invaders on the *Noche triste* (which began the "second phase" of the Conquest; Clendinnen 1991:67). Nevertheless, these descriptions of Moteuczoma's responses to the Spanish *entrada* have typically been taken as literal happenings that preordained the result of the ensuing conflict rather than as "the mythic constructs they largely are," in the opinion of historian Inga Clendinnen (1991:67).

Thus, despite all their evidentiary shortcomings, every popular and almost every scholarly account of the Conquest accepts that these narratives have a degree of historical veracity—that Moteuczoma did indeed exhibit certain personal failings and thus contributed to the rapidity of the Spanish takeover of his empire. Two major reasons have been given by various historians for believing Moteuczoma was reduced to if not terror, at least profound anxiety. First, a large number of written sources—both native- and Spanish-authored—mention the specific events that caused his panic. Although the information they contain is highly contradictory, their number is taken to indicate that they must contain some grain of truth (e.g., Colston 1985; León-Portilla 1974; Nicholson 2001). Second, the Aztecs are known to have been superstitious and to have interpreted various happenings as ominous auguries (e.g., López Austin 1969). These beliefs are considered to account for a certain level of foreboding, which seems necessary to explain Moteuczoma's otherwise irrational actions and thereby account for his easy capture (e.g., Martínez 1986:397–398; Padden 1967; Thomas 1993; Todorov 1985).

What we see in the present-day explanations of the Conquest is the persistence of the "positivist" (Fogelson 1989) and "literal-minded" (Burke 1990) approach in Western history, despite the fact that this mind-set has been under attack within the discipline of history since the 1930s. The positivist school assumes that historical events exist preformed within documents and merely have to be extracted through historians' methods of critical analysis, determining which events are more likely to be correctly represented, for example, by seeing their repetition across many historical records (Fogelson 1989:135; see, e.g., López Austin 1973:10–11). Raymond Fogelson (1989:135) recently accused fellow ethnohistorians especially of continuing to adhere to a positivist history, even as most others in the history profession have been abandoning it.

Two salient questions therefore arise from a serious consideration of the role of Moteuczoma's "terror and apathy" in the events of the *entrada* and Conquest. First, why does blame continue to fall on Moteuczoma today, given the very noncredible evidence for his personal failings? Second, why did the indigenous peoples assign such blame during the first century after the Conquest?

Given the lack of evidence for the many "events" said to have contributed to or represented Moteuczoma's weakness, we must consider the possibility that they fall into the category of "nonevents." Fogelson (1989) discussed the importance of "nonevents" in both Western and non-Western historiography, including a type of nonevent he calls the "imagined event." In some cases imagined events also become "epitomizing events," which are "narratives that condense, encapsulate and dramatize longer-term historical processes. Such events are inventions but have such compelling qualities and explanatory power that they spread rapidly through the group and soon take on an ethnohistorical reality of their own" (Fogelson 1989:143). Hence they will appear in the guise of historical fact in many different accounts.

From this perspective, the post-Conquest documents that fault Moteuczoma for the Aztec defeat can be seen as a subsequent re-envisioning of the Conquest, in part by the indigenous peoples themselves as part of their resistance and accommodation following the imposition of Spanish colonialism. This was an important aspect of the "transformation" that resulted from the invasion, but understanding this process requires us to consider central Mexican theories of history, not just our own—that is, an Aztec "ethno-ethnohistory" (following Fogelson 1989; Turner 1988). When we examine these accounts in terms of ethno-ethnohistory, we discover that the epitomizing nonevents salient to an indigenous comprehension of and explanation for the complex, long-term processes of invasion, disruption, defeat, subjugation, and iconoclasm focused on a singular image—the body and person of Moteuczoma. And the foremost mechanism employed to link these occurrences that were beyond Aztec control directly to Moteuczoma, as the embodiment of the Aztec state, was the later invention of cosmic portents—nonevents said to have heralded, if not caused, these events.

THE OMENS

It is commonly held today (Colston 1985:247; León-Portilla 1962:13; see also, e.g., Carrasco 1982; Collis 1954; Graulich 1994:232; León-Portilla 1974; Nicholson 2001; Padden 1967; Thomas 1993; Todorov 1985; this is not an exhaustive list) that Moteuczoma was *most* distressed because of his mistaken belief that Cortés was a god, in particular an ancient god who had left and predicted his return to retake the throne that originally belonged to him, the one Moteuczoma currently occupied. Although the Aztecs may have initially believed the Spaniards as a people, or Cortés as their leader, had divine qualities—just as Moteuczoma was a divine king—the notion that Cortés fulfilled some ancient prophecy, and in particular his identification with the Aztec deity Quetzalcoatl, was part of a millenarian movement that developed within the first two generations after the Conquest (Gillespie 1989; Stenzel 1980; see also Clendinnen 1991:69, 88; Cortés 1986:467–468).

More significant, in the accounts of the Conquest believed to be based on native perceptions and preserved in the writings of Sahagún, Durán, and others, the identification of Cortés as Quetzalcoatl is typically given relatively little importance as a cause for the fear and uncertainty that are said to have gripped Moteuczoma. Instead, much greater prominence is given to events interpreted as omens or portents of impending doom. Although these omens and the impact they had on the Aztecs in general and Moteuczoma in particular are found in many different documents authored by Spaniards, mestizos, and indigenous peoples, there are many discrepancies among them. At least three major series of omens that foretold the coming of the Spaniards can be discerned, and they are differentially distributed in the accounts, especially where later authors drew on a variety of earlier documents.

One of the earliest known detailed accounts of omens appears in the *Memoriales* of Friar Toribio Motolinia (1970:ch. 55), dating to the early 1540s (Fernández-Armesto 1992:288–289). Motolinia presented a list of several omens, all of which were said to have occurred before the Spaniards arrived in 1519, briefly described as follows: (1) there were visions in the air of people fighting with one another; (2) a man from Tlatelolco (the city adjacent to Tenochtitlan on the north), while waiting to be sacrificed, was visited by a bird from heaven wearing a crown, who told him that soon there would be no more sacrifices; and (3) for many days, two hours before dawn a light rose in the East over the sea and then disappeared. Toward the East some saw flames of fire, while others saw a great smoke that rose from the sea to the sky. The list of omens is followed by a description of their principal impact on Moteuczoma, who had experienced prognostications that white, bearded men would come from the East to rule his land and thus terminate the reign of the rulers of Mexico. Cortés's secretary, Francisco López de Gómara (1964:ch. 145, 294–295), writing the first history of the Conquest (1552), repeated Motolinia's list of omens—embellishing them somewhat—but in his story Moteuczoma ends up placating the fears expressed by others![2]

Despite the early date and later repetitions of some of Motolinia's portents in other accounts, most scholars have given greater attention to a numbered series of eight omens provided in Friar Sahagún's *Florentine Codex*, each with its own illustration (Figures 2.1–2.4). Sahagún claimed to have solicited information from surviving witnesses perhaps as early as 1547 and not later than 1555 and to have begun this part of his encyclopedic work while those participants (most of whom were likely Tlatelolcan) were still alive (Cline 1988:97), although the *Florentine Codex* appeared in final form decades later and some scholars consider it a "late work" (e.g., Clendinnen 1991:69; Fernández-Armesto 1992:289). The list of omens forms the opening chapter of Book 12, "The Conquest" (see also his 1585 Revision; Sahagún 1989). The entire list of eight, with much of their detail intact, is duplicated in a number of other sources, including the historical accounts of Diego Muñoz Camargo (1978:Bk. 2, ch. 1) and Friar Juan de Tovar (*Codex Ramirez* 1980:79–80), as well as in the works of two authors known to have copied from Tovar, Friar José de Acosta (2002:Bk. 7, ch. 23) and Friar Juan de Torquemada (1975:Bk. 2, ch. 110).

In briefest outline, these eight omens, said to have begun ten years before the Spanish arrival, are as follows: (1) a pyramid-shaped column of flames appeared before dawn in the East; (2) the temple of the god Huitzilopochtli mysteriously caught fire; (3) the thatch-roofed temple of the god Xiuhteuctli mysteriously caught fire; (4) a three-headed comet appeared in the daytime; (5) the lake waters boiled and foamed, flooding some buildings; (6) at night a woman's voice

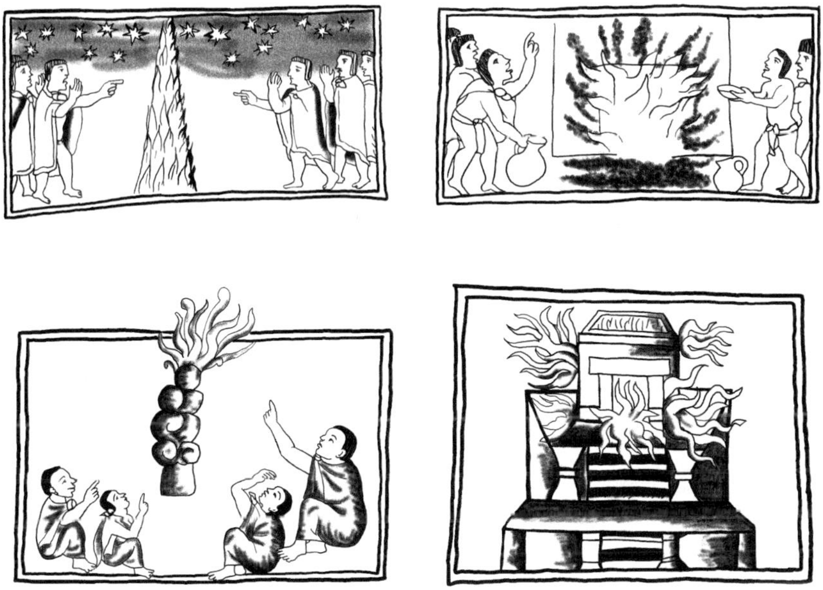

Figure 2.1. *Omens 1 and 2,* in Friar Bernardino de Sahagún, the *Florentine Codex.* Left: the first omen (top: Book 12, fol. 1r; bottom: Book 8, fol. 3v). Right: the second omen (top: Book 12, fol. 2r; bottom, Book 8, fol. 11v). Drawings by S. Gillespie.

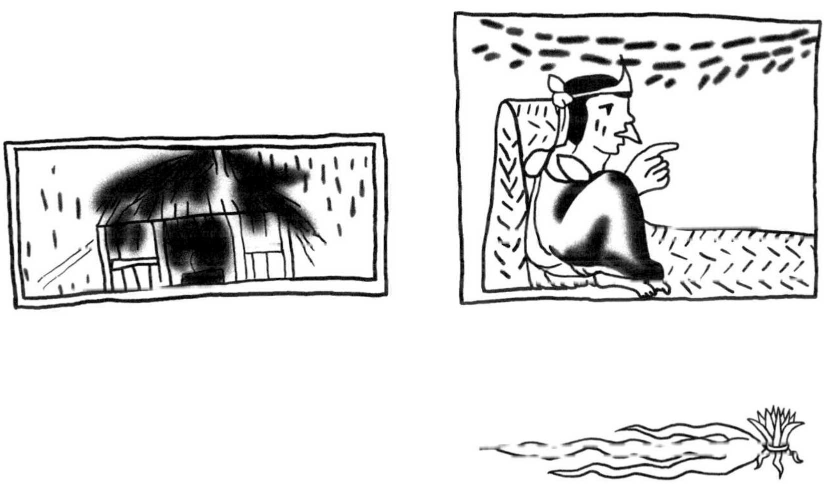

Figure 2.2. *Omens 3 and 4,* in Friar Bernardino de Sahagún, the *Florentine Codex.* Left: the third omen (Book 12, fol. 2r; not illustrated in Book 8). Right: the fourth omen (top: Book 12, fol. 2r; bottom: Book 8, fol. 12r). Drawings by S. Gillespie.

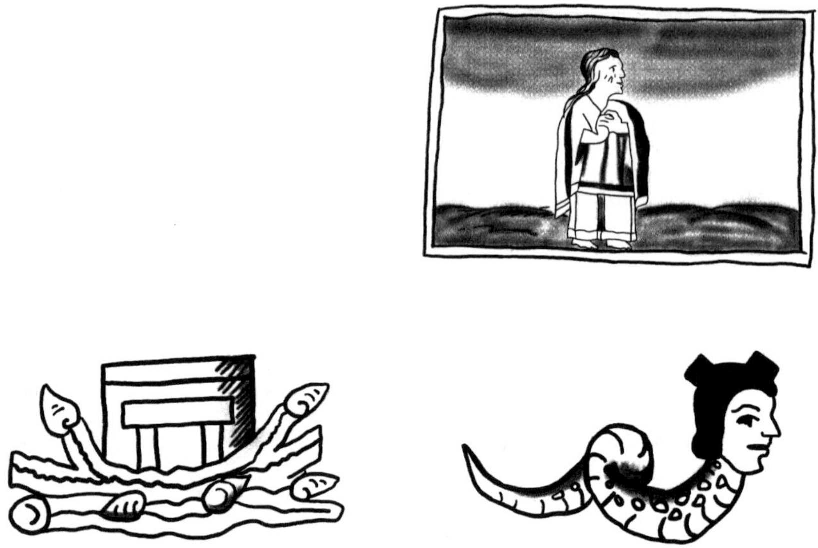

Figure 2.3. *Omens 5 and 6*, in Friar Bernardino de Sahagún, the *Florentine Codex*. *Left*: the fifth omen (Book 8, fol.12r; not illustrated in Book 12). *Right*: the sixth omen (top: Book 12, fol. 2v; bottom: Book 8, fol. 12r). Drawings by S. Gillespie.

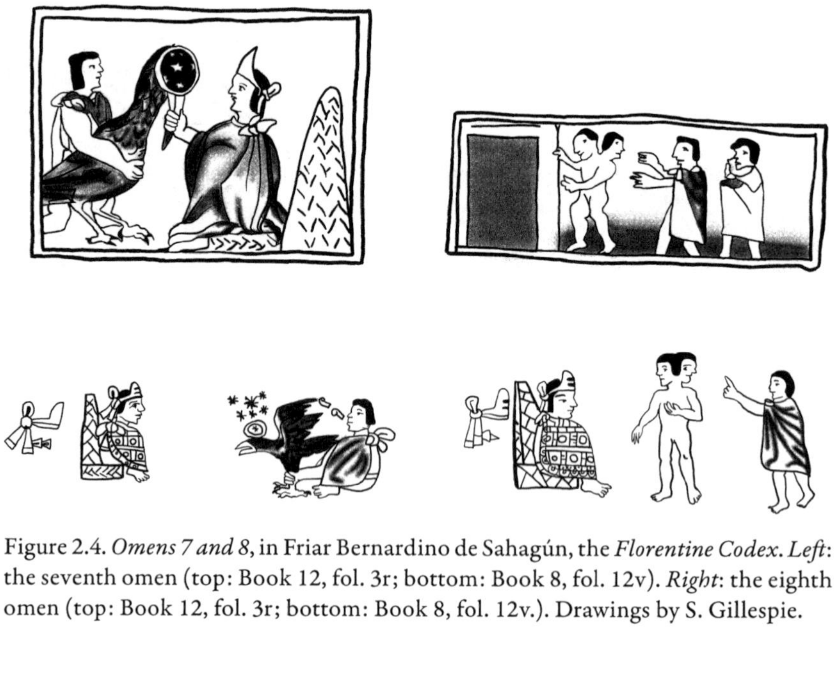

Figure 2.4. *Omens 7 and 8*, in Friar Bernardino de Sahagún, the *Florentine Codex*. *Left*: the seventh omen (top: Book 12, fol. 3r; bottom: Book 8, fol. 12v). *Right*: the eighth omen (top: Book 12, fol. 3r; bottom: Book 8, fol. 12v.). Drawings by S. Gillespie.

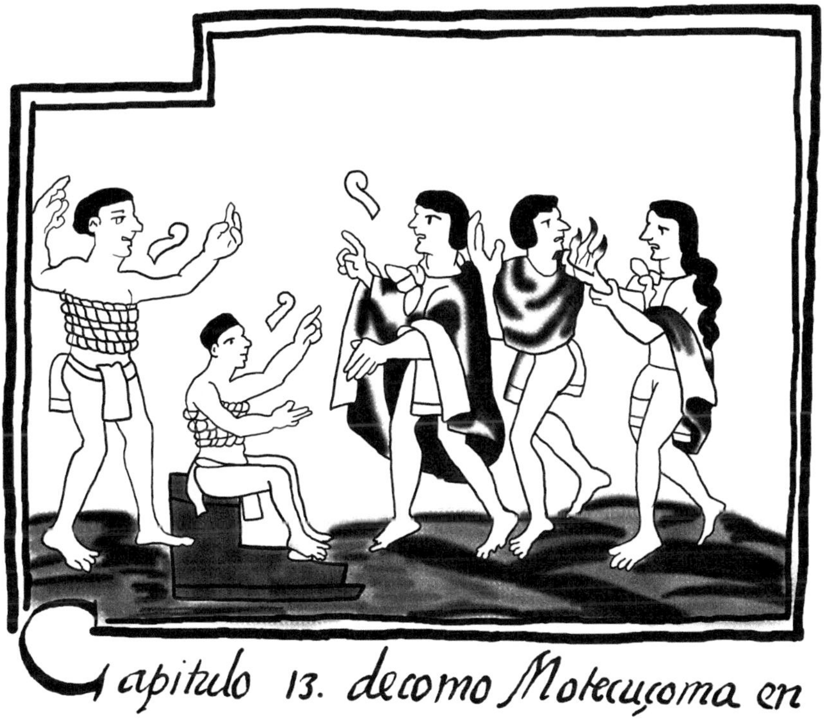

Figure 2.5. *The Omen of the Drunken Man of Chalco Bound with Rope*, in Friar Bernardino de Sahagún, the *Florentine Codex* (Book 8, fol. 18v). Drawing by S. Gillespie.

was heard wailing about the impending destruction; (7) lake fisherman caught a crane with a mirror in its head, into which mirror Moteuczoma saw stars and then an approaching army, after which the bird mysteriously disappeared; and (8) a two-headed man was taken to Moteuczoma but then vanished.

Sahagún also related another strange sign that appeared after Cortés was already on the eastern outskirts of the Basin of Mexico, so it is not numbered with the others. A drunken man from Chalco province (in the southeast area of the basin) appeared before the magicians and soothsayers sent by Moteuczoma to try to bewitch the Spaniards. The man, who was bound with rope around his chest, told the magicians they were all doomed and presented them with a vision of their city in flames (Figure 2.5). They recognized him as the god Tezcatlipoca and went back to Tenochtitlan (FC:Bk. 12, ch. 13, figs. 27–28). This story is also told in the *Codex Ramirez* (1980:86) of Tovar and Acosta's history (2002:Bk. 7, ch. 25). A final omen is mentioned in the *Florentine Codex* (Book 12, ch. 39), just prior to Cuauhtemoc's departure from his dying city. Deep in the night a fire, as if a blazing coal, came spinning out of the sky like a whirlwind and dropped into the water. But at this sign, unlike the others, the Aztecs remained silent.

It is less well-known that the list of eight omens is repeated and illustrated in Sahagún's Book 8, "Kings and Lords," and that there are discrepancies in the two chapters in which they appear (Figures 2.1–2.4). In Book 8 the omens are listed in a matter-of-fact style, with only a brief mention of how they caused Moteuczoma and his people to be afraid (ch. 7), whereas Book 12 describes in excruciating detail the extreme fright and paralysis they caused Moteuczoma. All eight appear in the same order in Book 8, chapter 6 as in Book 12, chapter 1, and six of them are illustrated in full color accompanying chapter 6 (FC:Bk. 8, figs. 56–61), unlike the cruder black-and-white illustrations of Book 12. However, in Book 8, chapter 1 there are only four omens, and they are somewhat different. Three are shown together in a single illustration (Bk. 8:fig. 10): (1) a beam in the "song house" (*cuicacalli*), a religious building, began to speak; (2) the goddess Cihuacoatl wept at night (she is the woman who wailed at night in the other lists because in the illustration for chapter 6 she is shown as Cihuacoatl, identical to this illustration for chapter 1); and (3) a woman who died and was buried came back to life to tell Moteuczoma that his reign was about to end. The last omen is illustrated separately (Bk. 8:fig. 11): (4) flames forming a pyramidal shape regularly appeared at night in the East for four years. Thus, only two of the four omens are repeated in the other series of eight. The story of the woman who came back to life received much more detail in Torquemada's *Monarquía indiana* (1975:Bk. 2, ch. 91), there identified as Moteuczoma's sister Papan (or Papantzin).

A third major series of omens is found in the related histories of Durán (1994: ch. 41–43, 46–48), Alvarado Tezozomoc (1980:ch. 100–106), Tovar (*Codex Ramirez* 1980:77–78), Torquemada (1975:Bk. 2, ch. 77–79, 91), and Acosta (2002:Bk. 7, ch. 23; the latter three also repeat the aforementioned Sahaguntine series). Besides being fewer and quite different than the earlier-described series, they are interspersed with other events in the narrative, especially in Durán's and Torquemada's accounts, rather than listed together as a series of the same kind of phenomenon. However, these accounts are no less elaborate in their descriptive detail or of the devastating impact the signs had on Moteuczoma's state of mind, especially in Durán's *Historia*, the only one of these documents that also provides illustrations.

The omens begin with the foretelling by the Tetzcocan ruler Nezahualpilli of the impending defeat of the Mexica Aztecs (in Durán and Torquemada; the *Codex Ramirez* and Acosta's account assign this role to Quetzalcoatl, the patron god of Cholula, as well as to Nezahualpilli). Nezahualpilli, *huey tlatoani* of the second-most-powerful city in the Basin of Mexico, predicted to Moteuczoma that he would be unable to win wars with Huexotzinco, Tlaxcala, and Cholula (enemy polities just east of the basin) and that he would see signs in the sky as an omen of what would come. Moteuczoma subsequently waged fruitless wars with Tlaxcala to determine whether Nezahualpilli was correct. As a later consequence, the Huexotzincans, allies of Tlaxcala at that time, burned the temple to the Aztec goddess Toci at Tocititlan (near the southern edge of Tenochtitlan), which Moteuczoma considered an ill omen (Durán 1994:ch. 62). In a Tetzcocan-biased account, *Historia de la nación chichimeca* (Ixtlilxochitl 1977:II, ch. 72), Moteuczoma and Nezahualpilli played a ball game as a form of divination to determine whether Nezahualpilli's prophecy was correct; not surprisingly, Moteuczoma lost the game.

While these particular omens caused Moteuczoma some anxiety, he was greatly frightened by what happened next. A comet appeared in the East (Durán 1994:pl. 48), which Nezahualpilli explained as a sign that indigenous rulership would soon be over, as decreed by the gods (see Figure 7.7). Time passed, but then another curious thing transpired that renewed Moteuczoma's fear. Moteuczoma desired a new stone to be used in rites of sacrificing war captives and ordered that a fine stone be brought from Chalco province to Tenochtitlan. However, the stone at first could not be budged. It then spoke to the masons and sculptors who had wrapped it in ropes to move it, telling them that their labors were useless for their destruction was at hand. When it finally agreed to be moved, the stone was dragged up the main causeway into the city from the south (in Durán's illustration [1994:pl. 51] one should take into account the anachronism of the wheeled cart) (Figure 2.6). Just as it reached the edge of the city, the stone broke through a bridge, dropping into the lake below. It was later discovered back where it had first been found in Chalco province, still bound with the ropes the sculptors had used to move it.

Several of the documents in this omen grouping follow the talking stone episode with a complicated story about a farmer from the Tetzcoco area, who was picked up by an eagle and carried to a cave. There he was directed to observe a vision of Moteuczoma sleeping. He was told to burn the emperor on the thigh with a smoldering tube of tobacco incense. This was to be a sign of the emperor's impending defeat, a punishment for his tyranny and oppression. The farmer did so, and after the eagle returned him to his field, he went to tell Moteuczoma what had happened. Only then did the *huey tlatoani* observe his burned thigh and realize his sorry future. Following these terrifying portents, Moteuczoma decided to flee and sought a cave at Cincalco near Chapultepec (a hill west of Tenochtitlan) where he could forever hide. This last act of cowardice is also related by Sahagún (FC:Bk. 12, ch. 9, fig. 23). In Sahagún's version Moteuczoma lacked the resolve to actually leave (see earlier excerpted quotation), but in Durán's account a

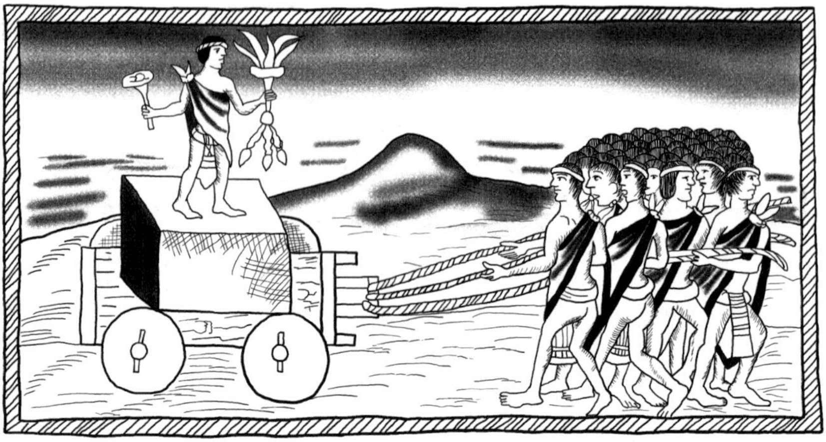

Figure 2.6. *Dragging the Talking Stone from Chalco to Tenochtitlan*, in Diego Durán, *Historia de las Indias de la Nueva España* (1994:plate 51). Drawing by S. Gillespie.

sleeping priest was awakened by a divine voice, telling him that Motecuzoma was indeed fleeing in a canoe across the lake to the west (illustrated in Durán 1994:pl. 52). The priest went after him to shame him into returning to accept his fate. In both episodes a humble and anonymous person brought down the great Moteuczoma.

THE ROLE OF THE OMENS IN THE AZTEC DEFEAT

Using a critical approach, most modern historians have tried by various means to determine the historical accuracy of these signs (e.g., Colston 1985; López Austin 1969) and thereby to understand how they might have affected Moteuczoma and the other native peoples. However, the issue of whether these omens actually occurred had been raised much earlier by the chroniclers themselves, some of whom suggested that the signs were real and were sent by God to signal the coming of Christendom (e.g., Acosta 2002:Bk. VII, ch. 23, 432; Muñoz Camargo 1978:Bk. II, ch. 1, 167). While this opinion is no longer popular in our secular society, it is still commonly held that most or even all of these omens did occur, were interpreted in a negative way, and hence were remembered for generations, in part because the Aztecs were already predisposed to anxious forebodings even before Cortés arrived.

Prescott (1873:1, ch. 6, 220), whose first edition appeared in 1843, was perhaps the first to suggest that rumors of white men in the Caribbean since Columbus's first voyage would have reached the Aztecs. He hypothesized that "[i]n the excited state of their imaginations, prodigies became a familiar occurrence. Or rather, events not very uncommon in themselves, seen through the discolored medium of fear, were easily magnified into prodigies; and the accidental swell of the lake, the appearance of a comet, and the conflagration of a building were all interpreted as the special annunciations of Heaven." Subsequent scholars have repeated this notion that native elites were already on edge because of strange peoples in their vicinity (e.g., Graulich 1994:233; Padden 1967:108; Thomas 1993:40ff), adding the detail that Moteuczoma was particularly dreading the upcoming year 1519 as symbolically associated with the god Quetzalcoatl (Collis 1954:56).

Other historians have suggested that only certain of these events are plausible—namely, those that conform to our understandings of the natural world, such as seeing the comet, the burning of the temples, the flooding of the lake, hearing voices in the night, the dragging of a large stone that fell into the lake, and so forth—and that because they are plausible, they probably did happen. Reasonable explanations have been proposed for some of the other signs as well. The light seen in the night could have been an aurora borealis, the two-headed man could have been Siamese twins (Thomas 1993:43), the woman who died and came back to life in her grave was actually only in a coma (Collis 1954:57). The few remaining non-plausible omens, such as the mirror-bird, have been attributed to "figments of the imagination of someone who had eaten sacred mushrooms" (Thomas 1993:43). Taking a different tack, Serge Gruzinski (1989:27–28) hypothesized that the omens were metaphoric renderings of the dissenting voices of both aristocrats and peasants against the growing domination of Tenochtitlan; hence they include the participation of Nezahualpilli, the Tetzcocan ruler, as well as an anonymous farmer from the Tetzcoco area.

Whatever their origin—actual or fabricated—it is widely accepted that something(s) untoward happened that distressed Moteuczoma and developed into a major contributing factor in the subsequent events of the Spanish *entrada*. In this common opinion, a very strong negative judgment of Aztec society is sometimes exposed: "Such unexplained, awesome events would have struck intense fear into the hearts of a people as ruled by fate as the Mexica" (Berdan 1982:141). R. C. Padden (1967:108) especially emphasized the psychological impact, considering all these portents—real or not—as the "product of mass hysteria" that infected the native population several years before Cortés showed up on the Veracruz coast. He further suggested that "the climate of hysteria that made possible such morbid hallucinating was the symptom of a sick and tortured society that eagerly awaited its own demise" (1967:108). This persistent negative stereotype of native American people is one answer to the first question asked earlier—why Motecuzoma still gets blamed for the Aztec defeat.

Moreover, while much contemporary historiography emphasizes the impact of these omens and portents on the Aztec state of mind, little has been said about the parallel information included in the writings of the Spanish conquistadors and missionary clerics. The Spaniards also claimed to have witnessed miraculous sightings and other happenings interpreted as signs from God that they were destined to be victorious. On the 1518 Juan de Grijalva voyage to explore the Mexican coast, Juan Díaz (1993:14) reported a comet that appeared and settled over a town. He described it as a "miracle" and one of the signs "by which we knew it was God's wish that we settle in that land." Bernal Díaz del Castillo (1994:ch. 34, 56) cited López de Gómara's account (1964:ch. 20, 46–47; see Cortés 1986:455) that St. James and St. Peter miraculously appeared to save the Spaniards in an early battle in Tabasco (on the Gulf Coast) but that as a sinner he was not able to see them. The conquistador Francisco de Aguilar (1993:141) recalled that once when Cortés's horse stumbled during a battle and his men interpreted this as a bad sign, Cortés, "with invincible courage and without a moment's confusion, kept right on going on foot"; that is, he ignored the inauspicious quality of the happening and refused to retreat, the very opposite of the picture of Moteuczoma.[3]

The existence of signs sent by God was integral to medieval Christianity. The Franciscan friars, such as Motolinia, Sahagún, and Mendieta—who avidly collected these omens from their informants—were much given to interpreting God's intentions through these means. As noted earlier, they and others believed Cortés was fulfilling the will of God in bringing Christendom to the New World and would have expected such omens and portents to be sent, even unto the Aztecs (Elliott 1967:55; Lafaye 1976:30–31; Phelan 1970). In addition, the missionary friars are credited with contributing not only an interest in portents but their specific content to their informants. Felipe Fernández-Armesto (1992:292ff.) has suggested that the eight omens in Sahagún's Book 12 were likely copied from three Greek and Latin books available to his chief informants, students in the Colegio de Santa Cruz in Tlaltelolco. In Europe of that era there was a similar recourse to Classical descriptions of omens and portents provided by such writers as Josephus, Plutarch, and Lucan (Fernández-Armesto 1992:293; see also Thomas 1993:42–43), including comets and visions of warring armies in the clouds. Torquemada (1975:Bk. 2, ch. 110) made the connection to the Classical authors in his recounting of Sahagún's eight omens. Fernández-Armesto (1992:295) noted that Sahagún's near-contemporary, William Shakespeare, drew on these same Classical sources to create the auguries of *Julius Caesar*.

Fernández-Armesto thus sides with a minority viewpoint that rejects the a priori notion that Moteuczoma was quaking in fear of the Spaniards as strange beings sent by gods, if not gods themselves. His opinion is shared by Inga Clendinnen (1991) and James Lockhart (1993). The latter two historians observed that in attempting to understand the Conquest, emphasis has always been given to its first phase, up to the Toxcatl massacre and the subsequent *Noche triste*. It is within this period of time that the narratives dwell on omens, the return of Quetzalcoatl, the terror of Moteuczoma, and the magicians and soothsayers—all of which seem to be late constructions (Clendinnen 1991:69, 88–89; Lockhart 1993:18). The reasons for such "unabashed mythic history, a telling of what 'ought' to have happened" (Clendinnen 1991:69), are quite straightforward in their perspective—the need "to explain the outcome of defeat . . . a concern for the construction of a viable and satisfying public history for the conquered" (1991:88–89). Fernández-Armesto (1992:295) arrived at the similar conclusion that the omens were the creation of a people "anxious to understand the conquest in terms of an alien heritage, and to re-express the Aztec experience in the discourse of Renaissance humanism."

In short, the standard portrayal of Moteuczoma decades after his death as fearful, indecisive, and cowardly can be attributed to "the classic reactions of a people after defeat, to blame their leader as a scapegoat" (Lockhart 1993:17), "a post-Conquest scapegoating of a leader who had indeed admitted the Spaniards into his city in life, and so was made to bear the weight of the unforeseeable consequences in death" (Clendinnen 1991:69). The descriptions of a tortured Moteuczoma likely reflected "the attitude of a whole cohort of Mexica smarting under their loss of preeminence and looking for someone to blame. Later generations, in need of symbols, gave both Cortés and Moteucçoma a meaning they hardly had at the time" (Lockhart 1993:18). Here is an explanation for the second question asked previously—the sixteenth-century indigenous blaming of Moteuczoma, although the issue of whether Cortés and Moteuczoma had such symbolic meanings "at the time" is less straightforward.

In this perspective, the omens represent an active response by subjugated peoples to their current circumstances—"the typical attempt of a vanquished group to explain, after the fact, what has happened" (Lockhart 1993:17). Tzvetan Todorov (1985) further explained the post-Conquest invention of these portents as an aspect of the Mesoamerican worldview, which was organized according to cyclical concepts of time such that the present and future must repeat the past. In his opinion, the dominance of cyclical time could ill accommodate the "radically new, entirely unprecedented situation" posed by the Spanish presence (Todorov 1985:87). Fabricating the omens that predicted what would occur was a reasonable recourse because "the present becomes intelligible and at the same time less inadmissible, the moment one can see it already announced in the past" (Todorov 1985:74).

Divination and prophecy form a major category of "imagined nonevents" in Fogelson's (1989) classification, as events that "never happened but could have occurred, or, according to the ethnologic involved, should have happened" (1989:142). Given that the Aztecs had experienced an event so horrific it was unthinkable—the rapid destruction of their most powerful city, Tenochtitlan, under the protection of the god Huitzilopochtli—this could only be the result of supernatural intervention, a major cosmic shake-up (Uchmany 1980:10). The ethnologic required divinely sent signs and portents of what was to come, an ethnologic shared in some ways by both the Aztecs and the Spanish invaders.

Nevertheless, once the portents have been categorized as an "emollient myth" designed for "the construction of a viable and satisfying public history of the conquered" (Clendinnen 1991:89), the Aztecs, and Moteuczoma more particularly, remain in our view as powerless—condemned by the inevitability of what was to come—as if the omens had really happened or their gods had actually turned against them (e.g., Colston 1985:240, 244). Moteuczoma and his people are portrayed as trapped in a worldview that could not accommodate the unexpected—hence the omens were needed later, if only to provide that expectation. In contrast (yet again), Cortés is said to have made adaptation and improvisation to changing circumstances "the very principle of his conduct" (Todorov 1985:87).

In sum, contemporary scholarship provides two stark alternatives to explain the omens and other events that conveyed a sense of supernatural intervention, superstition, and fatalism on the part of the Aztecs. Either there is a great deal of truth to these accounts, on the assumption that the impact they made on Moteuczoma was critical to the subsequent events of the Conquest, or they are the typical rationalizations of a defeated people thereby seen as less equipped to deal with events as they unfolded than their European counterparts. Neither alternative casts the Aztecs in a positive light against their opponents. Moreover, neither opinion gives much consideration to the substantive content and symbolic import of the omens themselves, despite the detail—in some cases quite extraordinary—that envelops them.

AN ETHNO-ETHNOHISTORY OF THE OMENS

A third alternative to account for these omens is to take an ethno-ethnohistorical approach. The happenings, actions, and emotions ascribed to the Aztecs in the later documents represent responses to the colonial situation—complex and emerging processes that came to be represented in narrative form as an iconic sequence of events and nonevents. To cite Terence Turner (1988:242), "To understand the terms in which other cultures have formulated their historical interaction with [European] society is to understand their ethnohistories of us—

to do ethno-ethnohistory." And it is precisely the cultural terms with which the Aztecs incorporated the Spanish into their own theory of history—and the role the omens and portents played in this capacity—that remain understudied.

Few historiographers—or mythographers, for that matter—have looked closely at the detailed descriptions of these omens to ask why they were given their specific form in the various traditions because such a question was irrelevant to their critical agendas. Among those who have, however, the symbolic qualities of these signs become readily apparent. Lockhart (1993:17), for example, called attention to the fact that Sahagún carefully listed eight omens in order; eight was "the canonical number of any set of things in the Nahua world." Stephen Colston (1985:240) observed that they incorporate the four elements of the universe (earth, air, fire, water). Michel Graulich (1994:227–228) took this quality farther, seeing in the omens' serial order the duality of oppositions characteristic of Aztec thought, one that contrasts celestial with terrestrial phenomena (although he also suggested that these were real happenings singled out precisely for their symbolic dualism; this aspect is further developed by Magaloni-Kerpel, Chapter 7, this volume). Even portents and signs that seem to be merely copied from European Classical sources by well-educated natives must nevertheless have had meaning for the Aztecs to have been incorporated into their native historical traditions.

Scott O'Mack (1990) has taken this type of analysis a step farther, observing that the omens should be interpreted as one means by which the Aztecs incorporated the Conquest into their own theories of history. In other words, what the Spaniards did or were believed to have done during the *entrada* and the Conquest subsequently became integrated into the signs and portents that seemingly predicted what they would do.[4] As Todorov (discussed earlier) and others have observed, time in the Mesoamerican worldview is ultimately more cyclical than lineal, and present circumstances are considered less a consequence than a repetition of past events. Nevertheless, the world of the Aztecs was far from being "overdetermined" and dependent on cyclical time to the point of being completely "foreseeable," hence incapable of adaptation and improvisation (contra Todorov 1985:66) when it clashed with unanticipated Spanish invasions. Rather than narrowly insist that the present must duplicate the past, another way to express this temporal aspect of Aztec cosmology is to say that precedence and antiquity are the basis for authority and legitimacy in the present. It was the chief function of the divine rulers, in their preeminent role as lawgivers, to *create* a link between past and present—that is, to establish precedence—through the medium of history. The indigenes' agency and inventiveness in comprehending and reacting to the present by drawing upon the past as a symbolic resource is revealed by careful examination of the "pre-Conquest" omens against the backdrop of analogous events, both earlier in time in Aztec historical traditions as well as during the *entrada* and the battle for Tenochtitlan.

To this end, O'Mack examined the place names associated with the "talking stone" episode, the specific places where it stopped on the journey. He observed that the route along which the stone was moved—from Chalco province in the southeastern corner of the Basin of Mexico up the southern causeway to the entrance to Tenochtitlan, where it fell through a bridge into the water—is exactly the path taken by Cortés when he first traveled to Tenochtitlan, as if the stone had predicted that route. More specifically, the place where the bridge collapsed and the stone fell is Xoloco (Alvarado Tezozomoc 1980:ch. 102, 665; Torquemada 1975:Bk. 2, ch. 79), precisely where Moteuczoma had his first meeting with Cortés (Caso 1956:14; FC Bk. 12, ch. 16). Durán (1994:chs. 66, 74) added further details to link the stone to Cortés through Moteuczoma's actions: when the stone was first dragged to Tenochtitlan, Motecuzoma ordered that all the people of the city should venerate it when it reached Tocititlan, the shrine of the goddess Toci, where the Huexotzincans had earlier burned the temple, taken as a bad omen. Later, when Moteuczoma set out to meet Cortés, he waited for him briefly at Tocititlan before going on to Xoloco. In addition, the same places to which the stone was moved were involved in a much earlier battle between Tenochtitlan and Chalco province during the time of a prior *huey tlatoani* also named Moteuczoma (Durán 1994:ch. 16), indicating that linking even earlier history to the "prophecies" of future events was at work in devising these omens.[5]

Although it is not my purpose here to delve into the complex symbolic significance of all these ominous signs, I call special attention to the links between the omens and Huitzilopochtli, the patron deity of Tenochtitlan. Described as a war god, Huitzilopochtli was also associated with the annual north-south movements of the sun (Gillespie 1999). In terms of the omens, the only direct link to Huitzilopochtli might seem to be the sudden bursting into flames of his temple, Sahagún's second omen. Nevertheless, this association is apparent in some of the details of this event and the other signs as well. The fire at his temple burned the location named Itepeyoc, where the image of Huitzilopochtli was placed during the fifteenth month of the Aztec year, Panquetzaliztli. The state ceremony of that month celebrated the annual rebirth of Huitzilopochtli (FC Bk. 2, ch. 34, app. 192, Bk. 3, ch. 1) in November. It occurred just prior to the winter solstice and marked the rebirth of the sun in the south, which would soon start to move north again, growing stronger each day to herald the coming summer and the main agricultural season (Gillespie 1999).

The bird with the mirror on its head—Sahagún's seventh omen—was also linked to Huitzilopochtli. This water bird, found in the lake, was taken directly to Moteuczoma, who looked into its mirror and first saw stars and then an approaching army before the bird mysteriously disappeared.[6] While most commentators emphasize the forebodings associated with an approaching army of men riding on the backs of what appeared to the Aztecs to be deer, the stars are more important. They were the stars of the "Fire Drill" constellation, called *mamalhuaztli* in Nahuatl (FC Bk. 12, ch. 1, 3, Bk. 8, ch. 6, 18) and *astillejos* (or *mastelejos*) in Spanish. They are usually identified with Caspar and Pollux of the Gemini constellation, stars that move near the Pleiades in the sign of Taurus (FC Bk. 7, app. ch. 3, 60; Sahagún 1989b:33; Milbrath 1999:267). Among later colonial writers who copied this information, only Friar Torquemada (1975:Bk. 2, ch. 110, 235) also identified the stars in the mirror, again as the *astillejos* constellation. He stated that this vision frightened Moteuczoma very much, while Sahagún (FC Bk. 12, ch. 1, 3) wrote that Moteuczoma "took it as an omen of great evil when he saw the stars and the Fire Drill." The *mamalhuatzli* drill is associated explicitly with Huitzilopochtli (FC Bk. 1, app. 67). As for Castor and Pollux, these two bright stars mark the northern extreme of the sun at summer solstice and were in conjunction with the sun on that solstice for over 1,000 years (Milbrath 1999:266). Thus, they too are linked with the annual movements of the sun and can be related to the complex celestial symbolism encapsulated by Huitzilopochtli.

Furthermore, Moteuczoma is said to have received the bird with the mirror (and the two-headed man, the eighth omen) while he was in the building named *Tlillan calmecatl*, roughly translated as "black palace" or "black chamber" (FC, Bk. 8, ch. 6, Bk. 12, ch. 1; Sahagún 1989b:Bk. 12, ch. 1; see also Acosta 2002:Bk. 7, ch. 23; *Codex Ramirez* 1980:79; Muñoz Camargo 1978:Bk. 2, ch. 1; Torquemada 1975:Bk. 2, ch. 110). A number of these late sources attempted to explain why this architectural location was mentioned. Sahagún (1989b) presumed that Moteuczoma was in his "black palace" because he used it as a retreat in times of adversity and sadness. Others picked up on this theme, and both Tovar and Acosta went so far as to say that Moteuczoma was sequestered in his black palace because his sorrow by then was so great, having interpreted the many omens as divine warnings.

However, the *Tlillan calmecatl* is described in both Sahagún's (FC Bk. 2, app. 182) and Durán's writings as a temple dedicated to the goddess Cihuacoatl. It was so-called because the inner chamber was always kept completely dark (Durán 1971:217), not because it was painted black (as Sahagún and others presumed). This was the place where the kings of Tenochtitlan were inaugurated, becoming the human incarnation of Huitzilopochtli (Durán 1994:297, 313). Durán (1971:217) stated that this temple was located adjacent to that of Huitzilopochtli because Cihuacoatl was Huitzilopochtli's sister. And Cihuacoatl was the wailing woman whose voice was heard in the night—Sahagún's sixth omen (explicitly identified as the source of the voice in Bk. 8, ch. 1, but not in Bk. 12). Such behavior was typical of this deity; elsewhere, Sahagún (FC Bk. 1, ch. 6, 11) stated that "[b]y night she walked weeping, wailing; also she was an omen of war."[7] Note that sisters of both Huitzilopochtli and Moteuczoma are among the personified omens.

As for the talking stone that would not budge, this omen was also linked to Huitzilopochtli. Durán (1994:477) stated that Moteuczoma ordered a new stone to be made for the "Flaying of Men" sacrifice, which would be a *temalacatl,* a large flat disk ornamented with the sun design upon which a captured warrior would stand to battle an Aztec adversary. However, Alvarado Tezozomoc (1980:ch. 102, 662) stated that it was destined to be a great sacrificial stone for the temple of Huitzilopochtli. Torquemada (1975:Bk. 2, ch. 79) and Tovar (*Codex Ramirez* 1980:77–78) intimated the same, that it was to be the principal stone of sacrifice. Durán, who provided the greatest detail concerning this event, elaborated how the stone's miraculous return to its place of origin terrified Moteuczoma, who went to Chalco to see it and make sacrifices. Afterward, Moteuczoma ordered his stonemasons to complete a different task instead—to carve his likeness in bas-relief on the face of the hill at Chapultepec, on the western side of the lake (Durán 1994:481). Chapultepec is also the location associated with the cave where Moteuczoma later attempted to hide to escape the doom that awaited him (Durán 1994:487; Sahagún 1981:Bk. 12, 35). Significantly, another document (a copy of the text of the *Codex Tudela*; Gomez de Orozco 1945:63) conflates these two episodes. It includes the story of the talking stone that broke through the bridge at the southern end of the city but states that this stone was being moved to Chapultepec to serve as the basis for Moteuczoma's portrait.

My point in bringing up these details is to demonstrate how the omens were directed very personally toward Moteuczoma. The ominous objects were taken first to Moteuczoma, after which they vanished. Moteuczoma personally played a ball game against Nezahualpilli to determine whether Nezahualpilli's prophecies would come to pass. It was Moteuczoma's sister who rose from the dead to tell him his reign was about to end. Moteuczoma was burned on his thigh in a vision. Moteuczoma ordered the stone to be moved, which at first would not budge and then refused to move further than Xoloco, where Moteuczoma would later meet Cortés. Moteuczoma attempted to flee, agonized over where he could hide, set out by canoe, and was brought back to face his destiny. These very personalized happenings are unlike the comets, lights in the sky, and visions in the clouds that characterize omens in European Classical tradition.

Furthermore, while nameless others are said to have been frightened by these portents, Moteuczoma's sheer terror is described in unrelenting fashion (especially in FC Book 12; see also Durán 1994; Motolinia 1970; Tovar's *Codex*

Ramirez 1980). There is more to these descriptions than just a man in fear of losing his throne or even his life. The close connections of a number of omens to Huitzilopochtli (and to gods related to Huitzilopochtli) further indicate the seriousness of what was at stake. Moteuczoma was a divine king, the incarnation of Huitzilopochtli (Cortés 1986:467; Durán 1994:ch. 53, 398, ch. 54, 406). These retrodictive (rather than predictive) signs demonstrate that the threat to Moteuczoma extended to Huitzilopochtli, and thus they impacted not just one man or the Aztec peoples but the maintenance of cosmic order itself.[8]

ANTHROPOMORPHIZING THE CONQUEST

The omens are therefore much more than imagined nonevents, occurrences that should have happened to provide a convenient scapegoat for the defeated Aztecs, divine justification for Spanish subjugation, and, more generally, a satisfactory historical explanation for the fall of Tenochtitlan. These signs were employed as a *mechanism* to very directly and personally involve Moteuczoma in what was actually a long sequence of complex happenings over a vast landscape involving thousands of players, beyond anyone's control. They reference an impending cosmic disaster while simultaneously centering it on one very important individual, even to the degree of laying all the fault for what occurred on his character. Moteuczoma's portrayals represent an oxymoronic mixture of arrogance, tyranny, and decisive, terrible punishments in dealing with his own people alongside cowardice, meekness, and indecision when dealing with the Spaniards. All of these details point to a significant aspect insufficiently addressed by historians, despite the emphasis in subsequent historiography on the contrast between Cortés and Moteuczoma—namely, the anthropomorphization of the Conquest. From the Aztec point of view, Moteuczoma literally embodied the state and hence its destiny.

I use the term "embodiment" very specifically because it is Moteuczoma's body that became a focus of attention in descriptions of the omens and their effects. He was burned on his thigh. He ordered his likeness sculpted at Chapultepec hill. And he attempted to flee his city, but only after he discovered that the Spaniards were enquiring about him in the most personal way—asking questions about his body, his appearance, his age (FC Bk. 12, ch. 9, 25–26; *Codex Ramirez* 1980:83). Completely terrified by this news, he tried to escape but found he no longer had the strength to act; he was immobilized. Like the talking stone that foretold his doom—and would go no further than Xoloco at the edge of the city—Moteuczoma could not move. And it was at that point that he was said to finally give up, to decide he could do no more than simply submit himself to what would happen.

Significantly, Moteuczoma's body was the subject of certain prohibitions, which were remarked by several of the conquistadors who wrote accounts of the Conquest, including Cortés. At their first meeting at Xoloco, Cortés moved to embrace Moteuczoma but was prevented from doing so by two lords who held the emperor's arms on either side (Cortés 1986:84; Díaz del Castillo 1994: ch. 88, 161); one of the lords was his brother Cuitlahuac, ruler of Itztapalapa, and the other was also a kinsman, Cacama, ruler of Tetzcoco. A further restriction was for anyone other than the highest lords to look at Moteuczoma in the face (e.g., Aguilar 1993:146–147; Díaz del Castillo 1994:ch. 88, 161; López de Gómara 1964:ch. 65, 139). Durán (1994:ch. 53, 398) recounted once asking an old man about Moteuczoma's facial characteristics, height, and appearance; the man replied that he could not honestly answer, never having seen his face, for it would have been death to have done so. But the Spaniards were not obliged to obey these rules, something that threatened Moteuczoma's ritual, and hence political, status. As Clendinnen (1991:75) astutely observed, their acts of gazing at, even eventually touching Moteuczoma contributed to his "desacralization," a process that accelerated when Cortés took physical custody of him. Such actions were emphasized by the native informants of Sahagún (FC Bk. 12, ch. 16, 45), who reported that at the first meeting at Xoloco, the Spaniards "grasped [Moteuczoma] by the hand. Already they went leading him by it. They caressed him with their hands to make their love known to him. And the Spaniards looked at him; they each looked at him thoroughly. They were continually active on their feet; they continually mounted, they continually dismounted in order to look at him."

With the diminishment of his sacred status came a loss of political power, the power to command obedience from the other lords. In fact, a few Spanish sources state that a successor, his brother Cuitlahuac, was designated ruler in his stead while Moteuczoma was still alive (Aguilar 1993:152; Díaz del Castillo 1994:ch. 126, 252). In another account it was his ultimate successor, Cuauhtemoc, who is said to have called Moteuczoma the "woman of the Spaniards" and to have proclaimed to a gathered crowd, "we do not want to obey him because he is not our king," just before a volley of arrows and stones killed the *huey tlatoani*. Although Cuauhtemoc was only eighteen, according to Tovar, the people already wanted to make him their ruler instead of Moteuczoma (*Codex Ramirez* 1980:89). And, of course, it was Moteuczoma's belief that he was about to be replaced—not by a younger successor but by the original inventor of kingship, Quetzalcoatl—that is said in later post-Conquest accounts to have contributed greatly to his "terror and apathy." It is hard to imagine a more dire situation—which is what is represented in these various documents—than for the cosmos to have been so threatened by the weakness and tyranny of a single king that kingship itself (and with it the cosmos) would have to be started anew, which is exactly what happened when the Spanish Crown took control of New Spain.

Moteuczoma's body also comes into play concerning his death in late June 1520 while in Spanish custody. There is a striking difference of opinion as to who killed him, with most native sources (including native informants of Spanish authors) insisting the Spaniards stabbed or strangled him, while most Hispanic sources state that he was killed by his own people, usually by stoning while attempting to speak to them on the Spaniards' behalf (see summary of these contradictions in FC Book 12, ch. 23, 65n). Díaz del Castillo (1994:ch. 126, 253) precisely locates where on Moteuczoma's body three stones struck and did mortal damage: on the head, arm, and leg; other sources mention the stone that hit his head. It is logical that Moteuczoma and the other lords in Spanish captivity would be killed at the point where Cortés determined he must escape Tenochtitlan as quickly and quietly as possible, while angry crowds cut off their supplies and daily threatened the Spaniards. Their anger is also a logical outcome of the massacre ordered by Pedro de Alvarado that prevented the main ceremony of the fifth month, Toxcatl, from being carried out in May of that year. As Sahagún explicitly recorded, the Toxcatl massacre was a turning point in events for the Aztecs (see earlier discussion). As a result, the invaders were forced to abandon the city, with disastrous results, on the night of June 30.

But in addition to such a logical cause-and-effect relationship among these events, we need to examine the further implications of Spanish interference with Aztec religious practices at this specific point in their calendar. The Toxcatl ceremony, which coincided with the first solar zenith passage, celebrated the annual ascension to power of Huitzilopochtli following his birth in the month of Panquetzaliztli, and FC Book 12 has multiple illustrations of the elaborate making and veneration of his image to be used in the rite. The failure to culminate this ceremony obviously would have called into question the fates of the cosmos more generally and of Tenochtitlan more specifically as the most important city under Huitzilopochtli's protection. Furthermore, Moteuczoma was supposed to have appeared at a precise moment in the ritual to renew his metaphysical link to his tutelary god (FC Bk. 2, ch. 24, 73), an annual reaffirmation of his sovereignty. However, he was prevented from doing so, which more immediately threatened his legitimacy as ruler of Tenochtitlan and its domain.

As with other divine kings symbolically linked to the sun—for example, in pharaonic Egypt, sub-Saharan Africa, Southeast Asia, and Hawaii (Beidelman 1966; Evans-Pritchard 1948; Feeley-Harnik 1985; Frazer 1940; Richards 1969; Sahlins 1985)—Moteuczoma's sacred status likely changed with the pulsing of the seasons. The Aztec emperor, like his counterparts elsewhere, "instantiate[d] different major gods or groups of their particularizations according to a precise ritual calendar . . . and also according to the vicissitudes of his reign" (Valeri [1985:142] for Hawaii). In the Aztec case, the changing relationship of the brother deities most closely associated with rulership—Tezcatlipoca (patron of Tetzcoco) and Huitzilopochtli (patron of Tenochtitlan)—as manifest in the annual calendar was preeminent to Moteuczoma's ritual status (Gillespie 1999).

It is also conceivable that, as with other divine kings, if Motecuzoma were seen as weak, his weakness would threaten the entire society, if not the totality of the cosmos itself. The ethnologic required that he be put to death and replaced so that kingship itself would not be further threatened. Indeed, it ultimately matters little whether the Spaniards or the Aztecs killed Moteuczoma; however, regicide for this purpose was more typically the act of the king's people.[9] Sir James Frazer discussed this topic at length in his chapter of *The Golden Bough* entitled "The Killing of the Divine King": "[I]f the course of nature is dependent on the man-god's [divine king's] life, what catastrophes may not be expected from the gradual enfeeblement of his powers and their final extinction in death? There is only one way of averting these dangers. The man-god must be killed, as soon as he shows symptoms that his powers are beginning to fail, and his soul must be transferred to a vigorous successor before it has been seriously impaired by the threatened decay" (Frazer 1940:265). Thus, in some Aztec histories we read of Cuitlahuac replacing Motecuzoma while he is most vulnerable but has not yet died or of Cuauhtemoc playing a direct role in denying Moteuczoma his status as a powerful figure to be unquestionably obeyed.

Finally, Moteuczoma's body continued to be an object of attention even after his death, as seen in the conflicting accounts of its disposal. Durán (1994:ch. 76, 545) reported two different versions—one that Moteuczoma received a rich funeral that lasted for days and was attended by many lords and the other that his body was unceremoniously cremated and his children and wives executed. The conquistadors' accounts typically state that his body was carried or even thrown out of their palace (e.g., Aguilar 1993:154; Cortés 1986:132; Díaz del Castillo 1994:ch. 127, 253). Sahagún (FC Bk. 12, ch. 23, 65), whose informants provided the most details, related that the Spaniards cast his body out from their palace at a place called Teoayoc, and people took it to Copulco, where it was cremated. As his body burned, it smelled foul. and the people castigated him and cried out their anguish and disapproval. The *Codex Aubin* (1963:59), however, relates a curious story that a man named Apanecatl took up Moteuczoma's body on his back and carried it to three different towns before the corpse was accepted and finally hidden; a man of that same name is said to have carried the image of Huitzilopochtli on his back in early Mexica history (Gillespie 1989:157).

All of these details suggest that the integrity, sanctity, and representations of Moteuczoma's body were essential not just to his own well-being but also to that of the kingdom he ruled and, ultimately, to that of the cosmos itself. In other ways, sixteenth-century documents indicate that, for all intents and purposes, the divine person of Moteuczoma literally did represent Tenochtitlan and the entirety of its domain. The name "Moteuczoma" was commonly used to refer to what we only much later called the Aztec Empire (Gillespie 1998:245), while a non-personal designation—the kingdom of Culhua—is rarely mentioned (e.g., Cortés 1986:173). Again, this is in keeping with the precepts of divine kingship elsewhere. As Valerio Valeri (1985:146) explained for the similar ideology underpinning Hawaiian divine kingship: "Since the king is identified with the cosmos, a fortiori he is identified with his kingdom, that is, with the land and its inhabitants. In fact, he personifies them; his kingdom is assimilated with his body or, what amounts to the same thing, is considered his child. . . . By appropriating the king's body, it is thus possible to appropriate his realm."

CONCLUSION

The blame assigned to Moteuczoma in the later recasting of the events of the *entrada* and the Conquest is not simply the result of a European historiography in which "great men" drive history, exemplified by Prescott's popular nineteenth-century history of the Conquest. Although weakness is a part of Moteuczoma's enigmatic character in the Spanish accounts, the native historical traditions provide the greatest criticism of his actions and inaction, as well as the most detailed descriptions of his dread and the reasons for it. These "remembrances" and reconstructions of history took shape as part of the post-Conquest processes of accommodation to invasion and subjugation. They incorporate various imagined epitomizing nonevents, things that ought to have happened, which have a certain logic in both Aztec and Spanish cosmologies and theories of history.

In particular, the omens and the prophecy of a returning god who would replace him served to focus the unfolding events in a very immediate and utterly personal way upon the body and sanctity of the Aztec emperor. They formed a means to directly fault him for this disaster, but then, as a divine king, the maintenance of cosmic and social order *was* his personal responsibility. Moteuczoma embodied the Aztec state in ways our secular society finds difficult to comprehend. If the empire and its capital city fell, it must have been because of his failings, but a strong successor should have set things right again. Cuauhtemoc did indeed attempt to fulfill that role, never yielding until absolutely everything was lost—to the great perplexity of Cortés (Clendinnen 1991)—and he remains a hero to the Mexican people today.

NOTES

1. Prescott (1873:I, ch. 6, 219) refers to the prophecy of the return of Quetzalcoatl and suggests that it was at hand, as indicated by "various preternatural occurrences, reported with more or less detail by all the most ancient historians." He goes on to list some of the reported omens, drawing them from Sahagún, Muñoz Camargo, and Acosta, among others. He also cites Friar Bartolomé de Las Casas's sixteenth-century *Apologética historia de las Indias* (Bk. 3, ch. 120): "segun sus próphetas agoreros le avian certificado, que su estado é rriquezas y prosperidad avia de perezer dentro de pocos años por çiertas gentes que avian de venir en sus dias, que de su felicidad lo derrocase, y por esto vivia siempre con temor y en tristeça y sobresaltado." Here Prescott also refers to Classical European sources, especially Lucan on Roman omens (1873:I, ch. 6, 220). He admits in a footnote that he omitted from this category of probable events interpreted as omens the resurrection of Moteuczoma's sister, Papantzin, as given in eighteen-century historian Franciso Javier Clavigero's account (whose source was the early-seventeenth-century *Monarquía indiana* of Friar Torquemada, discussed later in text).

2. Motolinia's description of the vision of armed men in the sky is repeated by Torquemada (1975:Bk. 2, ch. 110), who placed it in the year 1511. The latter two celestial omens (the rising fire and the smoke in the East) appear in the *Codex Telleriano-Remensis* (1995:fol. 42r, 1509, fol. 42v, 1512) and the parallel *Codex Ríos* (1996:fol. 87r, 87v). Similar information is depicted in two other parallel late-sixteenth-century pictorial documents, *Codex Aubin* (1963:78, for 1509) and *Histoire Mexicaine* (1998:fol. 14v) for the years 1509–1510. They are also mentioned in Chimalpahin's (1965:231–232) *Séptima Relación* (also for the years 1509–1510; more briefly in his *Tercera Relación* for 1510 [1965:120]) and Muñoz Camargo's (1978:Bk. 2, ch. 1) *Historia de Tlaxcala*, in the form of a bright cloud and a windstorm (although the last two authors reverse the order of these omens). Ixtlilxochitl's *Historia de la nación chichimeca* (1977:II, ch. 72, 181–182) speaks of the great light or fire that rose in a pyramidal shape in 1510 but only mentions, and does not further list, the numerous other signs and portents that announced the ruin and total destruction of all the land. The text of the *Codex Tudela* (Gomez de Orozco 1945:63) describes the smoke that rose in the mornings but says that it occurred in the year 1519, and this document also includes the talking stone omen (discussed later).

3. It has also been suggested that during the prolonged *entrada*, if any people were likely to have been "jittery and psychologically insecure," it would have been the Spaniards, trapped far from home in an alien and menacing environment with no clear way out (Fernández-Armesto 1992:301).

4. The same process happened in another world area two and a half centuries later, following British Captain James Cook's voyage to the Hawaiian Islands. Cook, like Cortés, was taken to be a god by the native peoples, possibly the one known as Lono. As Marshall Sahlins (1982:85, 1985:31) has shown, the Hawaiian rituals that could be interpreted as evidence for this mistaken identity were elaborated only *after* Cook's visit (and his death at the hands of the Hawaiians), becoming an "iconic representation of Cook's voyage" purposely forged to cement that identification rather than a mere coincidence.

5. Colston (1985:247) noted that the talking stone from Chalco was bound with seven ropes, while the drunken man from Chalco was bound with eight ropes, indicating

some symbolic connection between these two omens, even though they typically appear in different sources. The profound importance of Chalco as elaborated in these omens in terms of its historical links to Tenochtitlan and to the Conquest events cannot be further pursued here.

6. Furst (1995:32) identified the bird as the purple gallinule (*Porphyrula martinica* L.), called *cuatezcatl*, or "mirror-head," in Nahuatl. Sahagún's FC (Bk. 11, ch. 2, 32) describes it as a dove-sized migratory water bird, light blue in body color, with a round patch (of different color) on the crown of its head that was considered to be like a mirror. This bird was a sign of war, and it was said that one who captured it gazed into its "mirror." If he were to be unlucky in war, he would see himself taken captive, but if he were to have good fortune, he would see himself dragging his foe instead. While this folklore certainly may have played a role in the bird of omen brought before Moteuczoma—and the bird pictured in FC Book 8 is light blue—that bird is never identified to species. It is consistently described as the size of a crane, brown or ashen-colored (FC Bk. 12, ch. 1, Bk. 8, ch. 6; Muñoz Camargo 1978:Bk. 2, ch. 1; Torquemada 1975:Bk. 2, ch. 110). Acosta (2002:Bk. 7, ch. 23, 431) stated it was "the size and color of a crane but of a shape that was odd and outlandish." However, the Spanish version of Sahagún's FC (1981:Bk. 8, ch. 6, 292) describes the bird as the size and color of an eagle, one of the bird avatars of Huitzilopochtli.

7. Three other gods closely associated with Huitzilopochtli—Tezcatlipoca, Xiuhteuctli, and Toci—were also the subjects of omens, most explicitly the mysterious burning of Xiuhteuctli's temple, the "drunken Chalcan" identified as Tezcatlipoca, and the burning of the shrine of Toci at Tocititlan. Further explanation of the close symbolic linkages of Huitzilopochtli to these deities is beyond the bounds of this chapter (but see Gillespie 1999).

8. With Scott O'Mack, I have elsewhere (Gillespie and O'Mack 1991) developed the evidence that Cortés was likened to Huitzilopochtli, at least up to the time of the Toxcatl massacre. See also Cortés (1986:468).

9. In several accounts of Aztec historical traditions, earlier rulers of Tenochtitlan—Chimalpopoca and Tizoc, who are depicted as weak kings—were poisoned by their own people and replaced by more vigorous and successful kings (Gillespie 1989:16).

3

The Hero as Rhetor

Hernán Cortés's Second and Third Letters to Charles V

Viviana Díaz Balsera

Hernán Cortés (1485–1547) is one of the most legendary and controversial figures in the annals of early modern European and American colonial history. His inconceivable Conquest of Mexico with a few hundred Spanish soldiers and thousands of indigenous allies became a paradigm of heroism, ingenuity, and atrocity within his own lifetime.[1] Dauntless, bold, and with seemingly inexhaustible energy and an unswerving intent, he managed to subdue the greatest military power in Mesoamerica at the time, whose tributary states extended from central Mexico to the Peninsula of Yucatán. Penned by Cortés himself, the Second and Third Letters to Emperor Charles V narrate this colossal and violent Conquest that would change the destiny of civilizations. Able to grapple with the immensity of their epic subject matter not only at a descriptive level but also rhetorically, Cortés's letters are powerful pieces of writing. Thus, besides their value as historical and testimonial documents, they are also vital cultural texts. In this chapter I focus on Hernán Cortés's literary craft not only to show the rhetorical feats of the soldier but also to demonstrate why the Second and Third Letters to the emperor occupy a crucial place in the founding discourses about the New World.

In the Second Letter (1520), in which Cortés seeks to gain the favor and support of the emperor, he brilliantly constructs his own image as the supreme actor of a military campaign that led to the possession of the marvelous. The conquered city of Mexico-Tenochtitlan is implicitly portrayed in the Second Letter as the embodiment of Europe's most audacious dreams of faraway lands of unimaginable bounty. While the Second Letter has been frequently studied by literary critics because of its dramatic pace, its political treatment of prodigy, and the epic dimension of Cortés's self-portrayal,[2] the Third Letter (1522) has received undeservedly scant attention. More limited in its thematic range of action than the Second Letter, the Third Letter nonetheless registers how in winning back Mexico-Tenochtitlan, the author-hero of unbending intent was to lose it forever. It tells the story of unbreakable Mexica resistance in the face of the cataclysmic fall of their city to the Spanish and indigenous allied forces. It conveys the horror of a mode of annihilation heretofore unknown to the Christian world. I contend that only when the Second and Third letters are read together can the full impact of their double founding vision of the New World as the site of the marvelous and the horrific be disclosed. Vested with the immediacy of having been authored by the principal actor of the events at the time they were taking place, the letters of Hernán Cortés produce tales of uncanny plenitude and terror, domination and resistance, pain, might, and utter loss at the limits of the European imagination.

Before becoming a world-famous conquistador, both celebrated and vilified by his contemporaries, Hernán Cortés was just a shrewd colonist in Cuba, favored by the island's governor, Diego Velázquez. After two failed expeditions to the Yucatan Peninsula, during which the Spaniards received news of an immensely rich inland civilization, in 1518 a greedy Velázquez sought royal license to organize a third expedition and appointed Cortés its captain. In an unexpected flurry of activity, Cortés started buying ships, recruiting soldiers and sailors, storing food, getting firearms, procuring lavish objects for exchange, and sending Velázquez the bills. Angry at the high cost of the preparations and suspicious of Cortés's eagerness in putting everything together, Velázquez ordered his captain arrested. But it was too late. Cunning from the start, Cortés had befriended high-ranking officials and even relatives of Velázquez, and he was able to sail off to Mexico with ships, sailors, soldiers, horses, and all. Thus, when Cortés sat down to write his Second Letter to Emperor Charles V, he was a fugitive of the law. Cortés knew very well that since Velázquez had powerful influence at court, he would be accused of *alzamiento,* the Spanish legal term for any rebellious act against the king's law. In addition, the captain started to write shortly after his expulsion from Tenochtitlan on the *Noche triste,* or Night of Sorrows, a catastrophe during which he lost more than half his Spanish army to the Mexica. Thus, Cortés had a formidable rhetorical challenge in front of him. By virtue of the linguistic powers of his letter, the fugitive captain had to convince the king of his unswerving loyalty in spite of more than one insubordinate act. He had also to persuade His Majesty that it was in his utmost interest to legitimize a controversial enterprise on the verge of failing, and he had to move the king to provide material support to rescue it and put it back on track.

As is well-known, Cortés rose to the occasion, showing himself to be as much a consummate strategist of the word as he was of war. Commentators of Cortés's letters to Charles V have agreed that they are superbly crafted. Some have proposed that they are "splendid fictions" (Clendinnen 1991:68); others have pointed out that he almost invariably chose the "right word, the precise turn of phrase" (Coronado 1946:xii; translation mine), that he brought together power and the capacity to represent (Checa 1986:191), that "he excludes anything that cannot be suited to his objective . . . and carefully reworks the material selected for inclusion" (Pastor 1992:72) to obtain favor and fame. The concrete historical context of Spanish imperialist expansionism in the so-called New World made way for Cortés's narrative junction as protagonist, witness, and historian of great lived events. He even had an illustrious precursor in Latin antiquity: Julius Caesar's famous commentaries written to the Roman Senate in between battles in the conquest of Gaul. Wittingly or unwittingly, Cortés engaged the humanist imperative of the *imitatio* of the Greek-Latin models as he narrated events in which he was the principal actor (Díaz Balsera 1989:220).

Although both letters display Cortés's mastery of rhetoric, the second has higher stakes riding on an immediate response to its verbal powers. As stated earlier, the Second Letter tells the story of great and strange events leading to the possession of an object of European desire by a hero of unflinching resolve. But then, the precious object is lost. The burden of the text was to convey to its royal addressee overwhelming images of the heroic, the marvelous, and the pathetic, which were intended to nullify any looming questions about the hero's legitimacy and gather necessary support for the retrieval of the supreme lost object: Mexico-Tenochtitlan.[3] The Third Letter, on the other hand, is a magnificent narrative about the gruesome destruction of the great city. Its rhetorical challenges were of a more elegiac nature, since the coveted object was gone forever and the horrific spectacle of death had chastened desire.

One way in which Cortés achieves the effect of the heroic in both letters is by following strict chronological order in his narration. Although the act of writing comes months after many of the narrated events have taken place, seldom does the narrator anticipate what is coming or give any "synthetic or summarizing comment" (Merrim 1986:73) on what has been left behind. This temporal model meets the legalistic conventions of what the text claims to be, namely, a testimonial account, or *relación*.[4] Additionally, it cuts across the epic genre, as the latter tells the great deeds of a quasi-mythical hero who "performs superhuman exploits in battle or in marvelous voyages," who is protected by the gods, and whose unprecedented feats change the course of nations and civilizations (Baldick 1990:70). With an unmatched sense of heroic drama and suspense, the events are represented as if they were unfolding right in front of the reader's eyes. By never anticipating what the narrator already knows at the moment of the narration and by, in fact, being represented as written in the middle of military operations destined to re-conquest Tenochtitlan, Cortés's letter meets the epic convention of the *medias res*, of being in the middle of things. His heroic frame of mind is portrayed more powerfully this way, since in most difficult and extreme circumstances the captain is represented as not knowing what the outcome of the events will be.

And yet, the tone of the letters is quite temperate and restrained. Unlike the famous soldier of humble origins, Bernal Díaz del Castillo (1632), who is given to outbursts of self-praise and admiration in his monumental *Historia verdadera de la conquista de la Nueva España,* Cortés as a narrator is usually cool, focused, and determined.[5] The initial battles against the Tlaxcalans, in which Spaniards were overwhelmingly outnumbered by natives, are narrated in a dispassionate, almost detached manner:

> When night fell the enemy began to come down through two valleys, thinking that they were unobserved and could draw close to us the better to accomplish their purpose. But as I was well prepared I saw them, and it seemed to me that it would be disadvantageous to allow them to reach the camp; for at night they would be unable to see the damage my people inflicted on them and would be all the more intrepid. . . . Moreover, I was afraid they might set fire to the camp, which would have been so disastrous that none of us would have escaped. I therefore determined to ride out to meet them with all the horsemen to frighten and scatter them so they would be unable to reach the camp. . . .
>
> When we had rested somewhat, I went out one night, after inspecting the first watch, with a hundred foot soldiers, our Indian allies and the horsemen; and one league from the camp five of the horses fell and would go no further. . . . And although all those who were with me in my company urged me to return, for it was an evil omen, I continued on my way secure in the belief that God is more powerful than Nature. (Cortés 1986:61–62)

As we can see, control, restraint, and clarity of mind are enacted at the level of the enunciation of the narrative, as well as at the diegetic level of the narrated events.[6] Cortés does not doubt or hesitate for an instant in this situation, fraught with danger. Endowed with a privileged Christian faith, he casts himself as "a model of prescience" (Pastor 1992:86), able to foresee and plan for everything with an inexhaustible presence of mind. The disjunction between the impassive tone and the extreme danger of the narrated events again responds to the conventions of the unexcitable, legalistic language of the *relación* while at the same time conferring on Cortés epic dignity and aura. It is well-known that for Aristotle the most important use of rhetoric was to find the right means of expression for a particular situation. In the case of a hero, it would be unworthy to appear too frantic about the extraordinary deeds undertaken. The dispassionate and temperate tone is thus rhetorically appropriate for a narration of feats by the hero himself. It confers upon him further glory because it dramatizes yet another conquest: that of the vanity and elation that formidable deeds, along with the greatness of writing them effectively, would produce in any other man (Díaz Balsera 1989:222–223). Finally, this dispassionate tone also allows Cortés to show his fealty to the king. As critics have argued, Cortés depicts his depicted self in these letters as emptied of any personal ambition, purpose, or intention that may not fully coincide with the interests of the sovereign (Merrim 1986:63). In a last turn of the screw, Cortés's temperate tone shows off his strategic mastery as narrator, which reproduces his strategic mastery as conqueror of Mexico at the level of the story. This mirror effect creates an illusion of self-referentiality that adds credibility and authority to the story.

Another key passage that displays Cortés's calculated rhetoric is the one in which he convinces the Spaniards in Tlaxcala not to give up the enterprise in spite of the odds against them. Although this is not stated in the text, Cortés had lost 55 of his 300 Spanish soldiers in battles with the obdurate Tlaxcalans (Martínez 1990:214). Coming back to the fortress after raiding a nearby town, he overhears the Spaniards conspiring and complaining about the extreme dangers they faced. Cortés apparently comes out from hiding and tries to persuade them to go on:

> And I encouraged them by reminding them that they were Your Highnesses's vassals and that never at any time had Spaniards been found wanting and that we were in a position to win for Your Majesty the greatest dominions and kingdoms in the world. Moreover, as Christians we were obliged to wage war against the enemies of our Faith; and thereby we would win glory in the next world and, in this, greater honor and renown than any generation before our time. . . . I told them other things which occurred to me of this nature, with which and Your Highnesses's Royal favor, they were much encouraged and determined to follow my intentions and to do what I wished, which was to complete the enterprise that I had begun. (Cortés 1986:63)

In this passage Cortés deploys the themes of a providential conception of history, a Spanish universal empire, and a holy war against infidels. But such themes do not function in the text only as the ideological contents of the hero's beliefs. They are represented as rhetorical devices cleverly manipulated by Cortés to persuade the restive Spaniards to go on. Since the passage concludes by affirming that the latter did finally surrender to Cortés's will, it lends itself to be tested for its testimonial truth value. When Cortés represents himself trying to convince his soldiers and later claims that he, in fact, succeeded in persuading them with the arguments deployed, the reader can judge the degree of credibility he has as chronicler in this scene without ever abandoning the text. The more effective Cortés is at representing his rhetorical success over his soldiers, the more credibility and legitimacy the passage will obtain as testimony of the captain's alleged leadership. Indeed, the seductive, diegetic eloquence of the captain cannot be adequately represented without the eloquence of the chronicler. The power of Cortés's rhetoric in this passage lies again in the challenge of its self-referentiality. Thus, it does not even matter whether Cortés actually addressed the Spaniards with the Renaissance topics he discusses in the passage. What matters is that the way Cortés represents himself as convincing the Spaniards must be convincing to the reader. What matters is that the narrator in the text exhibits in all his narratological choices the strategic and linguistic brilliancy he attributes to his narrated self.[7]

On November 8, 1519, one month after having subdued the Tlaxcalans and made them the Spaniards' staunchest allies and barely two weeks after the bloody massacre of Cholula, Cortés made his entrance into the great city of Tenochtitlan. The latter sat in the midst of Lake Texcoco and served as fearful evidence of the Mexica's preponderance, might, and tenacity. Cortés's small Spanish army consisted of about 400 soldiers led by horsemen, then harquebusiers, crossbowmen, pikemen, and swordsmen, followed by 1,000 Tlaxcalans carrying cannons and supplies (Marks 1993:123; Martínez 1990:236). At the junction where the causeways of Iztapalapa and Coyoacán came together to lead into the Mexican floating city, Cortés was received by 1,000 noblemen, or *pipiltin,* who one by one, without haste or hurry, knelt in front of him, touched the ground with one hand, and kissed it as a sign of welcome. Walking further down into the straight causeway "as wide as two lances and well built so that eight horsemen can ride it abreast" (Cortés 1986:83), the Spaniards came upon 200 *pipilitin* of even higher rank than the previous thousand, standing in two orderly columns. In the midst of them, Moteuczoma descended from his litter. Leaning on his nephew and his half-brother, who flanked him, the great *tlatoani* (Mexica king) came forth to greet his obstinate guest Cortés. Not surprisingly, this momentous encounter that would change the destiny of peoples and civilizations was recorded in detail by Cortés and all subsequent chroniclers and historians of the Conquest of Mexico, as well as by visual artists, both native and European.[8]

Shortly after having been lavishly received and lodged in one of Moteuczoma's palaces, Cortés took the Mexica ruler as his prisoner. He justified this illegitimate act to Charles V by claiming that in this way he secured his men's safety, the Mexica Empire, and the interests of the Spanish monarch. A few days into his captivity, Moteuczoma called the lords of many principal cities and ordered them to give themselves over as subjects to the Spanish captain. Cortés depicts Moteuczoma as formally ceding the Mexica Empire to him in a public speech because the *tlatoani* believed the captain was a vassal of a descendant of the legitimate lord of the land, Topiltzin Quetzalcoatl. Yolanda Martínez San-Miguel and Ricardo Padrón have pointed out how only when Moteuczoma and the land are represented as under his control does Cortés finally engage in the *ekphrasis,* or vivid description, of the coveted Tenochtitlan (Martínez–San Miguel 2000:114, 116; Padrón 2004:108).[9] This is undoubtedly the culminating moment of the Second Letter. Cortés starts off with the size and geographic features of the province and then provides those of the lake in which the great city of Tenochtitlan sits, extending its three two-mile-wide causeways into the mainland. He moves on to the market square of Tlatelolco, where all that was produced in the land was exchanged by more than 60,000 people every day:

> There is a street where they sell game and birds of every species found in the land: chickens, partridges and quails, wild ducks, fly-catchers, widgeons, turtledoves, pigeons, cane birds, parrots, eagles and eagle owls, falcons, sparrows, hawks and kestrels and they sell the skins of some of these birds of prey with their feathers, heads and claws. . . . There are streets of herbalists where all the medicinal herbs and roots found in the Land are sold. There are shops like apothecaries', where they sell ready-made medicines as well as liquid ointments and plasters. There are shops like barbers' where they have their hair washed and shaved and shops where they sell food and drink. . . . There is much firewood and charcoal, earthenware braziers and mats of various kinds like mattresses for beds and other, finer ones, for seats and for covering rooms and hallways. There is every sort of vegetable, especially onions, leeks, garlic, common cress and water cress, borage, sorrel, teasel and artichokes. (Cortés 1986:103–104)

The *ekphrasis* presents the tempered splendor of the house of the idols and Moteuczoma's superb palaces:

> He also had another house . . . where there was a very beautiful garden with balconies over it and the facings and flagstones were all of jasper and very well made. . . . There were also ten pools in which were kept all the many and varied kinds of water bird found in these parts, all of them domesticated. For the sea birds there were pools of salt water and for the river fowl of fresh water. . . . Each species of birds was fed with the food which it eats when wild, so that

> those which eat fish were given fish and those which eat maize or smaller grain were likewise given those things. . . . There were three hundred men in charge of these birds who knew no other trade, as there were others who were skilled only in healing sick birds. (Cortés 1986:109–110)

Finally, Cortés dwells on the service to the great *tlatoani* of Mexico:

> Touching Mutezuma's service and all that was remarkable in his magnificence and power, there is so much to describe that I do not know how to begin even to recount some part of it; for, as I have already said, can there be anything more magnificent than that this barbarian lord should have all the things to be found under the heavens in his domain, fashioned in gold and silver and jewels and feathers; and so realistic in gold and silver that no smith in the world could have done better, and in jewels so fine that it is impossible to imagine with what instruments they were cut so perfectly. (Cortés 1986:108)

The description of the city and the things therein is considered by Cortés's commentators to have no match in the Chronicles of the Indies, even in the one composed by the Spanish genius of reminiscence, Bernal Díaz del Castillo. As if in a state of total alertness during the act of writing, the testimonial sharpness of Cortés's discourse almost never falters. He displays indefatigable mental energy, registering a seemingly endless flow of details with utmost precision while never losing sight of the larger picture. And yet, faced with this supreme object of European desire, the heroic narrator shows himself as losing his cool. The unshakable, almost infallible chronicler runs out of words to describe and understand some aspects of the magnificence of the city of Mexico. The fantasy of the prodigious becomes flesh for the hero-narrator in Moteuczoma's collections of perfect copies in gold, silver, and precious stones of all the things that could be found in his domain both in water and on land. Or perhaps the European subject loses his capacity to discern as he witnesses the inconceivable delicacy of a so-called barbarian, embodied in a city of feathers within a city. The New World is indeed the site of unimaginable bounty. What Columbus had prophesied with vehemence in his letters to the Spanish kings and to the world but had failed to deliver is what Cortés's unswerving intent had permitted him to witness and possess: *lo real maravilloso,* Europe's dream city of gold. In these passages of the marvelous, the hero-narrator allows himself to lose control over the object of his narrative. The rhetoric of his silence produces surplus meaning: it becomes the right figure of a greatness that will always exceed the boundaries of textuality (Martínez–San Miguel 2000:118). This unfinished text as metaphor of Tenochtitlan is then one of the hero-narrator's consummate linguistic performances, for one of the few things Cortés is able to offer the king at the time of writing is the discourse about the city. On the desire the possession of this verbal artifact may arouse in its royal receptor hinges the legitimation of Cortés's criminal actions, past and present, and the possibility of recovering its unspeakable object, whose awful loss will also be represented vividly shortly after.

Indeed, Cortés skillfully ties the disgraceful loss of Tenochtitlan to Diego Velázquez, who had sent a new expedition from Cuba to imprison the renegade captain. Having been informed by his people that Pánfilo de Narváez had disembarked in the province of Cempoala with a decree to hold the land for Velázquez, Cortés leaves the city to meet him. This proves an almost fatal error, for when he comes back, after having arrested Narvaéz and won over most of his soldiers, the prophesied city is in revolt. Pedro de Alvarado, the captain left in charge of the Spaniards by Cortés, had savagely massacred the cream of the Mexican nobility as they celebrated the feast of Toxcatl in the Templo Mayor.[10] I will not further describe this tragic event except to say that it was one of two principal accusations of open mass murder Friar Bartolomé Las Casas (1995) leveled against the Spaniards during the Conquest of Mexico in the *Brevísssima relación de la destrucción de las Indias*.[11] Cortés makes only a very elliptical reference to the issue since it clearly marred the image of an already illegal and controversial enterprise.

Six days after Cortés's return from Cempoala and the night after Moteuczoma's assassination, probably at the hands of the Spaniards, the latter are forced to abandon Tenochtitlan. More than half the troops perish in the retreat. The language that narrates the fateful *Noche triste*, or Night of Sorrows, while preserving its usual testimonial sharpness, is appropriately punctured by the immensity of the loss.[12] Having finally reached neighboring Tacuba and barricaded themselves in a fortified house, the Spaniards again left this city under the cover of night. But vigilant guards gave notice of their flight, and the Spaniards soon found themselves surrounded by multitudes of warriors:

> When I saw that the enemy was massing on all sides, I concentrated my people there, and from those who were still capable of action made squadrons, placing them in front and behind and on the sides with the wounded on the middle; and I distributed the horsemen likewise. In this manner we marched all that day, fighting on all sides and so fiercely that we covered no more than three leagues during a whole day and night. Just at nightfall our Lord showed us a tower and fortified house on a hill where we barricaded ourselves as before. That night they left us in peace, although shortly before dawn the alarm was raised, though for no reason save the fear which we all had of the great multitude of people who continued to follow us. (Cortés 1986:140)

Although according to the passage the Spaniards fought courageously and Cortés is still depicted as skillfully managing the dreadful situation, it also shows that the painfully moving troop was wounded at its very core, both literally and figuratively. The expulsion from the promised, but now prohibited, city of

Tenochtitlan plunged the daring conquistadors into misery, all but breaking them down. Not even the allusion to God helps temper the image of defeat, since His divine intervention, one could argue, is quite modest, seeming only to prevent total annihilation. At dawn, the terror that had taken hold of the soldiers formerly capable of killing without mercy was embodied in the jitters of the alarm raised for no reason. The tone of this section of the Second Letter is sober but not dispassionate. Sticking to the testimonial formalism of his account, Cortés offers image after image of the expelled Spaniards making their tortured way to Tlaxcala, conveying in this manner the enormous grief, humiliation, and even dishonor produced by the terrible loss of the great city of Tenochtitlan. Rhetorically speaking, the pathos of these images will be what justifies the headstrong Spanish comeback narrated in the last part of the Second Letter and what will serve as a befitting prelude to the ungodly thrust forward of the Third Letter.

After twenty days of rest in Tlaxcala and in spite of his weak and discouraged men's urgings to the contrary, Cortés slowly initiates the re-conquest of the land by attacking a region conterminous to Tlaxcala, friendly with the Mexica. There he founds the town of Segura de la Frontera, from which he will write the Second Letter. On several occasions Cortés mentions that he had to "lay aside all other business and dispatch which . . . [he] was writing for Your Majesty" (Cortés 1986:150) to go take care of the ongoing affairs of war. Because of the radical uncertainty surrounding the narrator at the moment of writing, Cortés's rhetorical correctness cannot but refer back to his heroic self within the text: the narrator reproduces in all his appropriate narrative choices the strategic brilliancy and clarity of mind he attributes to his narrated self. This mirror effect constitutes one of the rhetorical triumphs of the Second Letter and situates it among the most accomplished texts of the Chronicles of the Indies.

As historian Inga Clendinnen has observed, analysts of the Conquest of Mexico usually focus on the phase of the Conquest narrated by the Second Letter rather than on that narrated by the Third Letter (1991:67, 76–77). Although masterfully written, the Third Letter lacks the intrigue, cunning, variety, and self-referential drama of the Second. Cortés wrote it nine months after the fall of Tenochtitlan and almost a year and a half after he had received reinforcements and provisions from La Hispaniola. A royal treasurer had also arrived with the provisions, hinting at an initial royal recognition of Cortés's enterprise (Martínez 1990:295).

Much as in the Second Letter, Cortés reconstructs, distorts, and erases events in the Third and is extremely careful in managing his image for the king. But the text draws more attention to its narrated events than to its rhetorical, mirroring effects. Because of the catastrophic nature of these events, the Third Letter has more of an elegiac, mournful tone than a triumphal or even heroically dispassionate one. For in spite of the Spanish victory over the Mexica, the promised city of abundance of the Second Letter has been lost forever, and the human cost to win it over may have been much too high, even for the implacable hero. As Clendinnen has poignantly observed, there are signs in the writing and actions of the hero that indicate he has been changed by the final Conquest of Mexico (1991:90).

After the protocol of salutations to the king, the Third Letter starts off by stating that Cortés had written to His Majesty about his unshakable determination to subdue the Mexica: "I assured Your Majesty that until I had triumphed over my enemies I would not rest nor cease to direct my every effort toward that end, putting aside whatever dangers, hardships and expense I might have to face" (Cortés 1986:161). This statement anticipates what the narrator knows is the outcome of that effort and of all the dangers and hardships that were faced. It articulates briefly but effectively the total focus his resolution entailed. Since the passage speaks about facing the enterprise of war to the death, the statement also suggests other motives than just the acquisition of wealth and lands for His Majesty. To go back to retake Tenochtitlan was also a test of limits, a matter of civilizations: it entailed issues of honor, identity, blood, and religion. And sure enough, the hero-narrator brings back the memory of the expulsion from Tenochtitlan several times in the letter, as if justifying the immovable Spanish determination to conquer or die. Of course, this may be read just as a rhetorical, *a posteriori* statement, since very few Spaniards actually perished in the war. Throughout the letter the honorable determination to die defending the cause is enacted above all by the Mexica, the unconquerable adversaries whom Cortés, in spite of all his military power and his eloquence, was never again able to subject to his will after his expulsion from Tenochtitlan.

Just as in the Second Letter, Cortés's narrated or diegetic "I" in the Third Letter is fully epic. He oversees and foresees everything, he devises everything, he knows everything: he is in control of almost everything. Also, the narrator follows the strictly chronological order of the legal genre of the *relación*, which creates the epic effect of *medias res* discussed earlier. Again, this temporal model is clearly the narrator-hero's choice as the most appropriate to narrate the events to his royal audience.

The siege of Mexico started on May 30, 1521. Cortés's army consisted of approximately 800 Spaniards and 150,000 Indian friends from the provinces of Tlaxcala, Huejotzingo, Cholula, and Chalco (Martínez 1990:317). The Mexica and their principal allies, the Tlatelolca, had gathered approximately 300,000 men in Tenochtitlan and thousands of canoes to resist the siege (Martínez 1990:320). The war strategy was one of fearful simplicity. The Spaniards would attack Tenochtitlan from each of its four causeways, both by land and water.

Cortés divided his men into four groups, and each one settled its headquarters in towns close to the causeway entrances. Day in and day out they were to push their way into the city to burn down as many houses and cause as much harm as possible until the Mexica surrendered or the city fell.

Although Cortés narrates in detail the types of action taken, the representation of the notion of time is very rudimentary, as in a dream. Days are differentiated from each other only according to the barest chronological criteria: one event takes place after the other in a relentless, endless onward thrust. The text produces the illusion of a time warp, of being submerged in a nightmarish present with no end in sight.[13] Although the Spaniards were making important strides into the city and gaining increasing military advantage over the Mexica, the labor of war was incessant and exhausting. Narrating how he had sent Captain Gonzalo de Sandoval to subdue Matalcingo and Malinalco, small cities that were attacking neighboring towns allied with the Spaniards, Cortés remarked:

> God alone knows the danger in which they went and, indeed, that in which we remained; but as we had now to show greater courage than before and to die fighting if need be; we concealed our weakness from friend and foe alike. And not once but many times the Spaniards declared that they asked God only that they should live to triumph over the defenders of the city, even if this should mean that they gained nothing else in the entire land. From this may be seen the risks and extreme hardships our lives and persons were forced to bear. (Cortés 1986: 244–245)

In this passage, Cortés portrays honor as the Spaniards' fundamental motivation for fighting; honor is what they are heroically willing to suffer extreme hardship for without expecting anything in return. At other times, he presents the dissemination of Christianity and the augmentation of the king's lands as the ultimate motives that should give the Spaniards the desire "to conquer or die" (Cortés 1986:207). In the end, however, all of these motives turn out to be modest proposals of intent next to what the Mexica are shown to be doing so as not to surrender their city. After Sandoval comes back from defeating the rebel provinces, Cortés represents to the king his constant efforts to persuade the Mexica to recognize the unsustainability of their situation and surrender:

> Now, thanks be to God, all the lands round about had come over to our side. But when I saw how rebellious the people of this city were, and how they seemed more determined to perish than any race of man known before, I did not know by what means we might relieve ourselves of all these dangers and hardships and yet avoid destroying them and their city which was indeed the most beautiful thing in the world. They paid no heed to us when we told them that we would not strike camp, nor would the brigantines cease to attack them from the water, that we had destroyed the peoples of Matalcingo and

> Malinalco and that there was no one in all the land who could help them, nor could they acquire maize or meat or fruit or water or any other provision. The more such things were told them, the less signs they showed of weakening; rather, they seemed to attack each time with greater spirit. (Cortés 1986:247–248)

The predicament of Cortés in this passage is the impossibility of relieving his soldiers from so much fighting in the face of the resolute Mexica resistance and, thus, the almost inevitable destruction of Tenochtitlan and its inhabitants. He never considers the possibility of withdrawing his invading forces, and thus this wrenching dilemma has a false ring to it. The Mexica, on the other hand, are clearly shown to have no way out. Without allies, food or water, and access to the outside world, sooner or later they would fall. But rather than showing weakness or fear vis-à-vis this dreadful prospect, their determination not to relinquish their city seemed empowered by Cortés's admonitory words to surrender. The captain-general hints at another *episteme*, another way of seeing, knowing, and understanding the world, when he states that the Mexicas were "more determined to perish than any race of man known before" (Cortés 1986:247). It must be underscored that during the siege, Cortés was never able to break this otherly determination and the relationship to death and to the world it upheld. Thus, according to the narrative, despite Cortés's military gains, his time surplus, and the inevitability of a Spanish victory, the Mexica unhesitatingly held on to their deaths and to Tenochtitlan. The stronger Cortés's desire to possess again "their city which was indeed the most beautiful thing in the world" (Cortés 1986:248) and his urgings to the Mexica to give it up, the greater their resolve to prevent that from ever happening, even at the cost of collective annihilation.

And so, toward the end, Cortés climbs with Pedro de Alvarado to a tower adjacent to the market of Tlatelolco. He realizes that by then the Spaniards and their allies had seven-eighths of the city in ruins and under their control. Once again, Cortés exhorts the Mexica to give themselves up, as the Spaniards could hardly bear any longer the monstrous spectacle of the deaths of their indigenous enemies from starvation and epidemic disease. "But they replied that they would never on any account give in and when only a single warrior remained, he would die fighting. They also swore to burn or throw deep into the water all that they possessed so that we should not have it" (Cortés 1986:256). And indeed, that is what the resisting Mexica did.

The representation of the unshakable foe produces more than one possible reading of the text. If, as is most likely, Cortés wished to justify the total and brutal destruction of Tenochtitlan by claiming that its inhabitants never gave up, such a representation inevitably also offered an image of the Mexica as much more heroic and steadfast than the Spaniards. For if the latter claimed they were ready to die heroically fighting for honor, religion, and king, the trinity that marked the loftiest boundaries of European subjectivity of the period, the fact is that those who actually died for these values and with a heretofore-unheard-of capacity to endure suffering were the Mexica. The description of their demolished city—with survivors walking over their dead, the unbearable stench of rotting bodies, and women and children drowning in fetid lakes amid multitudes of corpses—is overwhelming (Cortés 1986:263–264). It is the hallucination of a limit, of an otherworldly human misery; it is a nightmare of mass destruction. If in the Second Letter Tenochtitlan had allowed the conquerors to behold a prodigious land of abundance, at the end of the Third Letter it offered them an unimagined vision of hell. In the fearful contest of wills entailed by the Conquest of Mexico, Cuauhtemoc's determination to resist until he was captured or killed and the city of cities was completely destroyed is what ultimately prevails in the text, not Cortés's unbending intent to possess it again. Only when the *tlatoani* was finally taken prisoner (he did not surrender) did the war cease on the spot. The siege had lasted seventy-five days.[14]

And yet, the Mexica's plight and unflinching resistance to the death are not represented by Cortés as the folly of barbarians.[15] Their determination to die defending their city is not portrayed as evidence of a lack of reason that proved the Spaniards morally, intellectually, and militarily superior. Instead, the vanquished Mexica are represented with dread: "The people of the city had to walk upon their dead while others swam or drowned in the waters of that wide lake where they had their canoes; indeed, so great was their suffering that it was beyond our understanding how they could endure it" (Cortés 1986:263). And finally, when the young *tlatoani* Cuauhtemoc is captured, he is represented with an unforgettable, tragic dignity that overshadows the somewhat trite consoling gestures of the conqueror-narrator: "I asked him to be seated, whereupon he came up to me and, speaking in his language, said that he had done all he was bound to do to defend his own person and his people, so that now they were reduced to this sad state and I might do with him as I pleased. Then he placed his hand upon a dagger of mine and asked me to kill him with it; but I reassured him saying that he need fear nothing" (Cortés 1986:264–265). Cuauhtemoc is depicted as believing he had done what was expected of him by resolutely resisting to the bitterest end and thus to ask for his turn to be put to death. Whether as a calculated narrative strategy or beyond the limits of rhetorical desire, the epic Conquest of the most precious city on earth is represented in the Third Letter as having led to a threshold of resistance, human agony, and destruction the Christian world had never witnessed or perpetrated until that moment.

If the Second Letter of Hernán Cortés is a triumph of rhetoric and self-referentiality fueled by an all-consuming hope to recover its narrated object, the Third

Letter is a grand narrative that depicts its monstrous, epic destruction. In both letters, Cortés shows himself to be a superb rhetorician, and both letters indeed helped to bring about the royal recognition he sought: reinforcements and a royal witness in 1521 and the *cédula real,* or royal decree, naming Cortés governor and captain-general of New Spain, signed in October 1522 by Charles V (although he would occupy the position for a very short time). Cortés's letters can be read, then, as powerful examples of the crucial role writing, rhetoric, and representation played in the Conquest of America right from the start. He and other conquistadors soon realized that to achieve the status, fame, and wealth they lusted for, they would also have to cross swords with bureaucracy at the tortuous battlefield of the king's court.

But something of much higher cultural import than the captain's personal rewards at court or his great manipulative powers are at stake in his well-written letters. The Second and Third letters of Hernán Cortés are founding texts of a Latin American imaginary depicting the New World as a site where the off-limits of the marvelous and the horrific could be experienced. They are testimonial renditions of implausible events leading to an eschatological imposition of European domination. At yet another level, they are monuments to the unbreakable, dreadful resistance of the masters of Mexico-Tenochtitlan, who resolved to perish in mass so they would never again see their city of cities possessed by an alien power. And finally, beyond their brilliance and rhetorical force, when read together the Second and Third letters ultimately convey sorrow for the fact that nothing would ever be able to summon the prodigious lost object of Mexico-Tenochtitlan back from its ashes.

NOTES

1. In his *Brevísima relación de la destrucción de las Indias* (1995:104–115) for instance, Friar Bartolomé Las Casas condemns Hernán Cortés as a criminal, looter, and assassin. Friar Toribio de Motolinia and Friar Jerónimo de Mendieta, both Franciscans, offer a very different view. Motolinia represents Hernán Cortés as a courageous soldier (1951:88), and Mendieta depicts him as a mirror image of Moses. Mendieta also represents Cortés as a counterfigure to Martin Luther because the former had brought to the church many souls (namely, those of the converted Mexica) to compensate for the ones lost by the latter's "heresy" (1993:174).

2. All critics who have engaged with Cortés's *Cartas de relación* (1983) have invariably pointed out that the author uses all his literary and representational powers to legitimate his figure and enterprise before Charles V, the royal addressee of the letters. In perhaps the most detailed study about fictionalization in the letters, Beatriz Pastor (1992) shows how Cortés carefully selected his narrative material to construct his figure as an ideal (read fictive) hero and vassal of the king and then model governor. Stephanie

Merrim focuses on the autobiographical ruses of Cortés in the Second Letter (1986), Viviana Díaz Balsera outlines its metatextual and performative strategies (1989), and Yolanda Martínez–San Miguel analyzes the correlation among desire, possession, and verbal production in the text (2000). Other critics have focused on the legalistic and imperial discourses manipulated by Cortés to legitimate his illegal enterprise (Elliott 1986); and, more recently, Ricardo Padrón has approached the Second Letter as an allegory of frontier that, at its fictional height, dissolves into a moment of full recognition of Spanish law when Moteuczoma sees himself and his people as already vassals of Charles V (2004).

3. The heroic is a category that pertains to great, noble, and courageous, if not superhuman, deeds, usually narrated in epic poems. The marvelous, as understood by sixteenth-century writers and theoreticians, was the sensation produced by novelty and/or the prodigious; the newly encountered lands of America were constructed over and over again by discoverers, conquistadors, and missionaries as a paradigmatic site of the marvelous. The pathetic is that quality of a literary writing that produces feelings of sorrow, pity, and compassionate sympathy (Baldick 1990:163).

4. The *relación de hechos* (report of acts) was a quasi-legal, factual record, letter, or deposition, usually of witnessed events (Pastor 1992:146–149; Merrim 1996:61). It was a genre widely used by conquistadors, missionaries, and colonists to solicit from the king rewards for services rendered. See Roberto González-Echevarría (1988), "The Law and the Letter," for a thorough analysis of the importance of the *relación* in the Spanish imperial bureaucracy.

5. Bernal Díaz del Castillo (1495–1564) was among the small Spanish army that accompanied Cortés in the daring Conquest of Mexico. Although Bernal had practically no education, he wrote (or dictated) the *Historia verdadera de la conquista de la Nueva España* (History of the Conquest of Mexico, 1632), considered one of the masterpieces of the Chronicles of the Indies.

6. The diegetic level is a category used in narratology. It refers to the depicted events of the story. The extra-diegetic level is the moment of the enunciation of the story. It usually lies in a realm outside the narrated events. We will see in the Second Letter, however, that part of the writing of the story is represented as one of the events within the story.

7. I take the discussion of the self-referential and performative aspects of Cortés's writing in this passage from my article on the Second Letter (1989:223–224).

8. Significant sixteenth-century visual representations of the encounter between Moteuczoma and Cortés can be found in the *Lienzo de Tlaxcala* (1979), the *Codex Durán,* and the Twelfth Book of the *Florentine Codex* (Sahagún 1950–1982), among others. In the seventeenth century, the most outstanding visual representation of this encounter is undoubtedly the painting *Meeting of Cortés and Moteuczoma*, the third of the remarkable eight-piece series about the Conquest of Mexico from the Jay I. Kislak Foundation Collection. Art historians posit that this sequence of paintings was produced toward the last quarter of the seventeenth century. And indeed, full of figures, curves, movement, and sharp contrasts of color, the facture of these paintings clearly corresponds to the Baroque aesthetic of the period. In terms of the representation itself, in *Meeting* the artist has taken liberties in the depiction of the place of the historical encounter, the dress of the actors

in the scene, and the protocol surrounding Moteuczoma. Rather than the straight causeway of Iztapalapa that led right into the island city, the meeting place seems to be a hill in the outskirts of Tenochtitlan, which downplays the urban backdrop of the encounter. The causeways, however, are evoked by the curved road at the right-hand corner of the painting. The Spaniards, particularly Cortés, are portrayed as donning handsome gilded iron helmets, armor, sashes, and cloaks, as if they were part of Charles V's imperial army. However, we know that the soldiers who accompanied Cortés had to pay for their own horses, weapons, and dress and that only the wealthiest soldiers and captains were able to afford armor and helmets. According to historian José Luis Martínez (1990), the majority of the soldiers wore hoods, long-sleeved shirts, doublets, and breeches. The footwear of most, if not all, Spaniards was the humble, universal *alpargata,* or shoe made of hemp. For their protection, most soldiers adapted indigenous defensive weapons such as cotton coats that would protect them from arrows and leather-skinned shields (Martínez 1990:223). However, in the indigenous visual representations mentioned earlier, particularly in the *Florentine Codex,* most Spaniards are represented as wearing at least gilded helmets. Regarding the dress of Moteuczoma and his retinue, perhaps the greatest liberty the artist takes is substituting the omnipresent indigenous *maxtlatl,* or cotton cloth covering male genitals and knotted at the front with hanging strips, with colorful feather skirts. These skirts remind the viewer of early-sixteenth-century German broadsheets and woodcuts, as well as of Albrecht Dürer and Hans Burgkmair's drawings of Amerindians. Rebecca Brienen has pointed out that although there is no evidence that natives of the Americas ever wore the aforesaid feather skirts, that "did not stop artists from picturing Indians, regardless of their national origin, wearing this article of clothing well into the nineteenth century" (2003:30). In an interesting mix of visual sources, Moteuczoma's feather headdress in the Kislak painting, although much more elaborate, resembles the one worn by the *tlatoani* in the drawings of the *Florentine Codex.* Moteuczoma, as well as his attendants in the painting carrying the canopy and the litter, are all shown wearing rich mantles in European fashion and not knotted at the chest or over the shoulder as was Nahua custom, according to the indigenous visual representations of the period that have come down to us. Last but not least, indigenous bodies and poses follow European Classical conventions of representation. All these points notwithstanding, or precisely because of them, Moteuczoma and the indigenous subjects are portrayed in *Meeting* with great dignity and majesty. Moteuczoma's prominence and hierarchy are highlighted by the green, richly ornamented pallium, as well as by his central and highest position in the painting, subordinating even that of Cortés.

9. The definition of *ekphrasis* is "an expository speech which vividly brings the subject before our eyes." *Ekphrasis* may refer to the description of works of art, such as paintings and statues; buildings, such as churches, palaces, and gardens; and *locus amoenus,* or amenable places (Race 1993:320).

10. The calendrical feast of Toxcatl was celebrated during the fifth month of the Mesoamerican eighteen months of twenty days each. The feast was dedicated both to the supreme god Tezcatlipoca and to Huitzilopochtli. See Sahagún (1989a:1, 115–122, 204–206) for a detailed description of this religious celebration.

11. The first one was the massacre at Cholula, mentioned earlier.

12. Appropriately entitled *The Sad Night*, the sixth of the Kislak paintings is perhaps the most powerful of the series. It masterfully portrays the Spaniards' defeat and flight from Tenochtitlan. A grim hue of gray, black, and brown covers the entire canvas except at the center, where the clash of forces is depicted. Light falls over the figures there, attracting the viewer's gaze right into the heart of the battle. The fighting parties are almost indistinguishable at the center, as if reproducing at a plastic level the deadly chaos of the portrayed situation. At the foreground of the painting, the figures of Cortés and his captains flee, although they look back to the center as if to assess the sorry situation. Falling bodies and weaponry can be seen behind the figures in flight. Intense dynamism and movement permeate the whole scene.

13. The seventh painting of the Kislak series represents the final Conquest of Tenochtitlan. Although the scene is obviously one of an impending, if not ongoing, battle, the painting does not give the sense of gruesome destruction Cortés records in his Third Letter. The Spaniards are seen to advance on three causeways into the Mexican city in unbroken military formation. In the foreground to the left, a group of Nahua allies is seen brandishing a Spanish flag. To the right, the Spanish cavalry is depicted again in full armor, with Cortés as the most outstanding and individualistic figure of the painting. It is significant that except for a small group on a canoe, the figures of the Mexica are hardly distinguishable. Visually, then, the Spaniards and their allies dominate in *Conquest* in terms of sheer numbers and—sometimes disproportioned—size. Very different from the battle scene of *The Sad Night,* order, not chaos, prevails in this painting. It is as if the Spanish invaders were ideologically portrayed as a structuring power, not as the annihilating force they turned out to be. The plastic representation of Tenochtitlan does not do justice to Cortés's splendid *exphrasis* in the Second Letter or to Bernal Díaz del Castillo's in *True History*. The pyramid of the Templo Mayor towering in the background notwithstanding, the buildings of the city look like those of an ordinary Spanish town of the period.

14. The last of the Kislak paintings on the Conquest of Mexico represents the capture of Cuauhtemoc. Much as in the previous painting, although the actual historical context is that of war and utter destruction, order prevails visually. The scene appropriately takes place in Lake Texcoco, where Cuauhtemoc was finally taken prisoner. The sails of the Spanish brigantines all point leftward, giving a sense of uniformity and pattern. In the background, canoes and Spanish brigantines sail freely on the lagoon surrounded by mountains; no clash among them is represented, although the military confrontation that has taken place is signified by Spanish flags standing upright as a sign of victory. At the foreground the figure of Cortés, in full armor with sash, is seen touching the *tlatoani*'s right thigh with his sword. Standing close behind each of the two figures is a Spanish captain, also in full armor. This is an artistic recreation because according to the Third Letter the captor was just "Garci Holguín, a captain of one of the brigantines" (Cortés 1986:264). Neither Cortés nor any of his principal captains was present at the moment Cuauhtemoc was made prisoner.

15. On this point I differ with Clendinnen (1991), who states that Mexican resistance was "to the Spanish eyes profoundly 'irrational' " (90), perverse, and obdurate (92).

4

Now You See Her, Now You Don't

Memory and the Politics of Identity Construction in Representations of Malinche

Constance Cortez

Malinche stands out as one of the most enigmatic figures of the Conquest of Mexico.[1] Eyewitness accounts of her are rare, despite her central position as Cortés's translator and, later, as his consort. She has been the subject of hundreds of books and articles, which explore not only her central role in the success of the Conquest of Mexico but her very character. Over the centuries, writers and artists have provided countless, sometimes contradictory representations of this complicated figure. Some have chosen to foreground Malinche's importance to the Conquest, while others have negated her role. Some have portrayed her as a woman of good character, while others have projected nothing but evil. Both the diversity and the abundance of extant representations of this Nahua-speaking woman beg a variety of questions. For instance, what can account for the visual liberties taken with Malinche's representations over the centuries? Was her role of translator and mediator between Mexico's indigenous peoples and the

Spaniards found too irresolute by artists? Why have artists and historians so often felt compelled to commit her to one side or another? Is there something larger than ambivalence at stake in these images? Perhaps a better to way to approach this subject is through memory and history: How did artists from different backgrounds and periods invoke the former to construct the latter?

The figure of Malinche as she appears in the seventeenth-century Kislak Conquest of Mexico series offers an important and, until now, overlooked opportunity to examine how sixteenth-century representations of this woman were modified to accommodate a re-visioned history. While change over 100 years is to be expected, Malinche's visual and ideological malleability was established even in her earliest portrayals. In this chapter, I will first address current scholarship regarding Malinche's construction in two indigenous sixteenth-century sources: the *Florentine Codex* and the *Lienzo de Tlaxcala*. This will be followed by my detailed analysis of her presence in the Kislak paintings. In contrast to the active role she plays in the sixteenth-century indigenous sources, where the intended audience included Spaniards, in the later Kislak canvases, likely made for a *criollo* audience in Mexico City, Malinche's image was pruned back to something resembling a handmaiden. As I will make clear, the portrayal of Malinche was dependent upon culturally defined notions of the past.

HISTORIC NARRATIVES GREAT AND SMALL

Records of Malinche are intimately linked to the Spanish Conquest of Mexico. Only a handful of primary sources mention her, with most of the information coming down to us from two sixteenth-century Spanish chroniclers: Bernal Díaz del Castillo (1963:85–87) and Francisco López de Gómara (1964:56–58). From them we learn that Malinche was a Nahua-speaking woman who was born around 1500 in the Isthmus of Tehuantepec in southern Mexico. Sometime around 1510 she was sold into slavery among the Maya of Potonchan and spent the next nine years in their service. It was during this time that she became fluent in Maya. In 1519, Hernán Cortés arrived on the shores of the island of Cozumel and was shortly thereafter joined by Jerónimo de Aguilar, a shipwrecked Spaniard who had been living among the Maya of Yucatán for eight years. During this time he had worked as a servant for a Maya lord and gained fluency in the indigenous language. After joining Cortés's group, his language abilities were utilized by the conquistadors in their dealings with the native population.

After the Spaniards arrived in Tabasco in 1519, Malinche (along with nineteen other women) was given to the Spaniards by the Maya and baptized under the Spanish name "Marina." As Cortés's forces moved away from the Maya-speaking area of the Gulf Coast, it became increasingly clear that Aguilar's language abilities had reached their limits. In the meantime, Cortés had noticed that Malinche was able to speak with representatives of a newly encountered indigenous group. The Spaniard found out that they were speaking Nahuatl, the language of the Aztecs and the lingua franca of sixteenth-century Mesoamerica. From this point, Malinche became an essential link between the Spaniards and the Nahua-speaking groups located in the interior and along the Gulf Coast.

Initially, translation was a three-way process: Malinche translated from Nahuatl into Maya, and Aguilar translated her Maya into Spanish for Cortés. As time progressed, however, Malinche learned Spanish, and Aguilar's services were no longer necessary. Malinche translated for Cortés throughout the Conquest, even aiding in conversations between the conquistador and the great emperor of the Aztecs, Moteuczoma II. Shortly after the Spaniards had subdued central Mexico, Malinche bore Cortés a son, Martín (1522). In 1524, while on an expedition bound for Honduras, Cortés forced Malinche to marry Juan Jaramillo de Salvatierra, one of his officers. The nature of the relationship between Malinche and her new husband is unknown, but two years later she bore him a daughter, Maria.[2] Little is known of Malinche's history after this point, but it is believed that she died sometime in 1528.

Writers and scholars who have studied Malinche agree that her translation work for Cortés was key to the success of the Conquest. There, however, agreement ends. Written descriptions of Malinche run the gamut from "mother of a new nation" to an Eve who allowed the serpent to pass into paradise (Lanyon 1999; Herren 2000). The modern and colonial ambivalence directed toward this woman has been addressed in detail by Angela Marie Herren, who cites a passage from Margaret Shedd's 1971 popular historical novel, *Malinche and Cortés,* as a negative extreme. Shedd asserted: "Malinche was a whore, but since everything this woman did was on a grand scale, so too was her whoring. She, a Mexican, made herself the honored concubine to Cortés, the Spanish conqueror of Mexico."[3] Shedd presents Malinche as an oversexed "other" who took advantage of the unwitting Spaniard by using her sexual prowess. This is, however, but one of many readings of Malinche. Other writers argue that she was a victim of love; a woman motivated by feelings of revenge against her parents, who had sold her into slavery; a paragon of pragmatism who waited to see which way the Conquest was going before finally committing to a position; or perhaps just a simple woman who survived the historic whirlwind around her by sheer tenacity, wit, and luck.

Whore, victim, avenger, stoic observer, survivor—all of these readings are dependent on the degree to which Malinche was a willing participant in Cortés's plans. Did this woman help destroy one of the largest empires ever known in Mesoamerica? Can we or should we view her, therefore, as one of history's most notorious traitors? Is she "*la chingada*," the violated mother who gave herself voluntarily to Cortés and, in doing so, turned her back on future generations of indigenous sons (Paz 1985)? Given the limited number of colonial sources on which modern interpretations of Malinche are based, these questions will likely never be answered. What remains evident from early written and visual sources, however, is that the imaging of Malinche was subject to the rules of memory as well as expectations regarding the unfolding of history. As I will show, the nature of both of these was culturally specific and politically laden in terms of power relations between different groups.

MALINCHE IN THE SIXTEENTH CENTURY

Generally speaking, during the sixteenth century Malinche is represented as both a mediator and an active participant in the Conquest. The two Conquest-period documents in which she appears most frequently in this capacity are the *Florentine Codex* (1558–1570; Sahagún 1950–1982) and the *Lienzo de Tlaxcala* (1979). With reference to the *Florentine Codex,* James Lockhart has noted that care should be taken when reading this or any other account produced during the sixteenth century (1993:5). Most of these narratives date from no earlier than 1545—twenty-four years after the Conquest. By that time, many of the principals involved in the war were dead. For both the text and the images, temporal distance facilitated the transformation of earlier events into the stuff of legend (Lockhart 1993:5).

Book 12 of the *Florentine Codex* presents the most detailed indigenous account of the Conquest from the sixteenth century. The *Florentine Codex* was produced in Tlatelolco, the sister city annexed and physically joined to Aztec Tenochtitlan in 1473. Tlatelolco was known for its huge market and its population of *pochteca*, the Aztec merchant class. After the Aztec defeat, Friar Bernardino de Sahagún gathered indigenous scribes from this city, and under his guidance they produced both the illustrations and the text that form this account. On the frontispiece to Book 12, Malinche is engaged in the triangle of translation among Aguilar, Cortés, and herself (Figure 4.1). Carol Maturo has identified the woman in the right middle ground as Malinche and has suggested that she is speaking Nahuatl to the man just left of her (1994:2). To her right, Aguilar is shown wearing Spanish garments. Presumably, Malinche was translating from Nahuatl into Maya, and Aguilar then translated from Maya into Spanish for the benefit of the scribe, who is shown seated in the process of writing. Maturo (1994) has posited that this seated individual may even represent Cortés.[4] The rest of the page has been organized into groups: Cortés's ships in the harbor, the unloading of goods from a docked vessel, and various groups of animals.

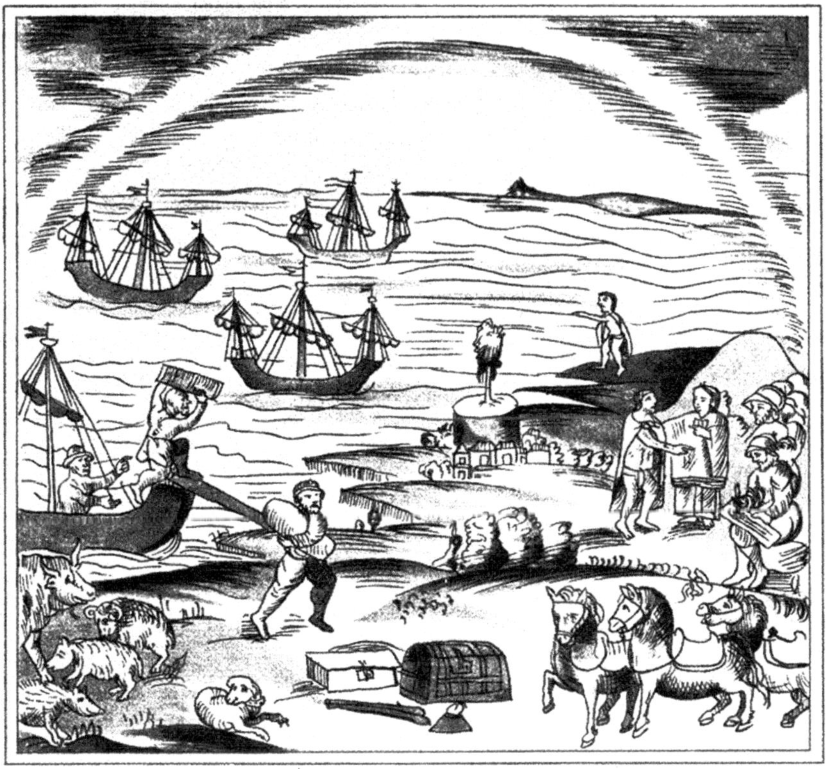

Figure 4.1. Frontispiece. *The Florentine Codex,* Book 12. Reproduced with permission from Bernardino de Sahagún, *General History of the Things of New Spain: Florentine Codex.* Translated from Aztec into English, with notes and Illustrations, by Arthur J.O. Anderson and Charles E. Dibble. Sante Fe, NM: School of American Research; Salt Lake City: University of Utah, 1950–1980.

The three decades between the Conquest and the volume's inception left their mark. Cortés's landing in Tabasco was restructured to fit both indigenous and Spanish expectations. For instance, the lack of modeling and the discrete placement of figures into groups of narrative action are in keeping with both native tradition and the Nahua sense of the episodic (Lockhart 1993:12). On the other hand, the diagonal of the shoreline is definitely borrowed from European sources and is an attempt by the indigenous scribes to render perspective. Additionally, the rainbow shape in the sky has its precedence in biblical accounts well established in European art. Rainbows and arcs are associated with new beginnings, as in the fulfillment of God's promise in the story of Noah and his ark. It is clear that the Spaniards understood the Americas as a kind of new beginning, a kind of Garden of Eden or New Jerusalem.

As both Lanyon (1999:99–105) and Herren (2000:161) have suggested, the differences in Malinche's appearance in the *Florentine Codex* and the *Lienzo de Tlaxcala* are a result of differing views of the Conquest. Most sixteenth-century indigenous renderings of the Conquest and Malinche's role in it are politically laden. The *Florentine Codex* was produced by the descendants of the defeated Aztecs of Tenochtitlan-Tlatelolco, many of whom had been children at the time of the Europeans' arrival. The *Lienzo de Tlaxcala*, on the other hand, was produced by people who had allied themselves with the Spaniards during the Conquest. It seems logical, then, that the Tlaxcallan vision of Malinche would be more flattering than that in the *Florentine Codex*. While this is not always the case, the most obvious area where differing attitudes toward the Conquest are borne out is in the frequency of representation. In Book 12 of the *Florentine Codex*, Malinche appears in only 7 of the 161 images (Lanyon 1999; Herren 2000). In the *Lienzo de Tlaxcala*, she appears in sixteen of forty-eight scenes. Both scholars note that this discrepancy can largely be credited to the fact that the Tlaxcalans, who sided with Cortés, were much more sympathetic and celebratory toward Malinche, Cortés's intermediary. The Tlatelolcan scribes, on the other hand, were less likely to represent Malinche, whom they viewed as one of the agents of their defeat.

There are also differences in the manner in which Malinche has been represented, from the way she engages those around her to the representation of her figure. For example, in the *Florentine Codex* she is depicted as a respectable woman (if we exclude images of her translating, which had the possibility of being viewed as an unseemly act for a woman). She wears the traditional hip-length *huipil*, the embroidered shirt associated with central Mexican women. Her hair is dressed in the two-horned hairstyle particular to Aztec matriarchs. As is consistent with her lower status as a female, she is consistently depicted barefoot and at the service of Cortés.

As Herren (2000:164) has noted, this representation is significantly different from the images of Malinche in the *Lienzo de Tlaxcala* (Figure 4.2). Here, Malinche is presented in a much more Europeanized manner. Her hair is down about her shoulders, and, while she still wears the three-quarter-length *huipil* associated with her people, she is also shown wearing European-style shoes. This latter aspect is in distinct contrast to the indigenous groups that appear in scenes with her, who are consistently shown without shoes or wearing sandals. Since shoes were viewed as elite-status goods, the implication here is that the *Lienzo* artists viewed Malinche as elevated in status and belonging, at least in part, to things associated with the Europeans. Nonetheless, in all these images her size is at least comparable to that of Cortés, and in some images she is even larger than he.

Herren also notes that in some representations Malinche goes beyond the role of mediator and takes on a far more active presence (2000:169–170). In one

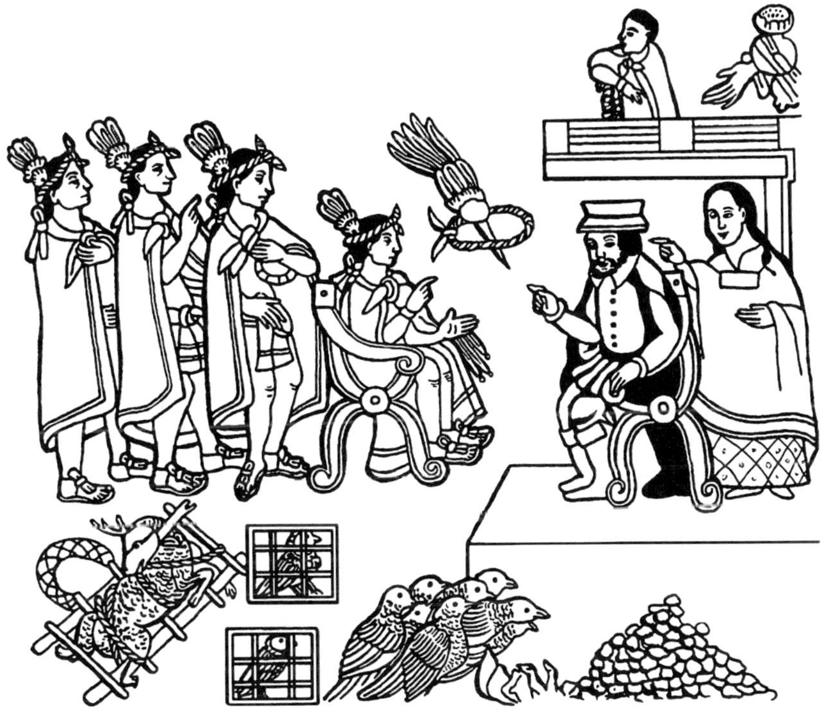

Figure 4.2. *Malinche Translating for Cortés*, in the *Lienzo de Tlaxcala*. Drawing by C. Cortez after *Lienzo de Tlaxcala* (Antigüedades mexicanas publicadas por lat junta colomina de México en el cuarto centenario del descubrimiento de América). México: Alfredo Chavero, 1892.

image from the *Lienzo de Tlaxcala* she is shown at the Battle of Tepotzotlan, where she has joined the Spanish vanguard as it attacks the city (Figure 4.3). She is located at the rear of the group and, like the soldiers before her, holds a European shield and sword. Even in the *Florentine Codex*, she often appears to exceed her role as translator by speaking for herself (Herren 2000:175–176). Many scholars have asked how it is possible to explain Malinche's inconsistent behavior in light of prescribed female roles as defined by both Spaniards and indigenous peoples during the sixteenth century. It is well known that when Aztec women vied for power or displayed destructive attitudes, they were categorized as "women of discord."[5] Only when they maintained their passivity and worked for the good of the Aztecs and family were they held as positive and regenerative in nature.

Alternative theories have been posited to explain how Malinche was able to transcend sixteenth-century models of passivity. All of them suggest that indigenous

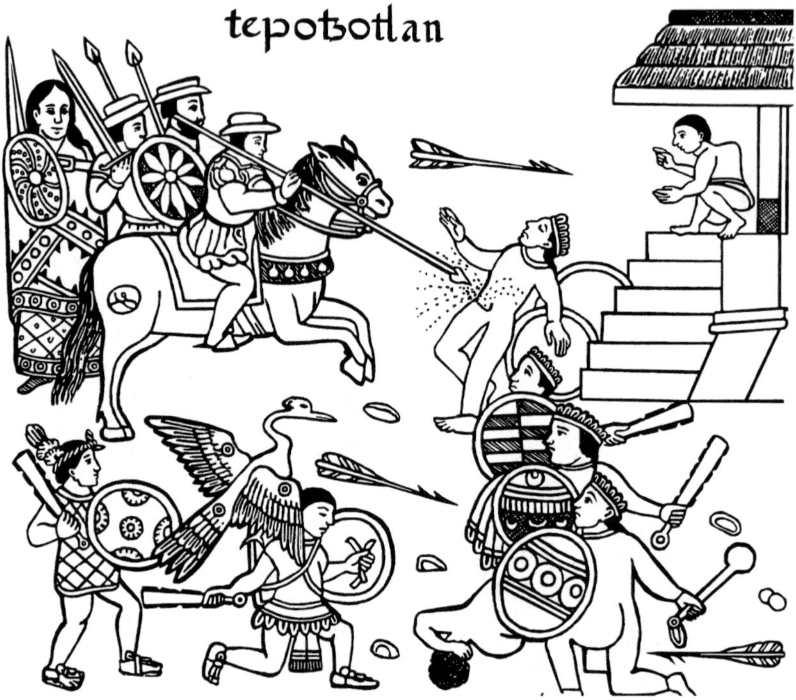

Figure 4.3. *Malinche at the Battle of Tepotzotlan*, in the *Lienzo de Tlaxcala*. Drawing by C. Cortez after *Lienzo de Tlaxcala* (Antigüedades mexicanas publicadas por lat junta colomina de México en el cuarto centenario del descubrimiento de América). México: Alfredo Chavero, 1892.

paradigms were in place to compensate for aberrant behavior. In this manner, behavior initially viewed as inexplicable could successfully be integrated into the preexisting structure of indigenous history and become part of an acceptable collective memory.

Frances Karttunen, a linguist of Nahuatl, has suggested that because of Malinche's position as translator and mediator for the Spaniards, her activities placed her in a special category of existence (1997:291–312). According to Karttunen, once transformed, Malinche was recognized by the Aztecs as belonging to a class of things that were *ixiptlayotl,* or "representation." Karttunen explains this concept as follows: in Aztec religious practice, chosen human beings served as temporary embodiments of deities, providing them with a conduit through which to speak and act in the world inhabited by humans. At the end of their service, some of these stand-ins would be flayed, and priests would dress in their skins to speak and act through them in yet another way. Perhaps the Aztecs and their neighbors perceived the Nahuatl-speaking woman as the *ixiptla* (the representative of a supernatural force) (1997:294). From this perspective, Malinche no longer fell into the category of human being but was instead the representative of a foreign and inexplicable presence. As such, the fact that she was a woman was irrelevant. Her actions were not subject to the same restrictions associated with common women.

Another perspective is offered by art historian Jeannette Favrot Peterson (1994:187–202). In her examination of Malinche, Peterson tries to explain her active role in Conquest imagery by looking to historical precedents in both European and indigenous sources. As far as the Europeans were concerned, an armed Malinche would fall into the well-known category of the Amazon, the archetype of a woman warrior. From the indigenous side, Peterson observes that, even prior to the Conquest, women were known to participate in and "lead violent uprisings." Peterson also notes that for the Aztecs, Malinche may have fallen into the category of supernatural and historical women known as "women of discord." According to Susan Gillespie's (1989) study of recurrent patterns in Aztec-produced histories, women of discord were periodically introduced into the narrative at significant junctures. Such women were inserted in strategic places to conceptually jump-start eras and natural cycles after cataclysmic events. Structurally speaking, these women acted as markers and mediators of extraordinary change. Given the parameters of this category, it seems clear that Malinche could be the quintessential "woman of discord."

In the *Florentine Codex* and the *Lienzo de Tlaxcala*, then, we are presented with sixteenth-century images of Malinche that emphasize her role as a mediator and an active participant in the Conquest. These images are inherently bilingual, bicultural, or both. They could be understood within the political and ideological realities of two different systems of signification and two systems of remembering: those of the indigenous peoples of central Mexico and those of the Spanish conquerors. If we believe Karttunen's and Peterson's hypotheses, Malinche as a warrior woman was an acceptable mechanism through which the Spaniards were able to conquer the unknown. At the same time, the Aztecs may have understood her actions as spiritually sanctioned and part of the preexisting and predictable structure of indigenous history. In other words, her predetermined structural presence as a woman of discord both anticipated the Conquest and explained and facilitated the transition into a new colonial era. As I will show, during the following century indigenous considerations fell by the wayside as Malinche was refigured to better correspond to European expectations and constructions of history.

SEVENTEENTH-CENTURY IMAGES OF MALINCHE: THE KISLAK PAINTINGS

By the seventeenth century, images of the Conquest had been codified according to changes in political climate and the dictates of taste. The Europeans who had witnessed or participated in the Conquest were replaced by or transformed into a new aristocracy. Indeed, the interests of seventeenth-century *criollos*, persons of Iberian descent born in the Americas, were quite different from those of their sixteenth-century predecessors. These well-heeled gentlemen were more interested in managing their lands and businesses and mining their mineral claims than in waging war or educating members of the indigenous population. Additionally, *criollos* were impacted by a sense of growing pride in New Spain, with its unique cultures, natural resources, and beauty. They began to develop a distinct sense of their place in this world. It was during this time that the stirrings of a singular national identity—one separate from Europe—began to formulate in their hearts.

Nonetheless, when it came to taste and the remembering and presentation of history, *criollos* relied heavily on Europe to provide the standard of representation. As a variety of studies have shown, *criollo* artists and writers borrowed heavily from Europe's Classical past and applied the same tropes of representation to their own indigenous characterizations.[6] The native past and the Conquest itself were refashioned into sagas of mythic proportions. Greco-Latin archetypes and allegories were supplanted by native American equivalents couched in classically inspired garb and poses. Just as Europe held claim to a glorious past, albeit one profoundly mythologized, so New Spain now held claim to its very own New World equivalent.

Artists trained in the European style also made use of a Classical system known as the "art of memory."[7] Having its origin in ancient Greece, this was a manner in which orators could jog their memory by using sequenced objects as mnemonic cues. By medieval times, the art of memory was widely used to teach sacred doctrine, and certain stories or doctrinal issues were associated with parts of buildings. By the sixteenth century the art of memory had made its way across the Atlantic, where it was intimately connected to ideological and actual architectural complexes and utilized to invoke memories that were sacred as well as secular.[8]

The Kislak "Conquest of Mexico" series is part of these classical traditions (Plates 1–8). The eight canvases are meant to be read sequentially, beginning with *The Entrance of Hernán Cortés into Tabasco* and ending with *The Capture of Cuahtemoc.* To understand the connection between these works and the art of memory, it is first necessary to imagine the paintings as they were probably meant to be presented—hung along the walls of a room in an upper-class home in

Mexico City. Viewers could read the works sequentially as they circumambulated the room, stopping at each painting in turn. They would read the glossed passages keyed into numbers distributed in strategic places in each canvas. Instead of mnemonic symbols, their eyes would find literal renderings of historic events on each of the canvases. Having completed one segment of the saga, they would move on to the next painting.

Malinche, as represented in the Kislak canvases, had become part of the (by now) heavily mythologized tale of Conquest. During the century that had passed since European contact, Cortés had become lionized in European and colonial sources. Malinche, in comparison to her earlier representations, had in turn taken on a much more diminished and passive role. In the first canvas of the series, *The Entrance of Hernán Cortés into Tabasco*, Malinche has been relegated to a small area in the middle right of the canvas (Plate 1). She is dressed in a half-length *huipil* and kneels, along with two other women, before Friar Bartolome de Olmedo. Her spotlighted baptism signals her conscious choice regarding the direction of her allegiance. This point of transformation is also indicated by other actions and her bodily position. As she touches the hem of the priest's cassock, Malinche faces her future, as indicated by the cross and Cortés. The conquistador stands on the other side of the altar, a symbolic mediator between past and future. Malinche's rejection of her past is indicated by the natives who stand amid the trees behind her. These are the lords of Tabasco. Dressed in indigenous garments and mostly standing in classically inspired *contraposto,* they watch from the shadows as events unfold before them.

The baptism group provides an island of calm in an otherwise violent scene of carnage. In the foreground, Spaniards are engaged in a battle to the death with natives dressed in a romanticized version of Aztec garb. Many of the Europeans appear to carry modified half-pikes, a European implement that did not become popular until the seventeenth century (Metropolitan Museum of Art 1990:426). The Baroque swirl of motion contrasts with the peaceful background, which contains a castle. The groupings of characters and their actions indicate the order in which the individual canvas should be read. Emily Umberger has shown that colonial imagery can generally be read both sequentially, in the manner of continuous narrative, and as a kind of morality play, reaffirming prescriptive and proscriptive behavior (1996:46–58). In this light, the violence in the foreground underscores the fate of the non-converted and those who resisted colonial rule. The idealized, peaceful background, on the other hand, foreshadows things to come. Here, Spanish civilization and order are to be understood as rewards for proper behavior and assimilation on the part of the indigenous people.

Likewise, the second canvas, *The Arrival of Cortés at Veracruz and the Reception by Moteuczoma's Ambassadors*, can be divided up in a similar way (Plate 2).

In the upper left corner, Spaniards and Aztec elite surround a table set with plates and vessels. Before them, other members of the Aztec entourage approach the table, two by two, offering gifts sent by their emperor, Moteuczoma II. Behind them horses parade, two by two. These ordered activities can be contrasted with the bedlam to the right. The chaos was the result of orders given by Cortés; he ordered cannon fire to impress and intimidate the Aztecs, rightly predicting that Moteuczoma's ambassadors would record the event and go back to the emperor with tales of amazing weapons. The contrast between Spanish and native reaction becomes an implied marker of each group's degree of civilization. The Spanish soldiers are shown to be relaxed and organized, their pikes poised in repetitive positions of ease. The indigenous warriors to the right, in contrast, form a chaotic mass of movement and confusion. Some fall to the ground, their weapons scattered about them in disarray. Surely, this is intended to prefigure the fall of the Aztec Empire.

A visual hierarchy of class and humanity plays across the surface of the canvas. The elite sit at a table in front of a meticulously manicured arbor and drink from gold goblets placed on a woven tablecloth. This group can be understood as having higher social standing than those who approach them by foot or horse. Malinche sits at the table adjacent to Cortés. She is dressed in white and demurely raises her left hand to her breast. Tilting her head, she directs her gaze at Cortés, to whom she listens attentively. (As the result of a past mishap, all we now see of Cortés in the painting is his right armored knee and part of his right arm and hand.) Also seated at the table are the Aztec ambassadors and other Spaniards, including Father Olmeda.

It is only in the third canvas of this series that we get our first, best, and last close-up view of Malinche (Plate 3). The large presence of Malinche in this canvas is a result of the importance of the theme: the meeting of Cortés and Moteuczoma. Here more than at any other time, her talents as a translator were essential to the success of the Spanish campaign. For the most part, the Aztecs and Spaniards are represented on equal footing—a decision no doubt meant to visually acknowledge the royal status of the great Aztec king, Moteuczoma II. He has just dismounted from a pseudo-Baroque throne supported by Aztec princes who wear European crowns. Now positioned under a bejeweled canopy supported by his four royal nephews, he uses his staff of office to support himself as he moves toward the Spanish entourage. Of particular note are the robes worn by the Aztec royalty; they seem to owe more to images of ancient Roman sculpture than to actual indigenous textiles. Cortés, who possesses an equally impressive demeanor, wears a silver suit of armor embellished with gold hardware. He moves forward to embrace Moteuczoma.

It is important to draw attention to both Malinche's physical position and her appearance in this image. Unlike many indigenous representations created during the sixteenth century, Malinche is not positioned between the two men. Rather, she stands behind Cortés. Further, although she is a translator, her mouth is closed. Gestures by the king and the conqueror indicate an ongoing conversation between the men, despite their language differences and Malinche's silence. Her function here, then, is more as a silent witness than as a mediator. Her secondary status is underlined by Cortés's body, which blocks most of Malinche's in a proprietary way.

Her appearance has also changed from earlier images. She no longer wears her hair in the traditional two-horned coiffure associated with indigenous women. Her hair flows around her neck and shoulders, and the artist has crowned her with a *xiuhuitzolli*, a crown generally associated with indigenous lords and their male descendants. Clearly, the seventeenth-century artist of this painting did not understand the headpiece's gender associations. Her garments have also been modified. While she still wears a *huipil*, it has been covered by a richly brocaded European vest of a type reminiscent of those worn by sixteenth-century European monarchs.

What is perhaps most disturbing about Malinche, however, is her skin color. Are we to understand that Malinche has spent so much time with the Spaniards that she has taken on not only the new religion and garb of the conquerors but also their pigmentation? Her skin color is significantly lighter than Moteuczoma's; in fact, she even appears to be lighter than Cortés. This kind of racial reassignment of exotic, compliant women appears during the seventeenth century not only in painting but also in plays associated with the Conquest.[9] As Stacie Widdifield has noted, by the eighteenth and nineteenth centuries, this kind of representation of indigenous women would become commonplace in nationalist images associated with the Conquest (1996). While Malinche is quite prominent on the Kislak canvas, there is no indigenous agency here, no mediation between cultures. Her function in the seventeenth century seems to be as a symbol of cultural hybridity and assimilation directed toward a single audience. In her new, redefined, and re-membered form, she can safely be consumed by the *criollo* gaze.

CONCLUSION

It is only in light of Malinche's ambivalent treatment in earlier documents that her new figuration in the Kislak canvases becomes understandable. Sixteenth-century representations of Malinche were directed toward two audiences: one indigenous and the other European. Logically enough, the images contain visual components derived from both groups. Nonetheless, these works were strongly impacted by the changing social and political circumstances of the native scribes who produced them, which is why pre- and post-Contact indigenous constructions and rationalizations of history and gender must be considered when examining images of Malinche. The pre-Columbian templates provided the parameters of definition and informed expectations for the post-Contact indigenous reading of Malinche.

As political and economic power shifted firmly into *criollo* hands in the seventeenth century, the evolution of a "new" past was inevitable. The need for a history that was, on the one hand, distinctly their own and, on the other hand, an ideological equivalent to that of Europe led to the use of Old World visual correlates. What was presented in the Kislak scenes of the Conquest was a new imaginary—a reconstruction of memory that was familiar yet essentially new. The accompanying changes in representations of Malinche were in keeping with the need to bestow upon her a level of respectability concomitant with seventeenth-century elite norms. The fact that artists in the seventeenth century felt comfortable taking liberties in manipulating her image is reflective of European organizational templates that validate elite expectations of memory, history, and gender.

In the final analysis, the paucity of written information on Malinche from the sixteenth century created a kind of tabula rasa, a blank surface on which future artists painted myriad Malinches. As a result, comparisons between sixteenth- and seventeenth-century images of the translator offer little disclosure as to her true character. While this may prove frustrating for biographers and art historians, these same differences offer the viewer a window into some of the processes involved in colonization. Multiple visions of the Conquest and the changing representation of Malinche are indicative of the artists' desires to validate their own societies' changing worldviews.

NOTES

1. I would like to thank Andrea Pappas at Santa Clara University and Brian Steele at Texas Tech University for their aid in clarifying various concepts addressed in this chapter. Also, many thanks to the editors of this volume, Rebecca Brienen and Margaret Jackson, for their helpful suggestions.

2. In *Malinche's Conquest* (1999:167–168), Anna Lanyon comments on the forced nature of the marriage and its possible repercussions when she notes that the relationship between Malinche and her husband was strained at best. She also strongly believes Maria may have been the child of Cortés, who assumed a paternal role in the child's life immediately after she was born.

3. See Shedd (1971). The passage constitutes the first words in Shedd's preface and is repeated (presumably for shock effect) on the back of the book's dust cover.

4. Although the seated position of scribe seems odd for Cortés, the identification makes sense, as Malinche is viewed as the mediator between Cortés and the indigenous

groups. With few exceptions, she is not depicted outside the presence of the conqueror in indigenous sources.

5. See Gillespie (1989:59). Gillespie derives this term from *yaocihuatl*, a Nahuatl word meaning "war-woman." See also Klein (1993, 1994) for a discussion of "women of discord" and Aztec gender categories.

6. See, for example, chapter 4, "The Influence of Classical Models on the Renaissance Image of the American Indian," in Moffitt and Sebastián (1996).

7. For a discussion of the art of memory and its Classical roots, see Yates (1966:1–49). For the integration of the art of memory into sixteenth-century Mexican *exconventos*, see Edgerton (2001:236–245).

8. According to Edgerton, in the colonial Mexican version of this, the clergy would aid the public in its process of memorization "by placing images of the holy stories in strategic locations along the liturgical procession routes within the church" (2001:239, cf. 4).

9. See Harris (1993:21). Harris notes the absence or downplaying of ethnicity, especially in women, when he examines William Hogarth's painting, *The Conquest of Mexico* (1732–1735), a work after Dryden's play *The Indian Emperour, or the Conquest of Mexico by the Spaniards* (1665). Harris states, "All the characters, whether they represent conquistador or Aztec, wear European dress. According to Frederick Antal, 'the children are wearing seventeenth century Spanish costumes.' Sixteenth century Cortez thereby suffers only a mild anachronism. But the three Aztec princesses, in elegant satin gowns, are denied all ethnic difference. A discreet feather in the headpiece of each actress is the only token of the exotic; otherwise the Indian princesses have been fully assimilated into the European world of their audience. It was apparently easier to reckon with the proximate otherness of a Spanish man than with 'the exterior and remote' alterity of the Aztec women" (1993:21).

PART II

THE TRANSFORMATION OF HISTORY

Painting the Conquest of Mexico

5

Spanish Creation of the Conquest of Mexico

Matthew Restall

The eight Conquest of Mexico paintings in the Kislak Collection contain a number of themes that were central to the way Spaniards in seventeenth-century Mexico viewed the Conquest. The paintings also reflect a number of larger cultural phenomena. Many of these are discussed elsewhere in this volume, but two are worth mentioning as significant backdrops to this chapter. One was the development of Baroque painting, specifically the ongoing popularity of battle scenes and the florescence of secular-themed paintings commissioned by local elites and executed on a scale suitable for elite homes (far larger than non-elite houses but offering smaller hanging spaces than churches and royal palaces). The second larger phenomenon of particular relevance here was the dawn in late-seventeenth-century Mexico of an interest in, perhaps even a preference for, local themes. This interest—which might arguably be seen as a kind of proto-nationalism—was manifested in the social topic of *mestizaje* and the historical one of the Conquest, both of which were explored in print (as in the writings of Sigüenza y Góngora) (Leonard 1959; Sigüenza y Góngora 1992) and on canvas (as in *casta* paintings and the Kislak series) (Carrera 2003; Katzew 2004).

It should be emphasized (as Schreffler does in Chapter 6 in this volume) that interest in local Mexican themes was still subsumed in the seventeenth century within a discourse and perception of the Spanish Empire that was celebratory, not oppositional. Indeed, the colonial Spanish view of the Conquest is the third larger cultural phenomenon reflected in the Kislak paintings—and it is the subject of this chapter. Spanish perceptions of their invasion and colonization of the Americas were not homogeneous, but by the turn of the seventeenth century a fairly coherent and consistent interpretive narrative had emerged. In this chapter I refer to that narrative as a "mythistory." The term was first applied to the Americas by anthropologist Dennis Tedlock (1985:64), referring to the blending of mythic and historical elements in the great written history of the Quiché Mayas. I use it here to mean a vision of the historical past heavily infused with misconceptions and partisan interpretations so deeply rooted as to constitute legends or myths. This mythistorical vision of the Conquest has its origin in the period of the invasion itself, but it subsequently evolved and, like a snowball rolling down the slopes of Popocatepetl, continued to grow over the centuries as it gathered new elements.

The principal way the conquistadors' own understanding of the Conquest was perpetuated during the colonial period was through official histories—official because they were either written by the royal chronicler or, at the very least, published only with Crown and church approval.[1] Each history drew upon previous ones, so that by the time Antonio de Solís y Rivadeneira (who became royal chronicler in 1661) published his *Historia de la conquista de México* in 1684, such a book contained a distillation of a century and a half of Conquest mythistory (Solís 1968; copy of the 1684 edition in the Kislak Collection, #1993.161.00.0008). It is possible that the Kislak paintings were created shortly after 1684 using Solís's history as a reference (Brienen 2003:34; Schreffler, Chapter 6, this volume); the paintings are narrative in structure, depicting sequences of events within each frame, and their selection of events and details is consistent with that of Solís (some examples of which I offer later).

In this chapter I focus on four aspects of the colonial-era mythistory of the Conquest: the portrayal of the conquistadors as soldiers in a royal army, the perception of native peoples and cultures by Spaniards, the granting of full credit to Cortés (and blame to Moteuczoma) for the fall of the Mexica (Aztec) Empire, and, finally, the theme of redemption.[2] Each of these is discussed in the form it had reached by the late seventeenth century, the same period in which the Kislak paintings were created and Solís's *Historia* was written.

SHOCK AND AWE

The first aspect of Conquest mythistory outlined here is the portrayal of the conquistadors as soldiers in a royal army. Modern images and accounts of the Spanish Conquest are full of references to "soldiers" and Spain's imperial "military operations" and "war machine," suggesting, if not stating, that the conquerors constituted an army sent by the king.[3] The first Kislak painting, *The Entrance of Hernán Cortés into Tabasco,* and the second, *The Arrival of Cortés at Veracruz and the Reception by Moteuczoma's Ambassadors,* reinforce this impression, presenting the Spaniards as a well-armed and well-disciplined military force (Plates 1–2). Although in *The Entrance of Cortés* the invasion force must fight to gain a foothold on Mexican soil (depicting events recounted in the final four chapters of Solís's Book 1), the theme of Spanish military might emerges very clearly in the emphasis in *The Arrival of Cortés at Veracruz* on the symbols of Spanish technological and organizational superiority (illustrating selected moments from the first ten chapters of Solís's Book 2). This is a seventeenth-century vision of a sixteenth-century display of "shock and awe"; the pictorial space is positively bristling with ship masts, lances, and cannons. There are eight ships, most of them large galleons, lying offshore, their gun ports open. Their masts cut the skyline, making them more visible, just as the lances of the Spaniards on horseback are highlighted against the sea and the open space onshore. All six cannons are in the process of being fired. The native audience is depicted as suitably prostrate with awe and fear at the far right, with Mexica ambassadors consequently acknowledging Cortés through the presentation of gifts on the left.

In fact, as primary sources clearly show, the conquistadors were not professional soldiers sent from Spain by the king but professionals from a wide variety of occupations who voluntarily formed and invested in companies of exploration and conquest. At times, the conquistadors were asked to state their occupations; such records for the invasions of Panama, Peru, and Colombia show that on average only 3 percent of conquistadors claimed to be soldiers or artillerymen (Lockhart 1972:38; Avellaneda 1995:91, 93; Restall 2003:35–37). Comparable records have not survived from the Conquest of Mexico, but biographies of Mexico's conquistadors constructed from various sources, such as their own merit reports (*probanzas de mérito*), show that in Mexico—as elsewhere in the Americas—the conquerors were mostly middle-ranking professional men, from merchants and notaries to artisans of all kinds (Thomas 2000). Such men acquired martial skills and battle experience in the Americas, but their goal was to settle and prosper in peace as beneficiaries of colonialism. Thus the Crown had no formal army in the New World; its role was merely to grant invasion licenses and confirm the privileges and status of these armed entrepreneurs should they be successful in founding a new colony.

Conquest accounts of the early sixteenth century, including those by participants such as Cortés, do not refer to company members as soldiers—although this is not always clear from English translations, in which Cortés's *trescientos peones*, for example, is glossed not as "three hundred men on foot" but as "three hundred foot soldiers" (Cortés 1983:32, 1986:50) (for more on Cortés's letters, see Díaz Balsera, Chapter 3, this volume). A 1528 writ of payment to three Spaniards, signed by Cortés and cataloged in the Kislak Collection as "Payment to two soldiers," does not, in fact, describe the men as such; one is given no label and the others are called *marineros* ("sailors") (Kislak Collection #1989.028.00.0002). Pedro de Alvarado does not use the term *soldado* in his letters to Cortés, written in the 1520s and describing his recent invasion of highland Guatemala (Alvarado 1924; Restall and Asselbergs 2007). Nor does it appear in the report of the *fundición,* or division of gold and silver, among the men at Cajamarca in 1533 (1557 MS copy in the John Carter Brown Library).

However, in the late sixteenth century, the term gradually begins to appear in Spanish sources. There is one use of the phrase *soldados españoles* in Friar Diego de Landa's brief account of the Conquest of Yucatan (in the surviving late-colonial copy of excerpts from a lost original manuscript composed in the 1560s; Landa 1982:29). In one collection of thirty-six letters written in the sixteenth century by conquistadors and other settlers, the term *soldado* appears once, in a 1556 letter written by a Spanish woman recently arrived in the colonies (Lockhart and Otte 1976:15). The term is common in Bernal del Castillo Díaz's narrative, written in the 1570s but not published until 1632. In seventeenth-century accounts, especially those by royal chroniclers, from Herrera to Solís, the conquistadors are as much soldiers in a well-organized and equipped army as they are in Kislak paintings such as *The Arrival of Cortés at Veracruz and the Reception by Moteuczoma's Ambassadors* (Plate 2). Although Cortés was merely a captain among other captains, albeit one with more political capital, Solís gives the impression of a general with supreme command over "his captains and soldiers [*sus capitanes y soldados*]" (Solís uses the phrase often, but, e.g., 1968:157). This shift in perception—the gradual mutation of conquistadors into soldiers—resulted in part from the impact of Europe's Military Revolution on Spanish military organization and capability (Parker 1996; Restall 2003:30–32) and in part from the institutionalization of Spanish activity in the Americas, as the period of exploration and conquest gave way to more conservative colonial times.

A BARBARIAN EMPIRE

The second aspect of Conquest mythistory illustrated in the Kislak paintings concerns how native peoples and cultures were perceived by Spaniards in midcolonial times. This is shown to some extent or another in the contrasting images of Spaniards and native people in all eight of the Kislak paintings but perhaps most notably in the first three in the series: *The Entrance of Hernán Cortés into Tabasco, The Arrival of Cortés at Veracruz and the Reception by Moteuczoma's Ambassadors,* and *The Meeting of Cortés and Moteuczoma* (Plates 1–3).

During the early decades of discovery and conquest in the Americas (1492–1519), Europeans tended to place native peoples into one of three categories, perceiving them as either lacking the attributes of culture and society, almost like animals; as innocent and childlike; or as savage and wicked (Restall 2003:103–107). The discovery of the Mexica Empire—as well as subsequent discoveries of complex native societies, such as the Mayas and Incas—altered and complicated Spanish perceptions of American natives, and the Kislak paintings attempt to convey something of the imperial importance of Moteuczoma and the Mexica (most notably in the depiction of the emperor receiving a half-bowing Cortés in *The Meeting of Cortés and Moteuczoma*). But elements of early perceptions lingered throughout the colonial period and can thus be detected in the Kislak paintings—in the prostrate, half-naked natives at the right edge of *The Arrival of Cortés at Veracruz*, for example. Even where the Mexica and other native warriors are painted wearing battle dress or other, more substantial clothing (examples are present in all eight frames), native men lack the civilized accoutrements of the Spaniards, such as horses, armor, swords, guns, and ships. Moteuczoma ruled an impressive empire (and the more impressive it was, the greater the achievement of its destruction), but it was still a barbarian empire.

One dimension of Spanish views of American natives, stemming from the perception of them as childishly naive and credulous, is the myth that native peoples took Spaniards for gods. There is evidence that this idea was circulating in Western European culture beginning in the sixteenth century, but there is no good evidence to suggest that natives in the Americas or elsewhere apotheosized European invaders. The myth of European gods still lingers today, mostly in the form of the apotheosis of Cortés—specifically the notion that Moteuczoma mistook Cortés for the returning Mesoamerican deity Quetzalcoatl. This idea, never mentioned by Cortés in his letters to the king of Spain, was promoted by Franciscans in the sixteenth century and was common currency by the time of Solís (1968: e.g., 96) and the Kislak paintings (Restall 2003:108–120). It was supported by the tendency in Conquest mythistory to reduce the Spanish-Mexica War to an encounter of two leaders, one noble and brilliant, the other weak and misguided. This interpretation found favor among Nahuas and Spaniards alike, as it blamed Aztec defeat on a scapegoated Moteuczoma (see Gillespie, Chapter 2, this volume) while glorifying Spanish imperialism through a hagiographic treatment of Cortés.

HERO AND VILLAIN

The Kislak paintings do not depict Mexicas or other natives as unambiguously believing the invaders were divine beings. But there is a tension in the paintings—as there is in Spanish written accounts, beginning with Cortés's letters—between magnifying the Mexica Empire (to highlight its defeat) and emphasizing its barbarian nature by showing that it was ruled by an emperor who was tyrannical, yet weak and credulous. Seventeenth-century viewers of the Kislak paintings would have brought from their reading of Solís or earlier accounts a mental image of Moteuczoma as impressed by the Spaniards from the very start (symbolized by the giving of gifts by his ambassadors in *The Arrival of Cortés at Veracruz*) and, before long, as overwhelmed by them. We might view the prostrate natives at the right edge of this painting as prudent warriors ducking at the sight of cannons being fired and the gift-giving ambassadors at the left edge as constituting a dignified diplomatic mission. But the paintings' audiences in the decades after 1684 were more likely to have been influenced by Solís's suggestion that the rituals depicted in the painting "confirmed their [the natives'] opinion that there came in the person of Hernán Cortés some kind of deity" and that the gifts given by Moteuczoma "were perceived by him as no less than sacrifices" (Solís 1968:96).

In *The Meeting of Cortés and Moteuczuma*, Moteuczoma does not seem to be surrendering to Cortés (on the contrary, the Spaniard seems to be deferring to the emperor), but illustrations of the meeting in some late-colonial editions of Solís's book portray Cortés as bolder and less deferential. Indeed, in these engravings the emphasis is on Cortés's attempt to embrace Moteuczoma, in violation of Mexica custom.[4] Furthermore, by the time of the Kislak paintings, the spin Cortés had placed on this diplomatic encounter—that it resulted in Moteuczoma's recognition of Spanish imperial sovereignty over Mexico—was deeply rooted. This distortion of the Mexica ruler's speech of welcome was echoed by chroniclers through to Solís and beyond and was a popular theme of colonial Mexican art—most notably in the form of the screen painting, or *biombo,* introduced to Mexico City by the Japanese ambassador early in the seventeenth century (for a discussion of *biombos*, see Schreffler, Chapter 6, this volume).

Finally, the colonial construction of the Moteuczoma story, as reflected in the Kislak paintings and in Solís's narrative, culminates in the emperor's murder by his subjects (Plate 4, *The Death of Moteuczoma at the Hands of His Own People*; Solís 1968:245). This ignominious fate undermines the impression of majesty given in the previous painting (Plate 3) and in Solís's Book 3 and much of Book 4. In the Solís account, the emperor's fatal wounding by arrows and stones is framed by his plea to Mexica warriors "to put down their arms," their dismay at seeing him "so humiliated" ("calling him coward, made a woman [*efeminado*] and a vile prisoner of their enemies"), and Moteuczoma's depressed spirits and his rejection of Spanish attempts to cure his wounds (*desviaba los medicamentos*), implying considerable complicity in his own death (Solís 1968:245–246).

Explaining the Conquest of Mexico as the achievement of one gifted leader was part of the larger myth crediting the whole phenomenon of Iberian settlement in the Americas to the genius of Columbus, Cortés, and, to a lesser extent, Pizarro and a handful of other explorers and conquerors. Solís summarized the Conquest of Mexico as a series of "admirable and heroic events," but the reader is left in no doubt as to which hero is most worthy of admiration; the sentence that introduces Cortés cites his bravery (*valor*) and intelligence (*entendimiento*) and asserts that in his handling of the Conquest lay "the success of his destiny" (*la felicidad de su destino*; Solís 1968:23, 41). Fundamental to the glorification of Cortés was the condemnation of Moteuczoma; the mistakes and weakness of the one underscored the genius and strength of the other. Inevitably, Moteuczoma's failings lead to his death and the empire's collapse (Gillespie, Chapter 2, this volume; Restall 2003:96–97, 113–115, 124, 134), while Cortés's destiny is to lead his men to victory. Cortés is featured and identified in the first three paintings and again in the fifth and sixth, but he is most prominent in the seventh painting in the series, *The Conquest of Tenochtitlan*, at the moment of his triumph (Plate 7). The largest figure in the frame, Cortés is shown on a rearing horse, sword held high, almost inviting the viewer to see what he has accomplished.

A coda to Cortés's triumph is *The Capture of Cuauhtemoc*, the final painting in the series (Plate 8) and likewise the event that closes Solís's account; Solís's last paragraph is framed with "Cuauhtemoc captured" and Cortés hailed as "illustrious captain" of an "admirable conquest" (1968:353). The contrast in the Kislak series between the fourth painting, *The Death of Moteuczoma at the Hands of His Own People,* and the last is most significant—more so than might at first be apparent. Although the two paintings were not intended to hang directly next to one another, the significance of the juxtaposition lies as much in what is missing as in what the paintings represent. To see how this choice of events serves the paintings' purpose in glorifying Cortés and the Conquest and illustrating the colonial Spanish understanding of events, we need only imagine the reverse depiction—the capture of Moteuczoma (defended by Solís as an unfortunate but prudent exigency; 1968:188) and the death of Cuauhtemoc (ignored by Solís). Cortés and other conquistadors successfully turned their tale of Moteuczoma's surrender, early house arrest, and later stoning by his own people into the conventional version of events. But an alternative story—in which Moteuczoma was seized once the situation of the invaders in Mexico-Tenochtitlan became desperate and then had his throat cut in secret by the Spaniards—circulated in the sixteenth century and is thought by most historians today to be closer to the truth

(Brooks 1995). Thus, the reality of the Spanish role in Moteuczoma's capture was ambiguous at best, if not dishonorable and treacherous.

Similarly, Cuauhtemoc's death would not have made a suitable subject for a painting intended to flatter Cortés and illustrate the glorious nature of the Spanish invasion; the last Aztec emperor was hanged from a tree four years after the empire's fall, hundreds of miles from Mexico, and following a hurried at-dawn judgment passed on trumped-up charges of a vague plot of revolt (Restall 2003:147–156). Such events did not fit well into Spanish Conquest mythistory and thus, not surprisingly, did not become the subject of one of the eight Kislak paintings.

REDEMPTION

It is important to pay special attention to the treatment of light when assessing the differences between these two paintings. The fourth painting is relatively dark, reflecting the difficult situation in which the Spaniards found themselves, while in the eighth the skies are cloudy but bright, representing the sunny aftermath of the Spanish victory. This stylistic dark-light contrast is paralleled by the starker contrast in *The Sad Night* and *The Battle of Otumba* (Plates 5–6). These two paintings illustrate the last of the four mythistory themes to be discussed in this chapter—the theme of redemption.

Central to Spanish imperial ideology, as it developed in the late fifteenth and sixteenth centuries, was the idea that all and any aspects of conquest and colonization were justified by the bringing of Christianity to the Americas and the subsequent redemption of native converts. The Franciscans promoted this idea most strenuously, portraying Cortés as a divine agent and, through that role, redeeming him and his fellow conquerors. The dark-light contrast present in *The Sad Night* and *The Battle of Otumba* is not just one of night and day (when these events took place) but also one of doom and desolation (albeit temporary), followed by salvation and redemption. As the battle turns in the sixth painting, the dark clouds to the left are pushed back by the white clouds and blue sky on the right, while one's eye is drawn both to the commanding figure of Cortés in the center of the picture and to the white horse immediately behind Cortés at the center of the action. The eye-catching white horse reminds viewers of the supposed appearance of Santiago, the patron saint of the (Iberian) Reconquest and the (New World) Conquest, at the battle's crux.

According to *The Battle of Otumba*, Cortés saved the day, but with the redeeming assistance of divine intervention. Solís similarly presents these events in juxtaposition to each other, ending Book 4 of his volume with a swift-moving narrative of the bloody escape from the city and the redeeming triumph over "all Mexican forces (*todo el poder mexicano*)" (1968:256–267). As in the Kislak painting, Solís places Cortés in a pivotal role, riding in "to rescue with his men those in most distress (*los mayores aprietos*) and bearing on his lance the dread and destruction of the enemy (*llevando en su lanza el terror y el estrago del enemigo*)" (1968:266).

The theme of redemption is carried over into the fifth and final book of the Solís account, which details the systematic subjugation of the Valley of Mexico, culminating in the inevitable fall of the Mexica capital city (1968:269–353). This theme is also central to the seventh Kislak painting, *The Conquest of Tenochtitlan*, in which Mexico-Tenochtitlan is not destroyed but saved, not consumed by disease and violence but overwhelmed by the forces of light. This is a more dramatically providential Conquest of Mexico than the one presented in comparable illustrations in native sources (such as the *Codex Mexicanus*, with its depiction of the smallpox epidemic as the prelude to defeat, and the *Codex Azcatitlán*, which includes native porters and an African slave or servant accompanying Cortés).[5] In reality, the Tlaxcalans outnumbered Spaniards during the siege by a factor of 400 to 1 (Hassig 1988:56; Oudijk and Restall n.d.), but in *The Conquest of Tenochtitan* they appear in the top right-hand corner, almost as an afterthought. Although black slaves and servants were few in number during the Spanish-Mexica War (there were many more on later Conquest campaigns), they played a significant role in the conflict. Yet no African figure appears in the Kislak series. In the Spanish vision of the Conquest there is little room for black conquistadors or native allies. Instead, the tale is one in which a glorious leader redeems a barbarous land, a perspective encapsulated neatly and simply in the caption to the seventh painting: *La caída de Tenochtitlan (The Conquest of Tenochtitlan).*

By the time Solís wrote his synthetic account of events, the redemptive rationale behind the Spanish Conquest had long come under attack from other Europeans—a criticism that would eventually become known as "the Black Legend" (Gibson 1971). Indeed, Solís began the first chapter of his book by stating that he had quickly dropped his original notion of picking up where Herrera had left off in 1554 because he soon realized that he had a more pressing "obligation" to illuminate earlier events (his book begins in 1517 but is almost entirely devoted to the invasion and war of 1519–1521). This obligation was a reaction to "the great daring and no small malice of foreign authors in inventing whatever they wish against our nation" (Solís 1968:25). Solís presents this need to impugn and argue against (*redargüir*) foreign authors as the primary motive for his choice of subject, thereby offering readers a tale of redemption with an additional contemporaneous jingoistic dimension.

The caption to the seventh painting—*La caída de Tenochtitlan*—encapsulates much of the mythistory of the Conquest that made up the conventional narrative of the event in the seventeenth century and beyond. Simply put: a man triumphs over an empire. The implications are equally simple: the superiority of what that man represents (a nation, a faith, a civilization) and the redemption, the divinely sanctioned rise, of the empire that replaced the Mexica. The success of that narrative, both when the Kislak paintings were freshly composed and in the centuries that followed, is eloquently captured by Prescott's words of homage to Solís's account. Solís "fixed his attention on one great theme—one that, by its picturesque accompaniments, the romantic incidents of the story, the adventurous character of the actors and their exploits, was associated with many a proud and patriotic feeling in the bosom of the Spaniard—one [that] afforded the brilliant contrast . . . of European civilization to the barbaric splendours of an Indian dynasty" (Prescott 1994:582).

NOTES

1. The best known of these were Francisco López de Gómara's hagiography of Cortés, first published in 1552 (Gómara 1964), and Bernal Díaz del Castillo's *Historia verdadera*, published posthumously in 1632 and much praised by Solís in 1684 (e.g., 1968:27) but not achieving the fame it enjoys today until the late nineteenth century (Díaz del Castillo 1963). Neither author was a royal chronicler; Gómara was chaplain to Cortés and later to his son, while Díaz del Castillo was a conquistador of Mexico. The most notable accounts of the Conquest by royal chroniclers were in the 1553 *Crónica de la Nueva-España* by Gonzalo Fernández Oviedo de Valdéz and in Antonio de Herrera's *Historia general*, first published between 1601 and 1615. Neither was as widely read in the seventeenth century as Gómara and Díaz, although all were superseded in the eighteenth century by Solís's account, which saw over eighty editions between 1684 and 1800 (Prescott 1994:287, 386, 472, 582; Few 2003:23). William Prescott, whose 1843 account has been enormously influential ever since it appeared, wrote that "the two pillars upon which the story of the conquest mainly rests, are the Chronicles of Gómara and of Bernal Díaz" (1994:471), meaning that subsequent historians, from Solís to Prescott himself, relied heavily on those two narratives.

2. A fuller articulation of the arguments in the "Shock and Awe" section may be found in Restall (2003:chapter 2); the section titled "A Barbarian Empire" is drawn largely from the same source, chapter 6; and the "Hero and Villain" section is more fully substantiated in chapter 1 of that source.

3. For sample quotes and sources, see Restall (2003:27–28, 169n2).

4. The illustration is reproduced in Brienen (2003:35). It was common in early modern Europe for illustrations to appear in multiple volumes; this one, for example, also appeared in John Harris's *Voyages and Travels* of 1748 (reproduced in Restall 2003:81). In Solís's account, Cortés is not attempting to embrace the emperor but merely to "throw over Moteuczoma's shoulders" the gift of a necklace of imitation diamonds and emeralds (1968:159).

5. These images are often reproduced in print and found easily on-line, but see, for example, Boone (2000:68–69, 228–229).

6

The Conquest of Mexico and the Representation of Imperial Power in Baroque New Spain

Michael J. Schreffler

Late-seventeenth-century New Spain was the setting for the production and circulation of a large number of paintings on screens, panels, and canvas depicting episodes from the Conquest of Mexico, with eleven distinct sets still in existence today. Art historians have seen the emergence of this Conquest imagery as evidence of a rising spirit of political autonomy and identity among Creoles, the descendants of Spaniards born in the Americas (Dujovne 1984:232–233; Vargas Lugo 1993, 1994, 2005; García Saíz 1994, 1999a; Cuadriello 1999). Such an interpretation is typical of a broader tendency in the literature, in which the visual culture of seventeenth-century New Spain is held up as an expression of proto-nationalistic sentiments that ultimately led to the establishment in the nineteenth century of the politically autonomous nation of Mexico (Toussaint 1948:191–289; Burke 1992:97–105). In particular, scholars have placed these late-seventeenth-century images of the Conquest within the context of that nascent nationalism, arguing that they represent a subtle act of resistance whereby the Creole elite began to wrest the writing of history, and, subsequently, the possession of political power and authority, away from the Crown.

Certain seventeenth-century retellings of the Conquest narrative may indeed function in this manner. As Matthew Restall (2003; Chapter 5, this volume) has shown, the narrative rapidly became a flexible "mythistory," which was modified and deployed to any number of ends. Nonetheless, a close examination of the imagery and provenance of the late-seventeenth-century Conquest paintings from New Spain tells a different story. In what follows, I consider some of the imagery from that corpus, arguing that this late-seventeenth-century iconography of the Conquest reveals a laudatory treatment of the theme that positions the work more squarely within a discourse about Spanish imperial power than within one of resistance or opposition to that power. The political tenor of these works is a matter of art historical interest, but it also has broader implications for the history of Spanish colonialism. As I shall suggest, these rhetorically complex images of the Conquest attest to the contested nature of history in colonial New Spain as well as to anxieties about the power and longevity of the Crown in the late-seventeenth-century Hispanic world.

CONQUEST AND THE TRANSFORMATION OF SPACE

One of the formats in which visual representations of the Conquest of Mexico appeared in late-seventeenth-century New Spain was that of the pictorial folding screen, or *biombo*. Such screens had a long history as bearers of visual imagery in Asia (Grilli 1970), but the use and circulation of the format in New Spain is a function of Spanish imperial expansion and trade. Decorative folding screens produced in Asia arrived regularly throughout the seventeenth century at Acapulco, the viceroyalty's principal Atlantic port. The demand for *biombos* in New Spain was both satisfied and fueled by the importation of works from Asia, and by mid-century, painters in the viceroyalty were producing their own pictorial screens on the model of the Asian imports (Castelló Yturbide and Martínez del Río de Redo 1970; Curiel 1999). The iconography of those New Spanish *biombos* was often similar in genre to that of their Asian counterparts, including panoramic views of cities, allegorical representations of the parts of the world, and notable historical events.

The extant corpus of seventeenth-century screens includes at least six that take the Conquest of Mexico as their subject. Of these, four juxtapose images of the Spaniards' campaigns against the Aztecs, painted on one side of the *biombo,* with a panoramic view of viceregal Mexico City and its environs, painted on its reverse.[1] Among the works in this remarkable genre-within-a-genre is a ten-panel *biombo* (Figures 6.1, 6.2), today in the collection of the Franz Mayer Museum in Mexico City, which represents the Conquest of Mexico as a sequence of discrete vignettes distributed across its leaves (Castelló Yturbide and Martínez del Río de Redo 1970:36–37; García Saíz 1994; Cuadriello 1999; Kagan 2000; Vargas Lugo 2005). The vignettes are labeled on the screen like chapters in a book, with the letters "A" through "I" keyed to a legend in the lower left corner. It would be reasonable to expect that both the painted vignettes and the legend would reconstruct for the viewer a chronological sequence of events in the conventional Conquest narrative, for example, as it was recounted in the contemporary texts of Bernal Díaz del Castillo (1632) and Antonio de Solís (1684), but that is not the case. Instead, the screen presents the viewer with a series of places that served as the settings for individual episodes in the Conquest narrative. For example, letter "C" in the legend reads "House and balcony where they stoned Moteuczoma."[2] It refers to a vignette at the lower center of the screen, but its phraseology emphasizes the existence and location of the house and its balcony over the historical act it claims took place there—the stoning of Moteuczoma. Similarly, letter "D" in the legend reads "Temple that was in the Plaza of Mexico, where today the Palace is located,"[3] referring to the polygonal structure in the upper center of the screen; the letter "E" reads "Temple that was in Santiago Tlatelolco, where today the church is"; [4] and letter "I" refers to "the causeway of Guadalupe, where the Spaniards and their allies, the Indians of Tlaxcala entered."[5]

The *biombo*'s pictorial rendition of the Conquest of Mexico, then, is an inventive representation of the campaigns of Cortés, the Spaniards, and their Indian allies against Moteuczoma II and the Mexica because it employs place rather than narrative as its chief compositional structure. But when regarded in relation to the imagery that serves as its foil on the screen's other side—the panoramic view of seventeenth-century Mexico City—the *biombo* becomes a more complex object whose dual images do, indeed, construct a historical narrative. The screen's image of the city is represented through the use of a pseudo-perspectival scheme in which the streets approximate orthogonal lines that recede into the distance and converge at what can be roughly understood as a "vanishing point." That point is also the location of the city's royal palace, a building that is painted white, thus contrasting with its neighboring structures. As the architectural representation of the king in the viceregal capital, the palace emerges from the landscape as an important and controlling entity in the city: the structure around which all other structures and institutions are arranged and the one to which the sharply curving aqueduct at the bottom edge of the screen leads the eye. The fact that the royal palace is given such compositional prominence in the image suggests something of the cityscape's—and, ultimately, the screen's—position in a visual discourse about imperial power in seventeenth-century New

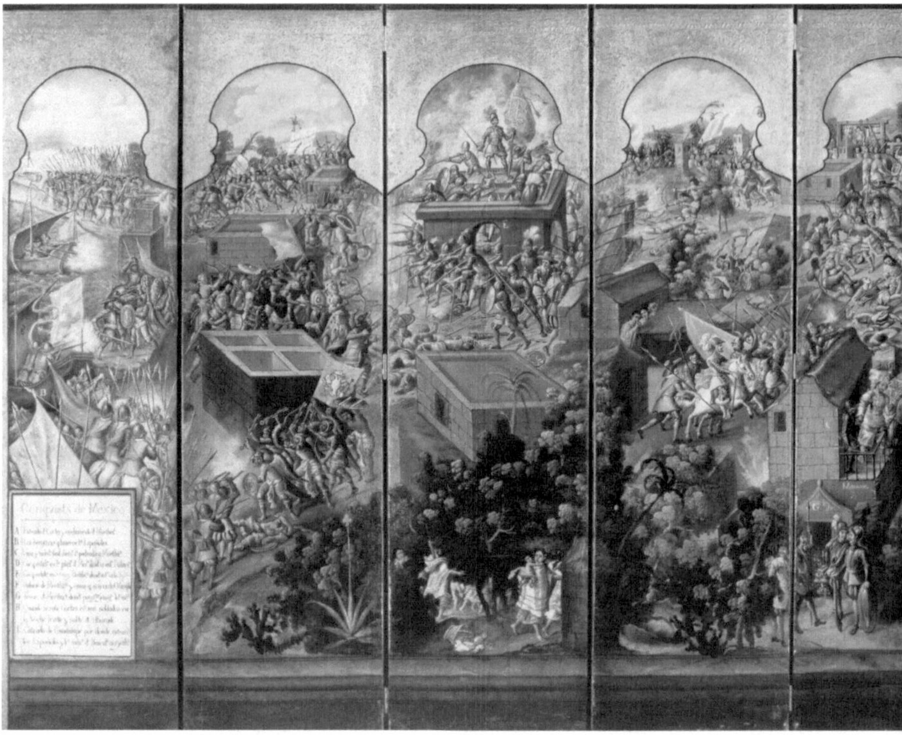

Figure 6.1. *Conquest of Mexico*, ten-panel biombo (view of front), late seventeenth century. Oil on canvas, 213 × 550 cm. Photo by Michel Zabé. Courtesy, Franz Mayer Museum, Mexico City.

Spain (Schreffler 2004, 2007). That discourse is referenced further by the title of the legend in the cityscape's lower-left corner, which identifies the screen's subject in imperial parlance as the "Very Noble and Loyal City of Mexico." The "loyalty" referenced in the legend is the city's loyalty to the Crown, a relationship of political allegiance and obedience rendered here in terms of surveillance and panoramic spectatorship.

The *biombo*'s juxtaposition of these images, the Conquest of Mexico and the City of Mexico, is neither accidental nor whimsical, for each employs a number of interrelated compositional and rhetorical devices that link one to the other. Most obviously, and as scholars have noted, the two sides of the screen represent a single space at two distinct moments in its history (Cuadriello 1999; Kagan 2000). The Conquest side represents Aztec Tenochtitlan in the early sixteenth century as the geographic and architectural setting for certain events in the Conquest of Mexico, while the cityscape side represents a utopic vision of the built environ-

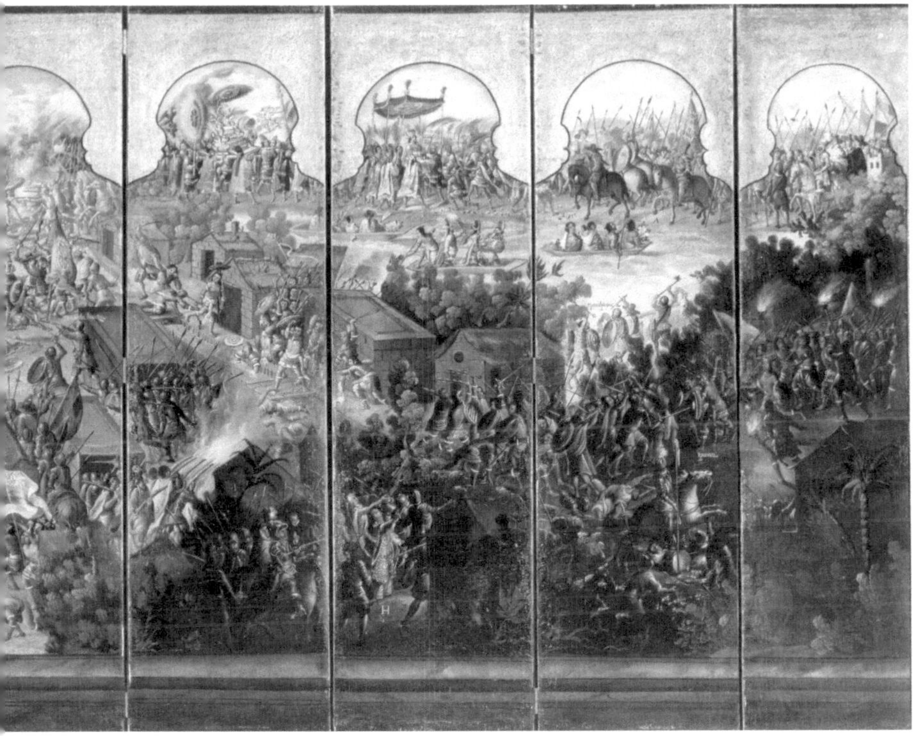

ment of seventeenth-century Mexico City under Spanish rule. The royal palace, positioned near the top and center of the screen, is literally superimposed upon its architectural antecedent, the polygonal structure identified on the Conquest side of the screen as the "Temple that was in the Plaza of Mexico, where today the Palace is located." This, in turn, solidifies the panoramic cityscape's relationship to the Conquest imagery painted on its reverse.

Read in relation to one another, the two sides of the screen conceptualize the history of the Crown's rule in New Spain in terms of the transformation of geopolitical space: Aztec Tenochtitlan, rendered as compositionally chaotic and nearly illegible to the casual viewer, becomes Mexico City, depicted as a civic space that is orderly and geometric as well as "noble" and "loyal." The contrast the screen establishes between the sixteenth-century past and the seventeenth-century present suggests that its inventive vision of the Conquest is one told from a particular perspective. Like the text of Bernal Díaz (1632), it is a memory. Here, through a

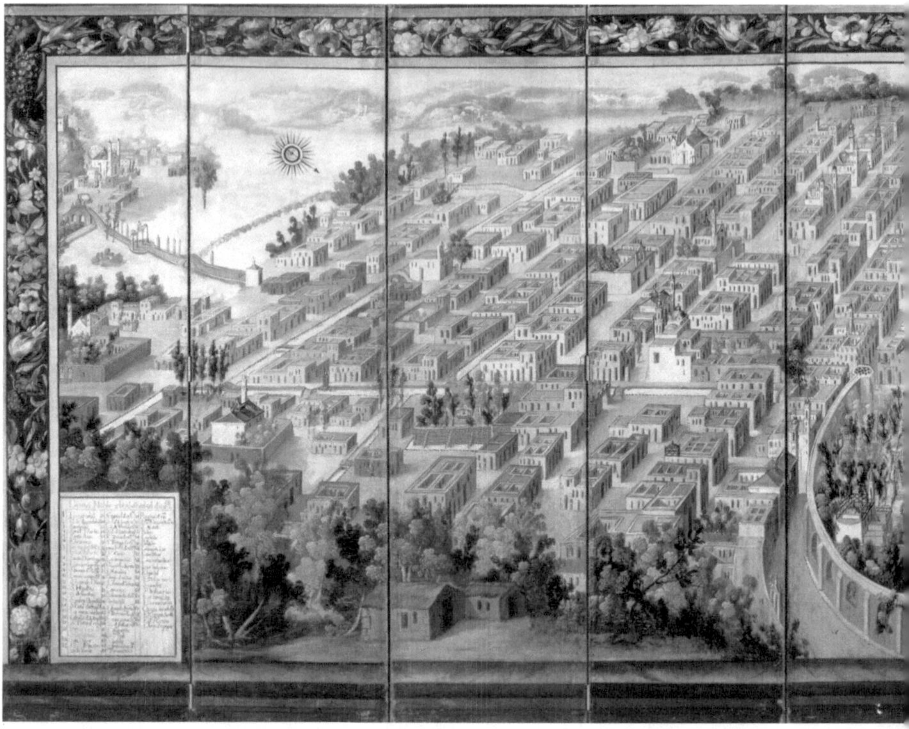

Figure 6.2. *The Very Noble and Loyal City of Mexico*, ten-panel biombo (view of back), late seventeenth century. Oil on canvas, 213 × 550 cm. Photo by Michel Zabé. Courtesy, Franz Mayer Museum, Mexico City.

panoramic survey of the structures built over the ruins of Aztec Tenochtitlan, a vision of the events of the early sixteenth century can be recalled through tactics similar to those of the ancient art of memory (Yates 1966).

In addition to presenting the history of Spanish imperialism in the Americas in terms of the transformation of space, the narrative as represented on the *biombo* forcefully asserts that it was the power of the Crown that brought about that transformation from Aztec Tenochtitlan to the "noble and loyal" City of Mexico. Indeed, on the cityscape side of the screen, the presence and power of the Crown is symbolized by a highly ordered composition and the royal palace, while on the Conquest side its force is indicated by the numerous standards of Castile and León, which, carried by Cortés and his men, emphasize that their enterprise was one undertaken in the name of the king and that the spoils of war would ultimately belong to him. As such, the screen's imagery resonates with the rhetoric of Antonio de Solís's 1684 *Historia de la conquista de Méjico*, an account that

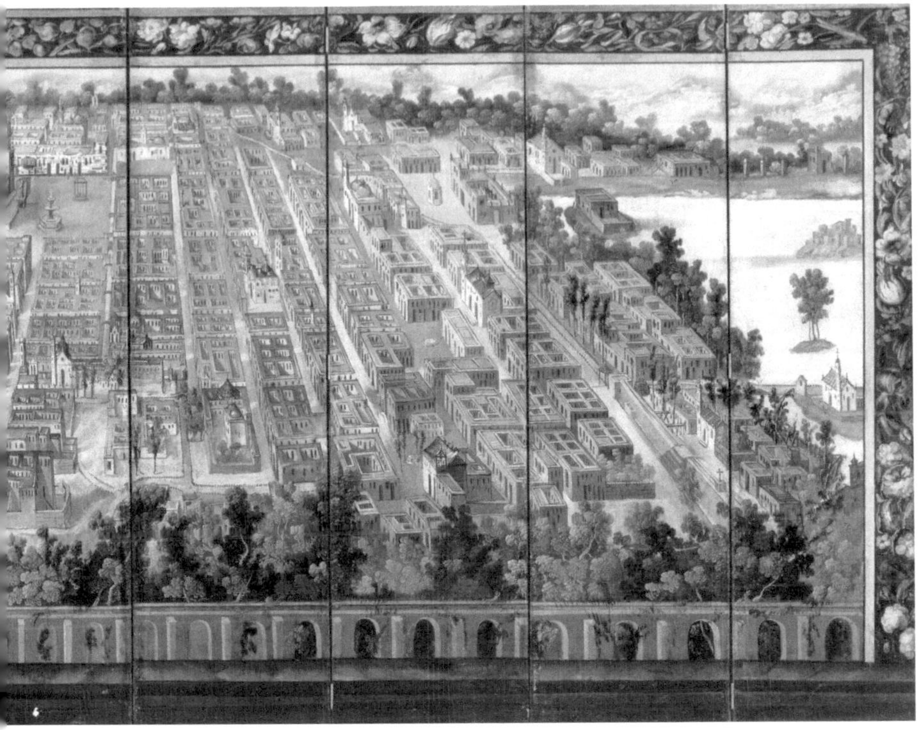

glorified the events of 1519–1521, extolled the loyalty and bravery of Hernán Cortés, and, ultimately, credited the Holy Roman emperor, Charles V, with having brought about the Conquest of New Spain. As Solís wrote: "The Influence of the new King [i.e., Charles V] quickly arrived in the Americas, his name functioning there just as his presence did in Spain. Men's minds became disposed to great undertakings; the soldiers' courage grew and they put into action the operations that preceded the Conquest of New Spain, whose empire heaven had destined to exalt the beginnings of the reign of this august Monarch" (Solís 1684:I, Bk. 1, ch. 5).[6]

Like Solís's *Historia*, the *biombo*'s laudatory treatment of the Conquest theme partakes of what David Brading (1991:50) has called the "Imperial school of New World History," an official mode of historiography that squares with what is known about the social lives of the Conquest/cityscape *biombos*. Although there are few concrete provenance data for the screens, anecdotal evidence suggests that at least some of them circulated in the ambit of the Spanish and New Spanish nobility, perhaps within the families from which the viceroys and other political appointees to New Spain had been drawn.[7] The screens' deployment of that laudatory, "imperial" mode of historiography is precisely the version of the story one might expect to have been promoted by that social group, dependent as it was on royal favor for its very survival. As such, the nobility's apparent embrace of an official, imperial retelling of the Conquest narrative suggests the degree to which a shared history, presented on these *biombos* as collective memory (Halbwachs 1992), constituted a common point of identification for a geographically scattered community of imperial subjects.

CONQUEST AND THE PRODUCTION OF LOYAL SUBJECTS

The Conquest of Mexico is also the subject of the imagery on at least five distinct but stylistically similar suites of seriated panel paintings produced in late-seventeenth-century New Spain (Dujovne 1984:117–218; García Saíz 1999a). This corpus of Conquest paintings is characterized by the prevalence of gold, red, and black pigments in its imagery, the use of mother-of-pearl mosaic to adorn certain areas of the composition, and the appearance of a lacquer-like layer on the panels. Because of the artists' inventive use of shell (*concha*) mosaic in their compositions, these panels are often referred to as *enconchados* (or "shell-encrusted objects") in the art historical literature. On the basis of provenance, data, and the appearance of the date 1698 on one of the panels in the corpus, the entire body of Conquest *enconchados* is generally dated to the late seventeenth century. Similarly, because of the appearance of the names Juan González and Miguel González, who may have been brothers, on several of the panels, the works are associated with these artists, their workshop, or both. Scholars have further suggested that Juan and Miguel González were descendants of Asian immigrants, a hypothesis that squares with the materials, style, and formal characteristics of the works attributed to them (Dujovne 1972:15; Armella de Aspe 1990; Tovar de Teresa 1990; Rivero Lake 1994; Ávila Hernández 1997).

As in the case of the Conquest *biombos,* scholars have consistently argued that the use of historical narrative in the Conquest *enconchados* is evidence for a nascent Creole patriotism and identity within the viceroyalty (Dujovne 1984:233; Vargas Lugo 1994:122–123; Cuadriello 1999:69–70; García Saíz 1999a:113–114, 117, 121, 134). But here, too, an examination of their imagery reveals a laudatory treatment of the theme that parallels the one found in both Solís's *Historia* and the Conquest *biombos,* thus positioning the *enconchados* within a world of ideas about imperial power. The following analysis focuses on images from two sets of Conquest *enconchados* (each having twenty-four panels), one in the collection of the Museo Nacional de Bellas Artes in Buenos Aires and the other in the Museo de América in Madrid.[8]

Like the Conquest *biombo,* the Conquest *enconchados,* too, represent the campaigns of Cortés and his men in Aztec Mexico as a radical transformation of space. Such transformations are depicted quite literally on some of the panels. For example, the fourth panel on the Buenos Aires series (Figure 6.3) depicts a sequence of episodes whose juxtaposition rehearses that of the two sides of the folding screens. As described in the circular cartouche at the top of the panel, the uppermost scene is one in which "The soldiers of Capitan Cortés work in the construction of Villa Rica, [and] the Totonac Indians help them."[9] The image depicts the construction of several buildings including, most conspicuously on the right, a church, identified as such by its large portal and tower. Its bell rests on the ground in front of the structure, waiting to be installed. Complementing that image of construction is the one of destruction that dominates the panel's lower sector. There, as recounted in the cartouche, "Capitan General Cortés orders the destruction of the idols that were in the town of Cempoala."[10] The image shows Cortés, at the right, pointing toward the platform where his men use tools to demolish an image, part of which has fallen from the raised area and rests at a soldier's foot. At the center of the panel, two scenes of religious conversion mediate between the episodes of construction and destruction, intimating that in the New World, the transformation of space accompanies a spiritual transformation.

Other panels in the corpus, however, fuse the transformation of space with changes in political subjectivity. Such is the case in a series of vignettes on the panels depicting scenes in which conquered natives perform ritualized expressions of loyalty to the Spanish Crown. For example, the sixth panel in the Madrid series (Figure 6.4) depicts a scene in which, according its accompanying text, the Indians of Cholula "give obedience to the king of Spain."[11] The obedience scene is presented as the aftermath of warfare in Cholula, seen at the center of the panel; it appears in the foreground and shows the figure of the conqueror Hernán Cortés, who points to a red flag bearing the royal insignia as the conquered Cholulans kneel before it. Similarly, the fourteenth panel in the Buenos Aires series (Figure 6.5) depicts a scene in which the emperor Moteuczoma is seated between Cortés and the royal standard in an enclosed space in the midst of a large number of onlookers, where, according to the accompanying text, "The emperor Moteuczoma gives obedience to His Majesty."[12] Here, too, the obedience episode appears in the foreground, where the defeated Moteuczoma appears in a moment of subject re-formation. Seated in the center of a crowded room, he is no longer the crowned king of his own empire. Instead, he is shown in the process of becoming a subject of the king of Spain, an obedient vassal whose crown has been removed from his head. Cortés, seated next to him, gestures toward a standard bearing the arms of Castile and León, indicating that Moteuczoma's allegiance is now to the Spanish Crown.

The representations of the royal standard and the figure of Cortés in both images are the primary means by which the presence of Spanish imperial power is marked. At the same time, however, the panels represent in more subtle ways the transformation of subjugated peoples into subjects loyal to the Crown. Through the graphic representation of bodily gestures and the transformation of pictorial space, the ritual formation of loyal subjects is foregrounded in each panel. Consider, for example, the episode on the Madrid panel (Figure 6.4). The Cholulans kneel in their expression of allegiance in a dark, open space marked by the Cortés figure and the flag at the center of the panel. The space is graphically differentiated from that of the episode pictured above it. That scene, the war in Cholula, occurs in the chaotic pictorial space of the Cholulans, in which weapons clash, horses rear their heads, and the Indians of Cholula fight to their deaths. In contrast, the loyalty scene occurs in a newly produced, orderly space—that of the Crown—with the royal standard and insignia presiding over the events below. Within this space, the Crown enacts a political transformation of the conquered subjects of Cholula. Two Indians kneel, lay down their arms, and prostrate themselves before the standard that marks the king's presence.

This simultaneous transformation of space and subjects is also seen in the Buenos Aires panel (Figure 6.5), in which the Aztec emperor Moteuczoma swears his allegiance to the Crown. The artist's depiction of the first of the panel's episodes, in which the Lord of Texcoco is taken prisoner by order of Moteuczoma, appears in the panel's upper register in a complex, composite space that is expansive—outdoors and boundless to the viewer's left and restricted and enclosed on the right. The boundless space to the left is occupied by a crowd of Indians. It is both the place where the Texcocans comply with Moteuczoma's order and the space in which the authority of the Crown has not yet been made present. In contrast, the space to the viewer's right in that upper register is a darkened, interior setting echoing that of the loyalty scene at the bottom of the panel. It is in that built and enclosed space that the Lord of Texcoco meets Cortés, the figure who stands in for the power of the Crown. The graphic distinction between the dark and enclosed space of Cortés and the Spaniards and the lighter, open space of the Texcocans is strong, juxtaposing a built environment with the space of the natural world. An even more detailed representation of an enclosed space appears at the bottom of the panel. Here, thick red and gray lines double as the rooftop of that space, in which the ritual of loyalty to the Crown takes place. That latter space is further represented as having a textured floor and furniture; it is emphatically depicted as a space produced through human labor rather than as the space of the natural world.

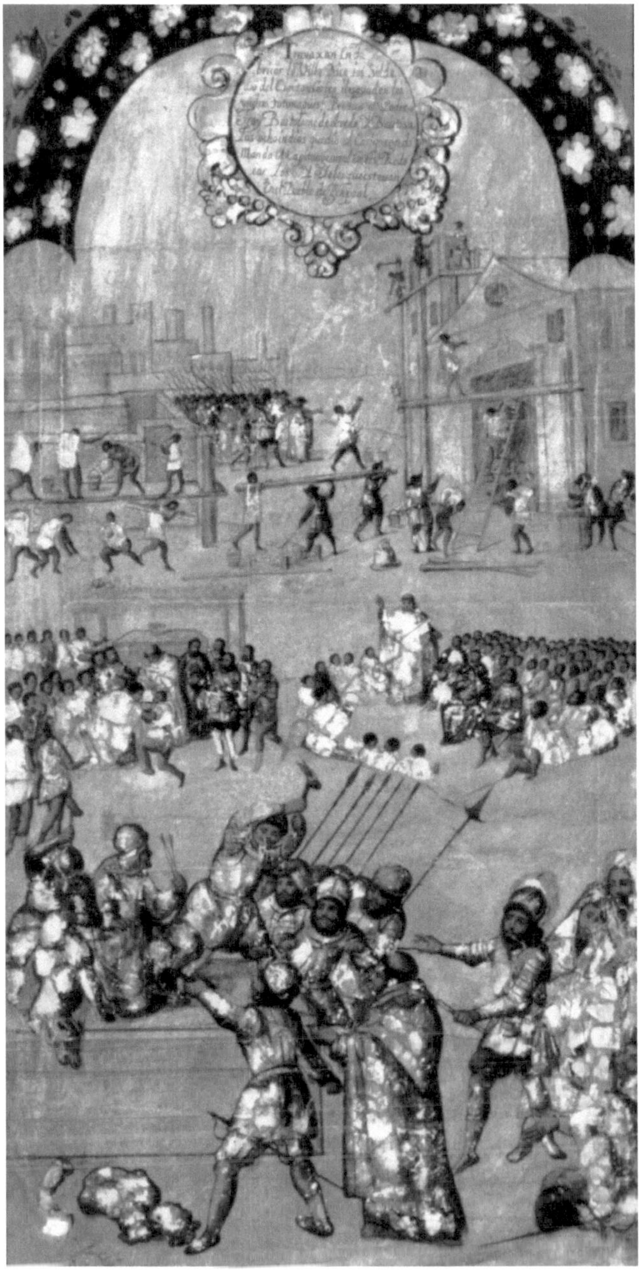

Figure 6.3. *The Soldiers of Capitan Cortés Work in the Construction of Villa Rica,* from *Conquest of Mexico*, late seventeenth century. Ink, paint, and mother-of-pearl on fabric mounted on wood, 100 × 50 cm. Photo by Horacio Mosquera. Courtesy, Museo Nacional de Bellas Artes, Buenos Aires.

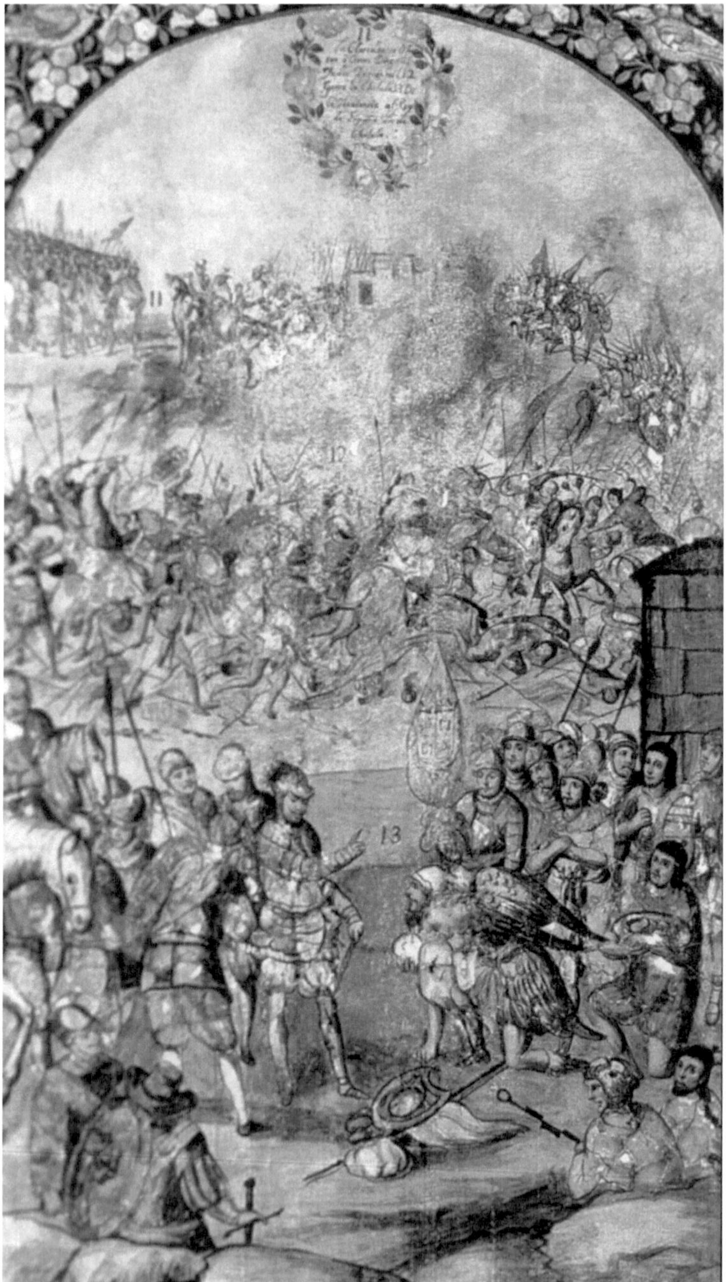

Figure 6.4. *The Indians of Cholula Give Obedience to the King of Spain*, from *Conquest of Mexico*, late seventeenth century. Ink, paint, and mother-of-pearl on fabric mounted on wood, 100 × 50 cm. Courtesy, Museo de America, Madrid.

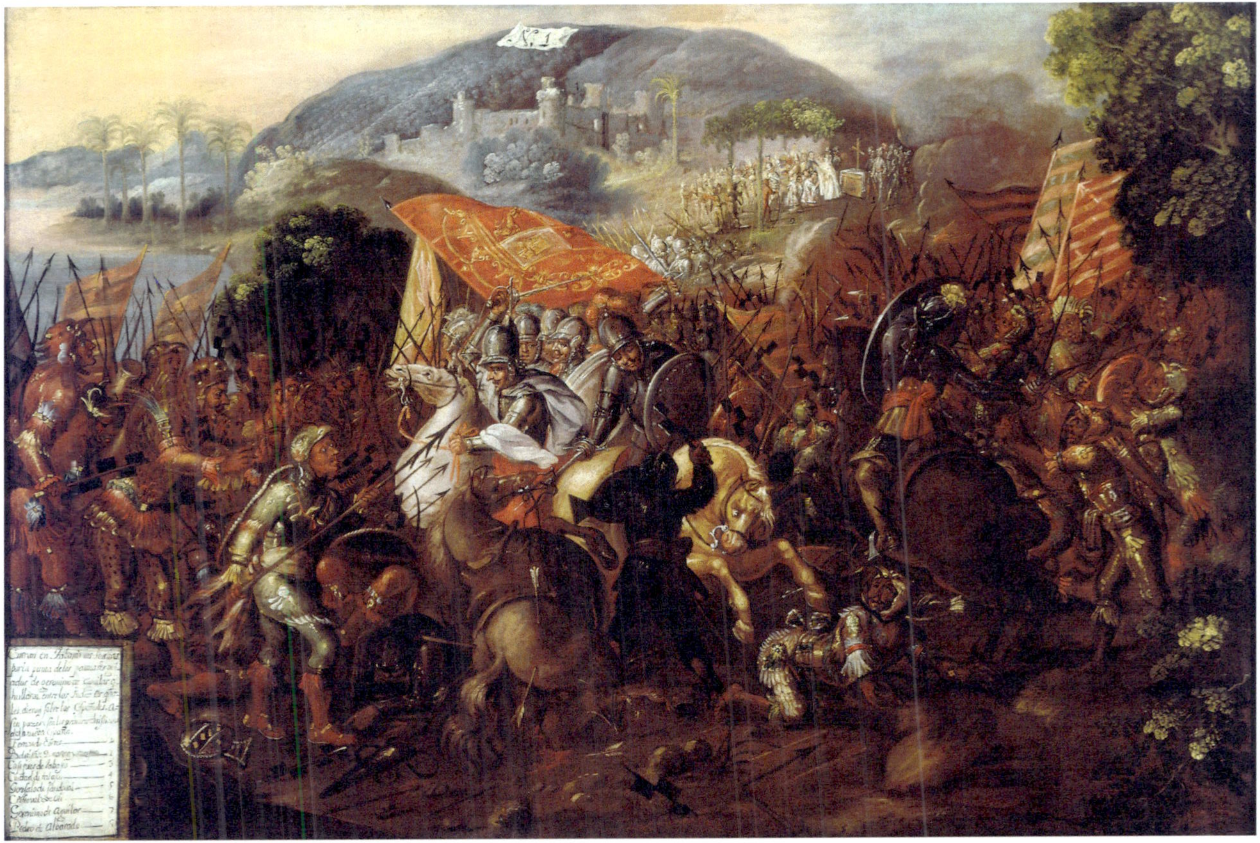

Plate 1. *The Entrance of Hernán Cortés into Tabasco* (La Entrada de Cortés en Tabasco), second half of the seventeenth century. Oil on canvas, 48 × 78 inches.

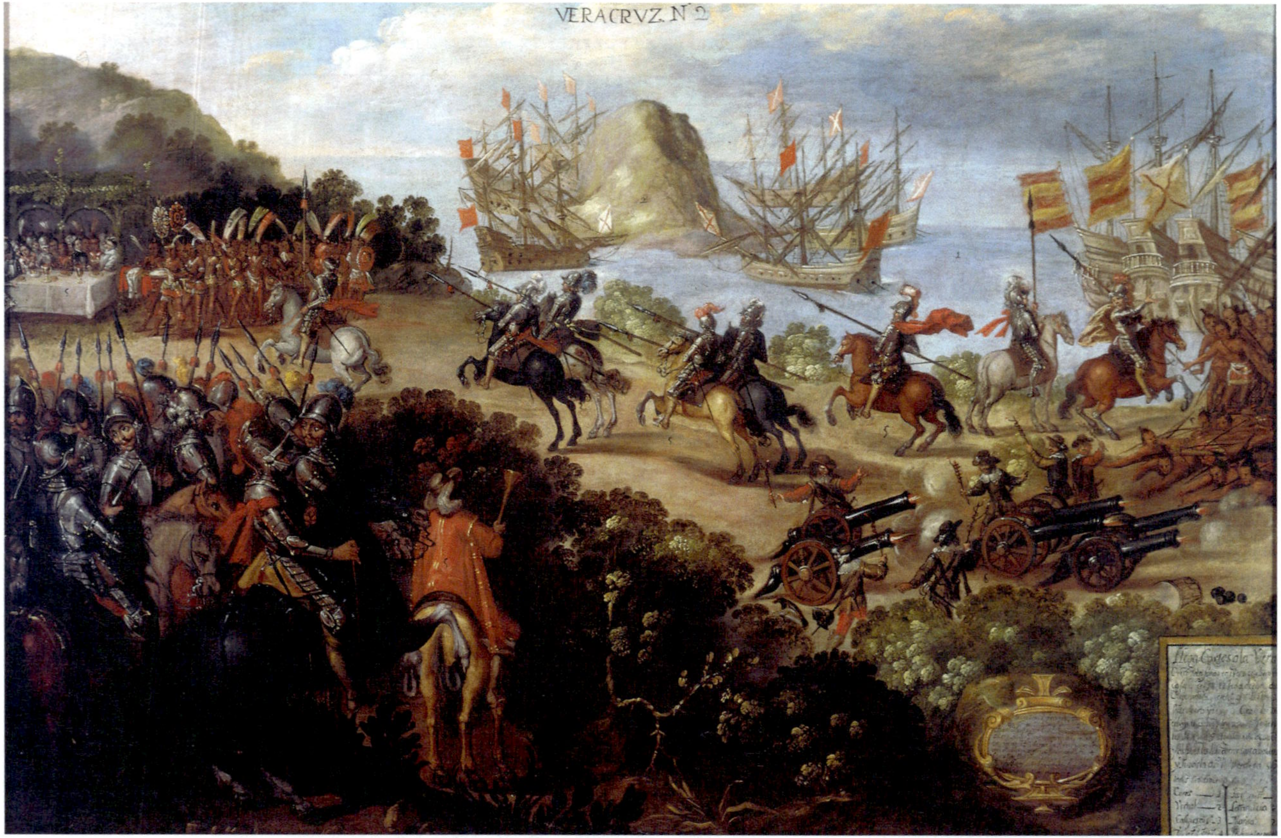

Plate 2. *The Arrival of Cortés at Veracruz and the Reception by Moteuczoma's Ambassadors* (La llegada de Cortés a Veracruz y la recepción de los embajadores de Moteuczoma), second half of the seventeenth century. Oil on canvas, 48 × 78 inches.

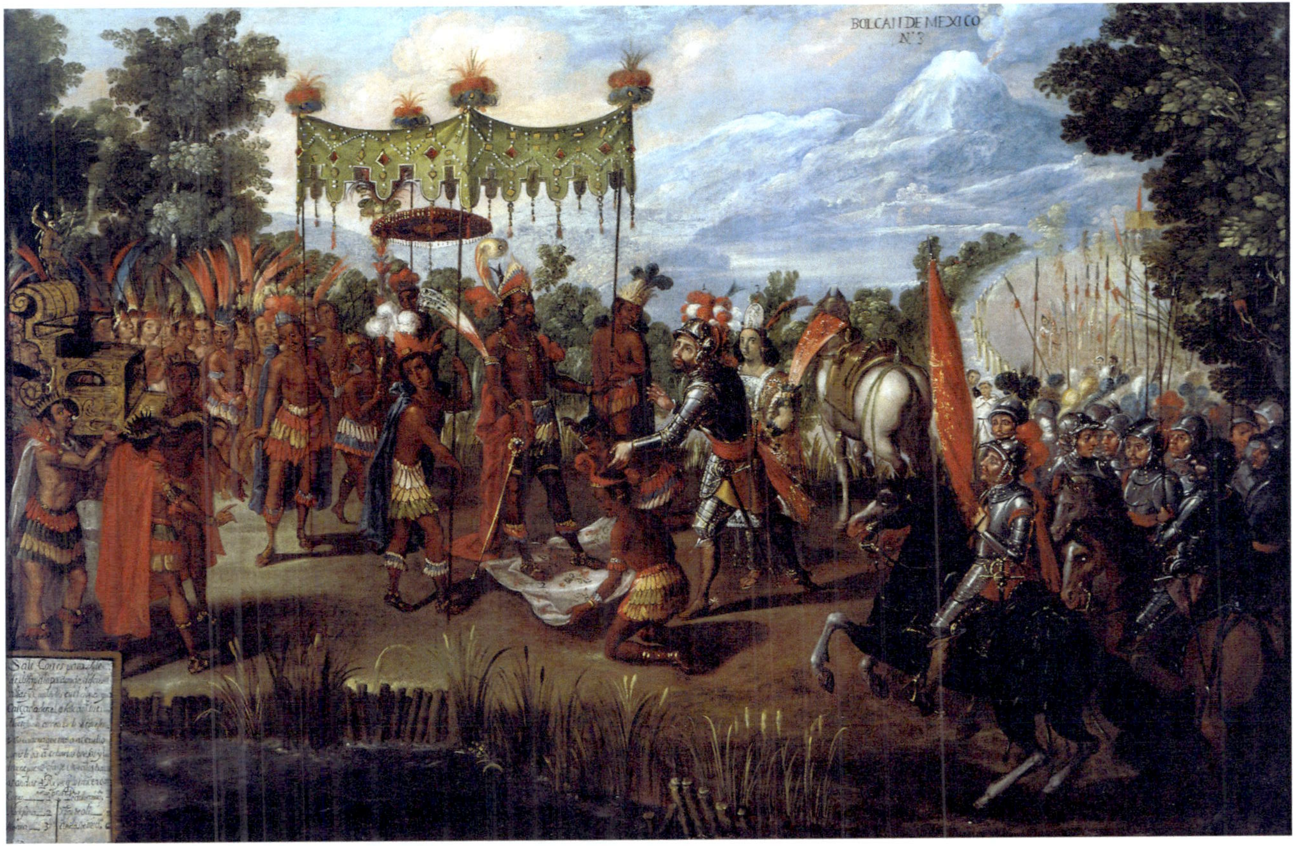

Plate 3. *The Meeting of Cortés and Moteuczoma* (El encuentro de Cortés y Moteuczoma), second half of the seventeenth century. Oil on canvas, 48 × 78 inches.

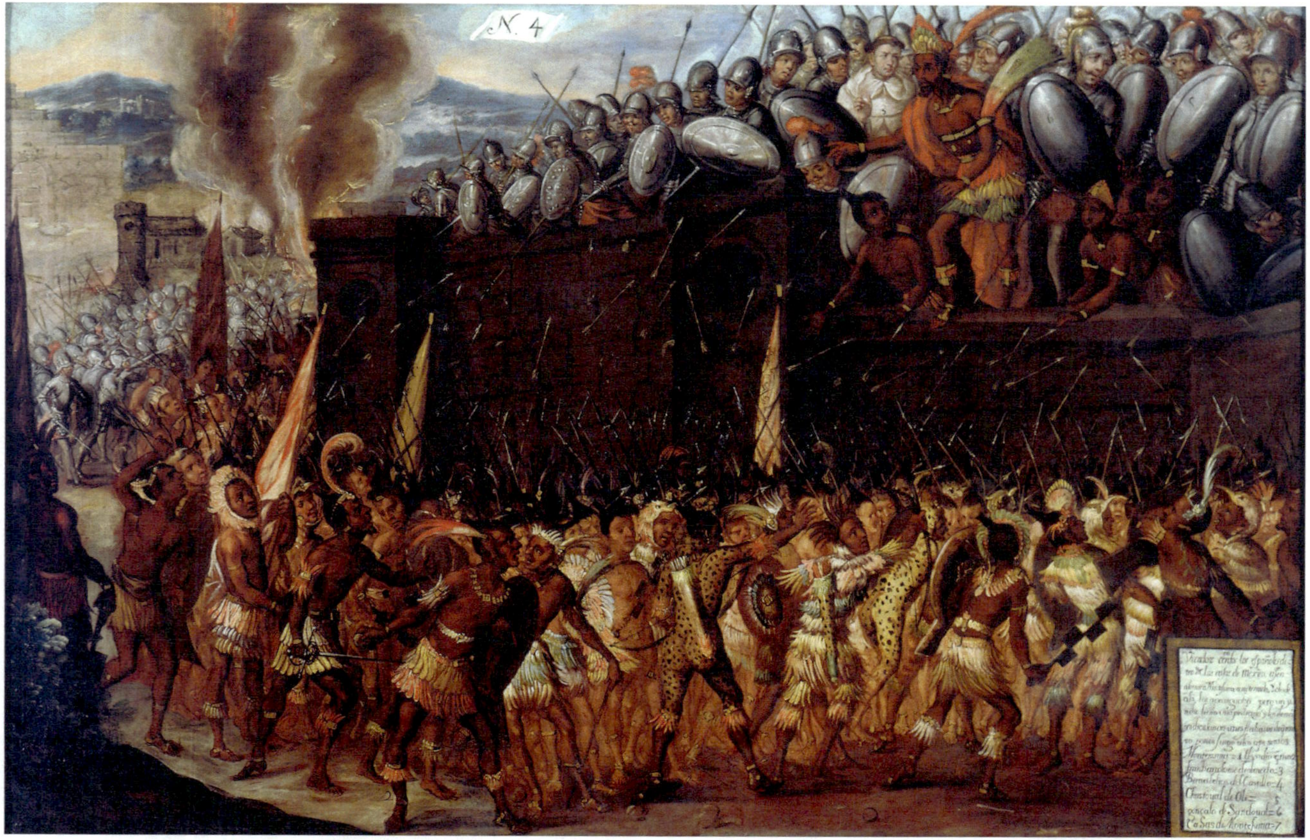

Plate 4. *The Death of Moteuczoma at the Hands of His Own People* (Moteuczoma lapidado por su pueblo), second half of the seventeenth century. Oil on canvas, 48 × 78 inches.

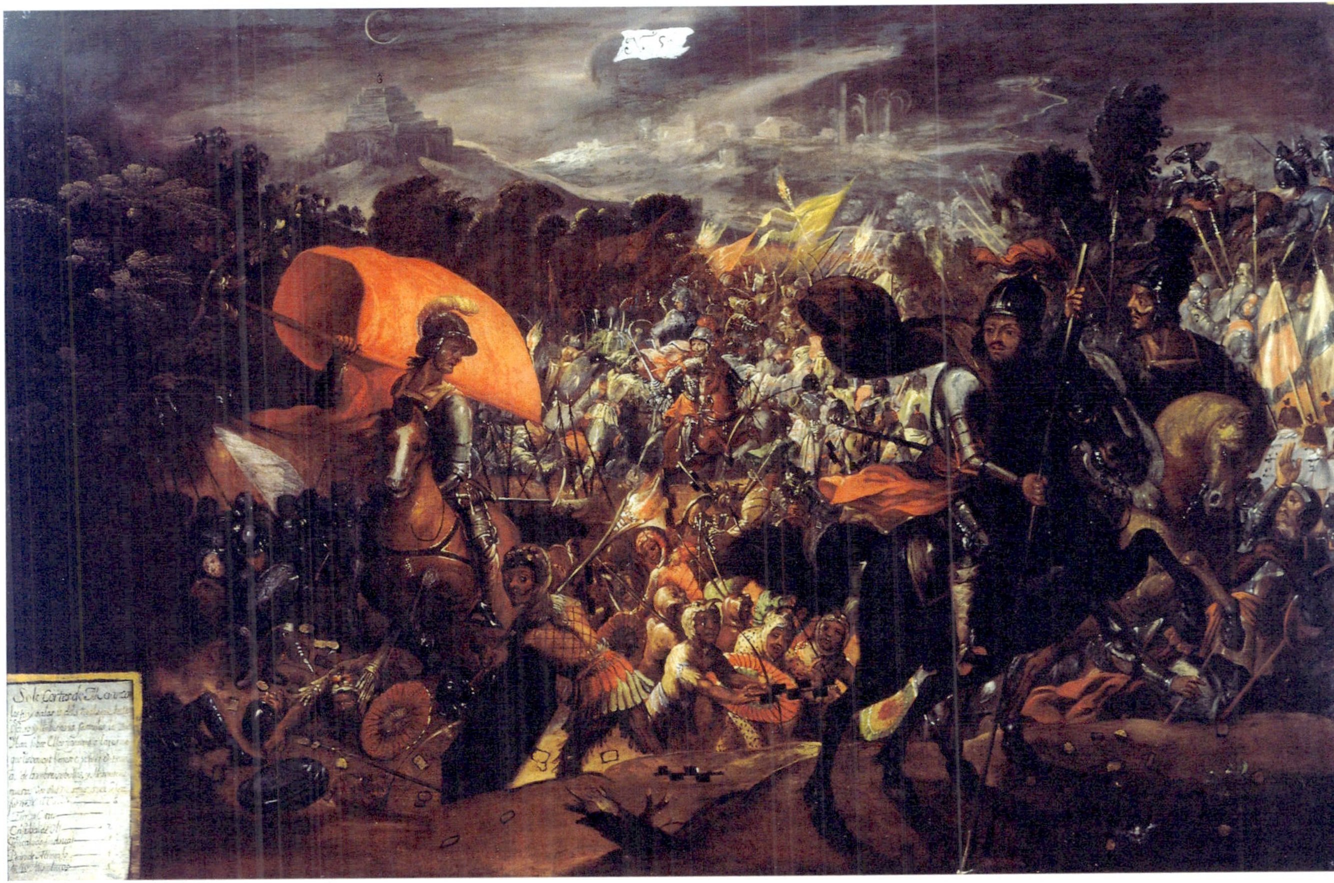

Plate 5. *The Sad Night* (La Noche triste), second half of the seventeenth century. Oil on canvas, 48 × 78 inches.

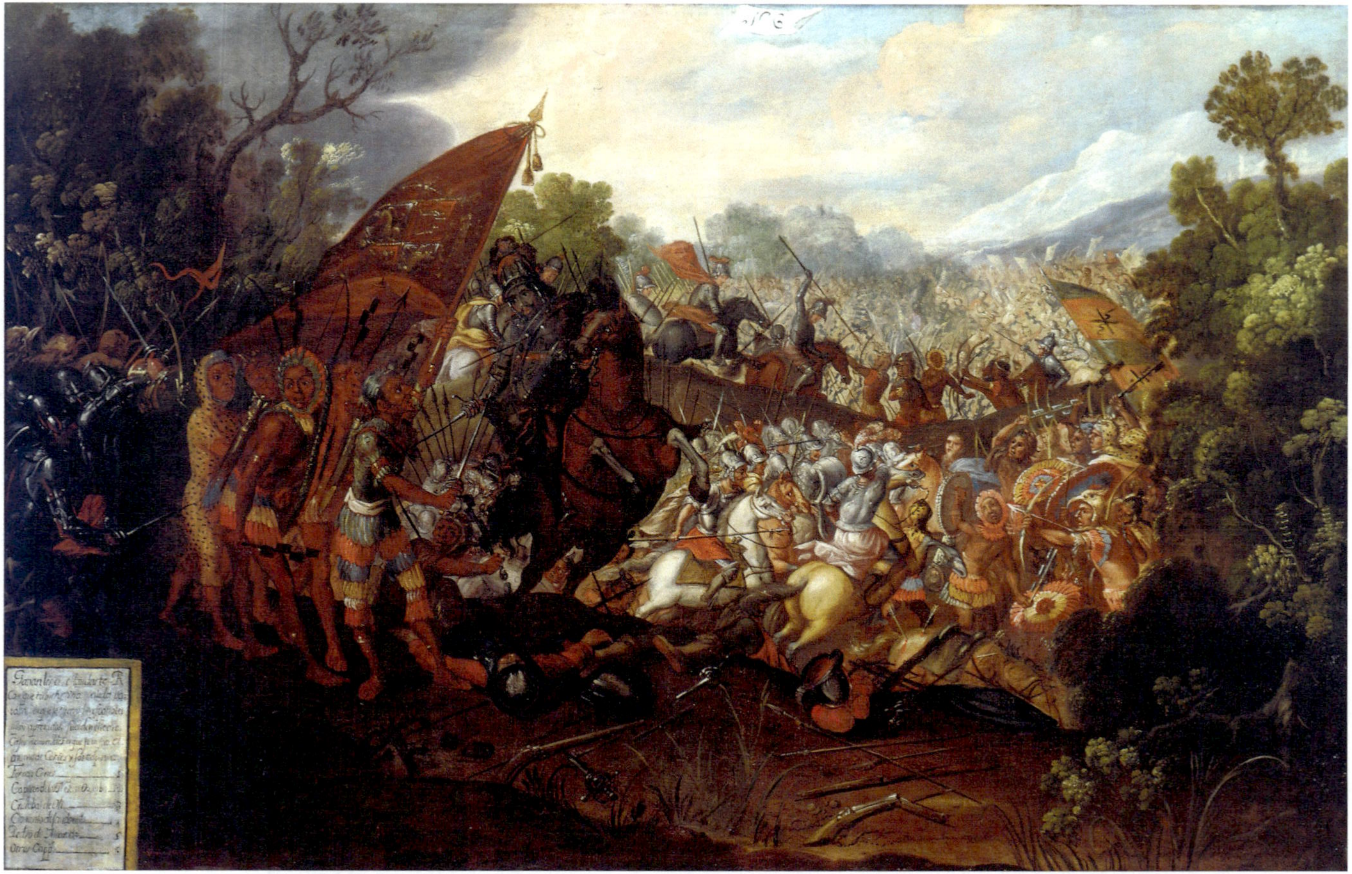

Plate 6. *The Battle of Otumba* (La batalla de Otumba), second half of the seventeenth century. Oil on canvas, 48 × 78 inches.

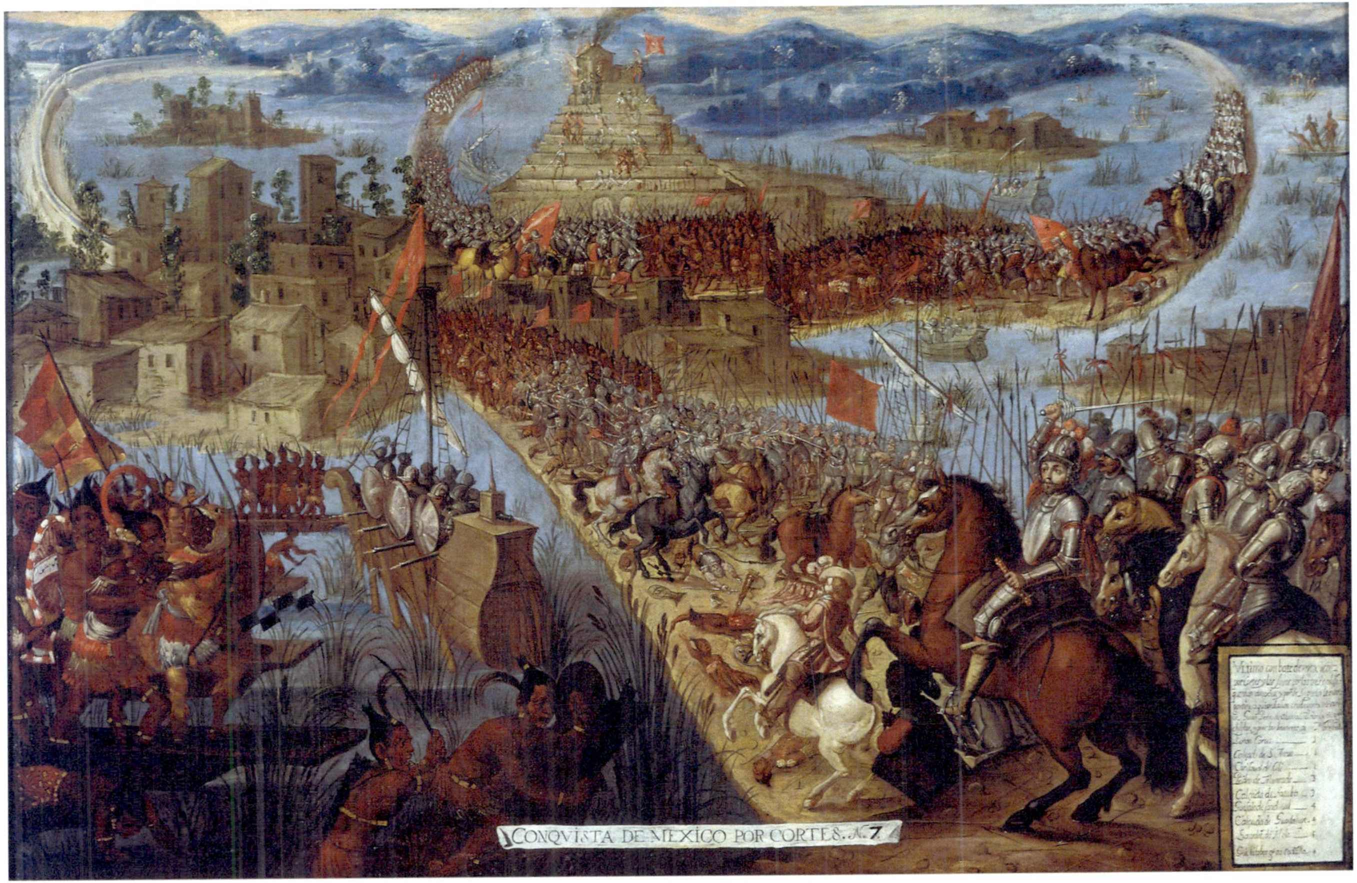

Plate 7. *The Conquest of Tenochtitlan* (La caída de Tenochtitlan), second half of the seventeenth century. Oil on canvas, 48 × 78 inches.

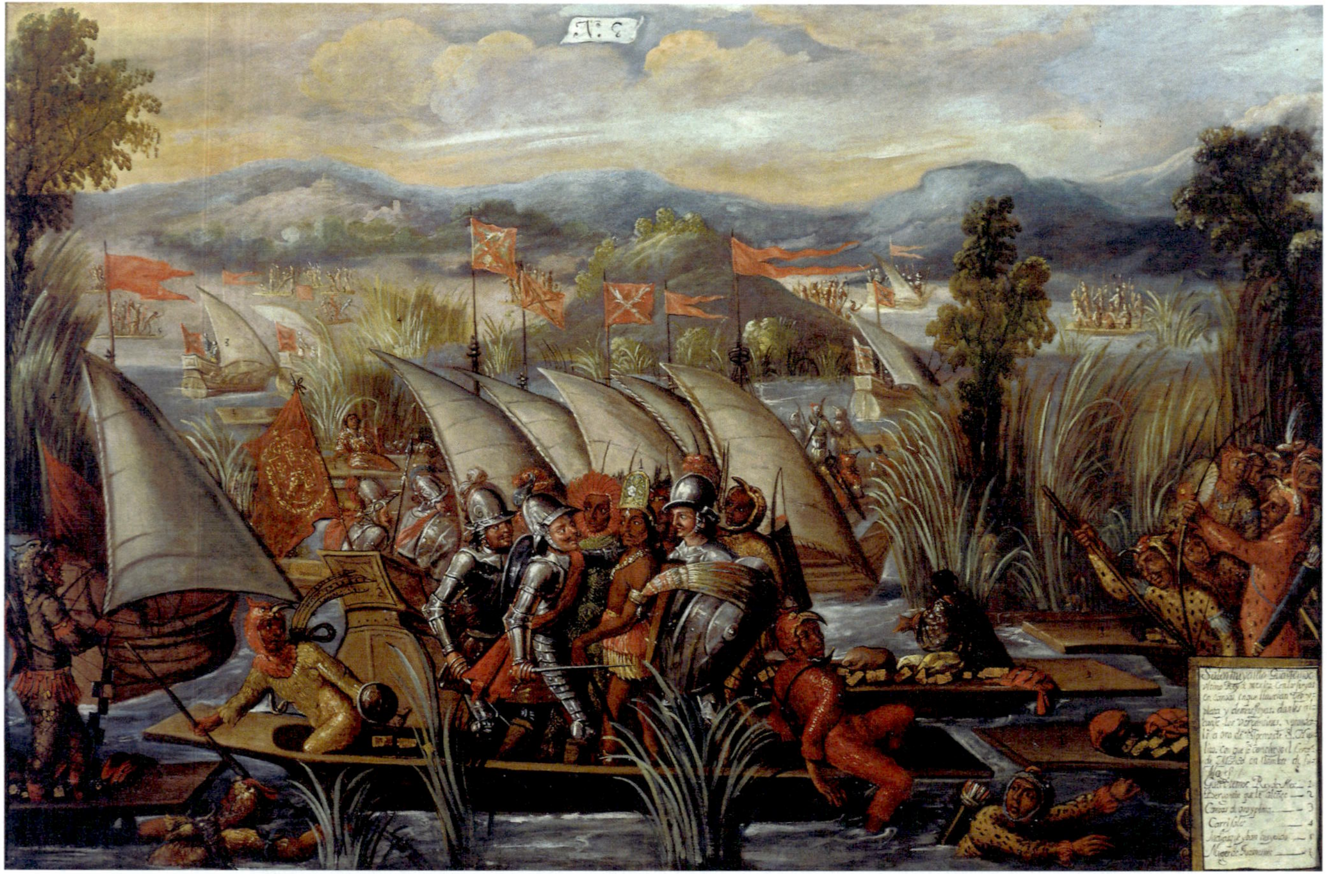

Plate 8. *The Capture of Cuauhtemoc* (La prisión de Cuauhtemoc), second half of the seventeenth century. Oil on canvas, 48 × 78 inches.

Like the complementary imagery on both sides of the Conquest *biombo,* the loyalty scenes on the Conquest *enconchados* use built and structured space as a metaphor for political transformation and, as such, are effective in their demonstration of the Spaniards' victory in Aztec Middle America. But the presence and prominence of these scenes on the panels are even more remarkable for their demonstration of a process of editing and revising of the story of the Conquest of Mexico by the painters and designers of the imagery.[13] The story of Moteuczoma's loyalty is recounted in the texts of both Bernal Díaz del Castillo (1632) and Solís (1684), but its position in the foreground of the panel gives it greater visual importance than the scenes that accompany it. In fact, this story becomes a kind of resolution to the subplot of which it is part. In the case of the scene of the Cholulans' loyalty, an image that also appears in the foreground of this panel, contemporary texts have little to say about the incident. Díaz (1963:ch. 82, 157–158) wrote that Cortés requested that the Cholulans render their obedience to the king and noted that they "gave their word that they would do so, but not before a scribe." In the text, however, there is no scene in which they ritually demonstrate their vassalage. Solís, in his account (1968:III, ch. 4–8, 138–154), makes no mention of the incident.

How can this editing and revising of the Conquest narrative be explained? The answer may relate to the particularities of the production and social lives of the Conquest *enconchados.* As with the Conquest *biombos,* much remains to be discovered about the provenance of these works, but evidence suggests that one or more of the sets was involved in an economy of gift exchange that would have called for the promotion of a laudatory, imperial version of the Conquest narrative. As García Saíz (1999a:112–113) has noted, the inventory taken in 1700 at the royal palace of La Granja, near Madrid, indicates that a set of Conquest *enconchados* was in the royal collections by that date, for they are described in one of its entries as "twenty-four lacquered, mother-of-pearl encrusted panels that can serve as a back wall or low folding screen for the dais" (Fernández Bayton 1975:I, nos. 125–127).[14] This set of Conquest *enconchados* had likely been given to King Charles II as a gift, and it is probable that a viceroy or another high-ranking Spaniard was involved in its patronage and presentation to the king. Scholars have hypothesized that the gift giver may have been José Sarmiento de Valladares, the Count of Moteuczoma and thirty-second viceroy to New Spain, a man who has also been associated with at least one of the extant Conquest *biombos.*[15] Such a transaction between a viceroy and a king would not have been unique in the early modern Hispanic world; paintings and other art objects were customarily given to the king by members of the nobility as expressions of gratitude and loyalty and with the expectation that their gifts would generate the counter-gift of continued favor (Morán Turina and Checa 1985:284; Brown 1995:112, 114–116, 131, 138–139, 141).[16]

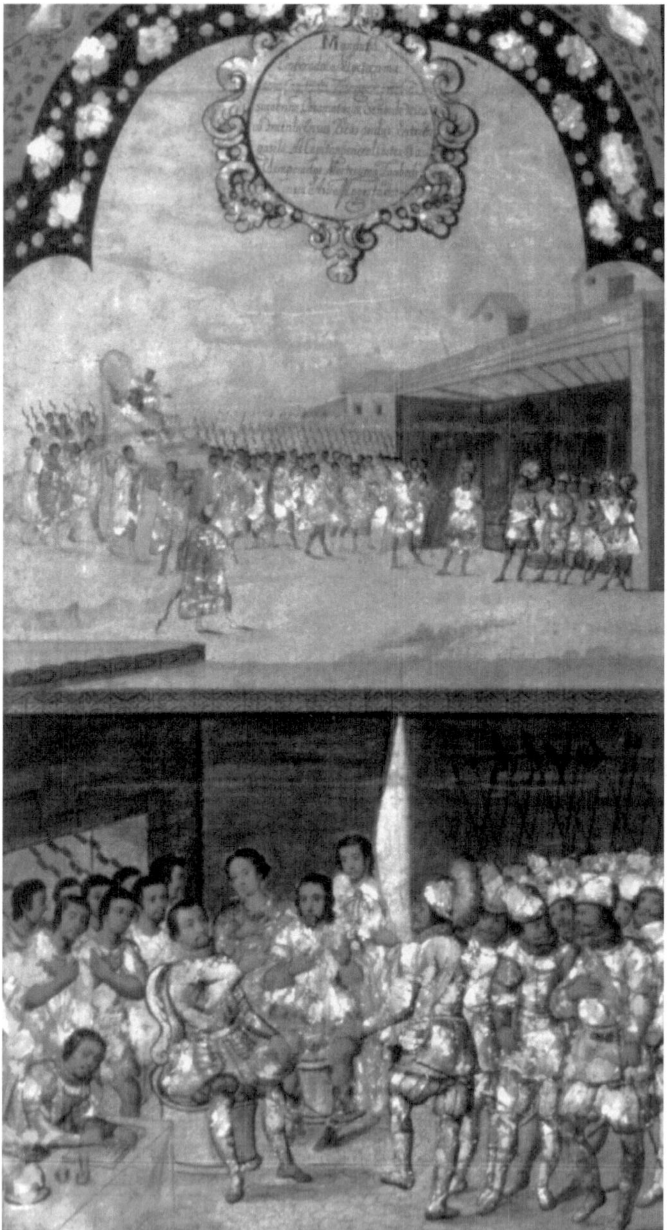

Figure 6.5. *The Emperor Moteuczoma Gives Obedience to His Majesty*, from *Conquest of Mexico*, late seventeenth century. Ink, paint, and mother-of-pearl on fabric mounted on wood, 100 × 50 cm. Photo by Horacio Mosquera. Courtesy, Museo Nacional de Bellas Artes, Buenos Aires.

CONQUEST AND KINGLY PRESENCE

The embrace of this mode of imperial historiography is also evident in the set of eight Conquest paintings, formerly owned by the Jay I. Kislak Foundation and now part of the Kislak Collection of the Library of Congress. Like the Conquest *biombos* and *enconchados,* the Kislak paintings emphasize the transformation of the space of the Aztec Empire in Middle America into a piece of the empire of the Spanish Habsburgs. The works in the series construct a coherent narrative, moving through time and space from the arrival of Cortés and the Spaniards on the Gulf Coast to the eventual siege and overthrow of Aztec Tenochtitlan (Cuadriello 1999:85–91; Jackson and Brienen 2003:57–72; Ángeles Jiménez et al. 2005). The narrative is organized in relation to a series of places, each of the pictures emphasizing in different ways the settings in which the battles and other events of the Conquest occurred. The first canvas (Plate 1) depicts a battle fought in the vicinity of the fortified city of Tabasco. The city, portrayed anachronistically as a massive stone fortress, is positioned prominently at the top of the painting. It is described in the legend in the lower left corner as *Ciudad de Tabasco* (City of Tabasco). The next canvas (Plate 2), the second in the series, depicts events that occurred in Veracruz, a place whose name is inscribed across the painting's upper edge. The third canvas (Plate 3) depicts the meeting of Cortés and Moteuczoma as occurring in yet another place, in the vicinity of the Valley of Mexico. That location is acknowledged at the upper right sector of the painting with the words "*Bolcan de Mexico*" (Volcano of Mexico), a reference to Popocatepetl, a prominent geographic feature in the central Mexican landscape.

The Kislak paintings employ place names and landscape elements, such as volcanoes and bodies of water, to represent and define the locations in which the events of the Conquest occur, but they also indicate pictorially the transformation of space through acts of military conquest. One of the ways they do so is iconographically, through the use of royal standards and other military flags, symbols that appear throughout the larger corpus of seventeenth century Conquest imagery. For example, in the first painting in the series, the city of Tabasco is represented architecturally at the top of the canvas. Its impending political transformation is indicated by the billowing royal standard of Castile, which echoes the walled city compositionally and threatens to obscure it from view. Similarly, the royal standard occupies a prominent place on the seventh canvas in the series (Plate 7), where it is held by the conquistador Pedro de Alvarado, who stands at the apex of the temple-pyramid in the upper center of the painting. Emphasizing that the flags are representations of the presence of the king, the accompanying text reads "Pedro de Alvarado wins the high temple of Huitzilopochtli and places the flags of His Majesty."[17]

An ensemble of other kinds of flags establishes the political status of Veracruz, the setting for the second painting in the series, as a conquered place. Prominent among the numerous banners that adorn the masts of the Spaniards' ships lining the coast in the background is the Raguly Saltire of St. Andrew, a flag that consists of a red "X" shape positioned against a white field. This flag was understood in the early modern Hispanic world to have been used in various sixteenth-century military campaigns of Charles V (Smith 1975:124–125; Calvo Pérez and Grávalos González 1983:58–59). On the eighth and final canvas in the series (Plate 8), the Saltire of St. Andrew appears together with the royal standard, where both flags indicate that the main subject of the painting—the capture of Cuauhtemoc—was an act undertaken and accomplished in the name of the Crown.

In giving pictorial prominence to the royal standards and other devices that emphasize the role of the Crown in the radical transformations of space and place they depict, the Kislak paintings are ideologically similar to the Solís text. As noted earlier, Solís emphasized the role of Charles V in the Conquest of Mexico, "his name doing as much [in America] . . . as his Presence did in Spain."[18] A discursive relationship between these two representations of the Conquest is evident in other ways as well. For example, the spatial and narrative trajectory of the Kislak paintings is identical to that of the Solís text, beginning on the Gulf Coast in Tabasco and ending in central Mexico with the capture of Cuauhtemoc in the eighth painting in the series (Plate 8).[19] In this, they differ from the text of Díaz (1632), whose memoir begins on the island of Cuba, and from the Conquest *enconchados,* whose stories begin in Veracruz and Cozumel.

As others have posited (Cuadriello 1999:85; Jackson and Brienen 2003:57, 96), the similarities between the representation of the Conquest in the Kislak paintings and in the Solís text suggest that the two representations of the Conquest were produced at the same time. If this hypothesis is correct, then the Kislak canvases would also be contemporary with the Conquest *biombos* and *enconchados,* paintings consistently dated to the 1690s in the art historical literature (De la Maza 1968:13; Kagan 2000:153, 217n12; García Saíz 1999a:109–114).[20]

How can this apparent enthusiasm for the Conquest theme at this historical moment be explained? The concentration of these representations of the Conquest at the end of the seventeenth century may relate to the political fears and anxieties of the Spanish nobility at that time. The 1680s and 1690s saw economic and political crises in the empire, as well as numerous challenges to its territorial integrity (Elliott 1963:359–367; Kamen 1980:381–389; Rubio Mañé 1983:II, 92–151). Adding to this atmosphere of imperial decay, Charles II was widely perceived as a weak and ineffectual monarch. The biographical literature abounds with examples of his physical and mental weakness. He is said to have begun to walk only at four years of age, and he is described as illiterate even at age nine. Reports stated that he was unstable on his feet and required constant support; he almost never traveled, and he never produced an heir (Kamen 1980:21).[21]

These troubles may explain the nearly overwhelming presence of regal symbols—in the form of mirrors, eagles, lions, and orbs—in the official portraits of Charles II by Juan Carreño de Miranda (Figure 6.6)—symbols whose presence contrasts sharply with the more austere and understated portraits of his father and predecessor, Philip IV (Gallego 1984:197; Brown 1988).[22] The abundance of those kingly symbols in the Carreño portraits resonates with the concentrated use of royal standards and other flags in the corpus of late-seventeenth-century New Spanish Conquest imagery and, particularly, in the Kislak Conquest of Mexico paintings. In the eighth painting in the series (Plate 8), for example, kingly presence is symbolized by no fewer than fifteen red flags and pennants that adorn the vessels framing the scene of Cuauhtemoc's capture. This profusion of symbols suggests that the works may have emerged in an environment in which it was necessary to articulate the Crown's power in unambiguous terms. Certainly, the final years of the seventeenth century were such a time. In a world where Spanish imperial fortunes were fading, boundaries were shrinking, and the continuity of the Crown itself was in question, the narrative of the Conquest of Mexico may have emerged as a convincing alternative to reality—one that rehearsed the early-sixteenth-century successes of the ruling monarch's namesake, the Holy Roman emperor, Charles V, and that ultimately served as a convenient vehicle for the redirection of the nobility's fears and anxieties.

The version of the Conquest narrative told in the seventeenth-century New Spanish paintings also allowed those loyal to the Crown to project the indignities of the reign of Charles II onto the figure of Moteuczoma II, the king depicted in all late-seventeenth-century visual representations of the Conquest as enduring the ultimate disgrace: that of being killed by his own people. In the Kislak series, Moteuczoma's death appears on the fourth canvas in the series (Plate 4), where the Aztec emperor stands precariously at the edge of an elevated stone structure. Surrounded by Spaniards, he faces a mass of Indians, identified as such by their clothing of feathers and animal skins, standing on the ground below him. Numerous arrows fly through the air toward Moteuczoma, thus reiterating the text in the legend at the bottom left of the painting, which asserts that "An Indian hit him [Moteuczoma] with a stone and the other Indians threw arrows, by which he died."[23] Like representations of the event on the other late-seventeenth-century Conquest paintings (García Saíz 1999a:132–134), the Kislak canvas depicts the Aztec emperor's death as an act of betrayal by his own people. Similar versions of the story are recounted in the sixteenth- and seventeenth-century

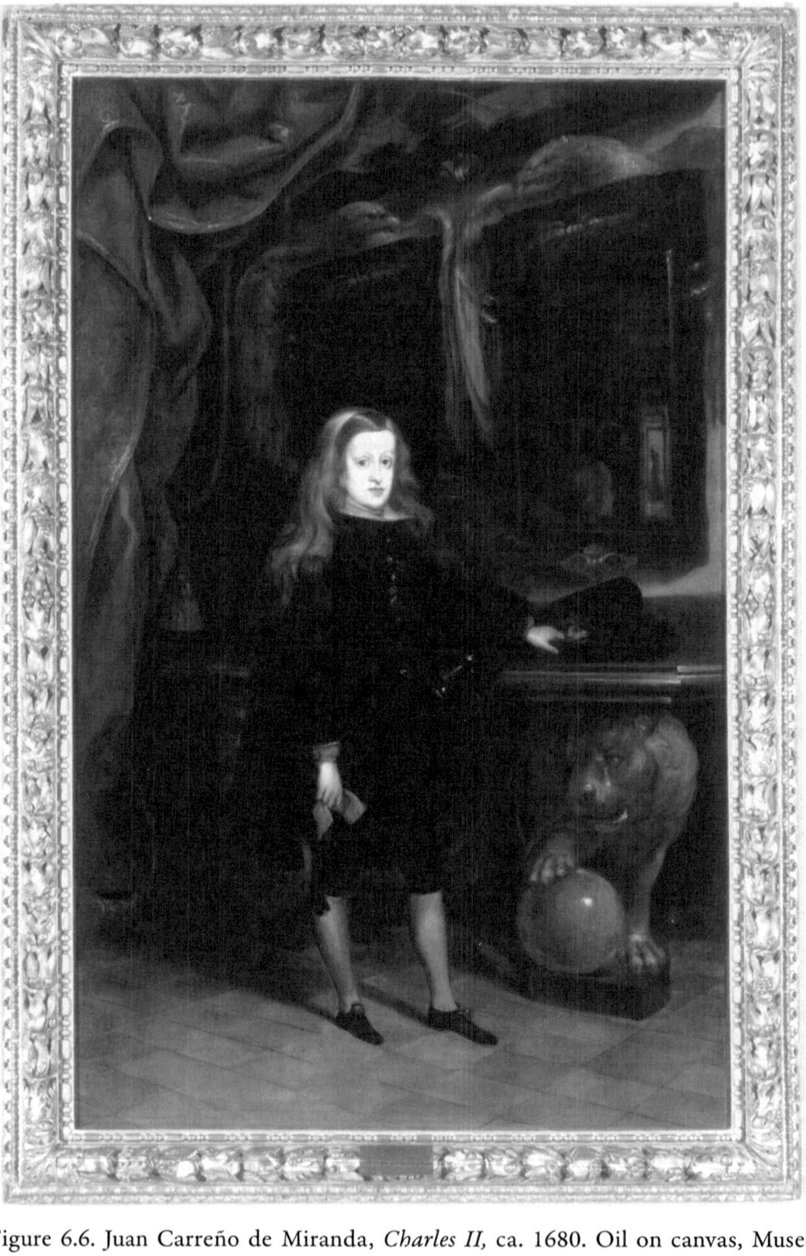

Figure 6.6. Juan Carreño de Miranda, *Charles II,* ca. 1680. Oil on canvas, Musee des Beaux-Arts, Valenciennes. Photo credit: Réunion des Musées Nationaux/Art Resource, New York.

Conquest texts, including that of Solís, but this narrative is by no means the only version of the story in circulation in the early modern empire of the Spanish Habsburgs. Other accounts, for example, identify the Spaniards as the assassins of the Aztec king, the narrative thus casting the scene as an act of enemy aggression rather than one of disloyalty (Cortés 1986:477–478n89). Like the representations of the event on the *biombos* and *enconchados,* the Kislak painting tells the story of the king's death from a particular point of view and, in doing so, turns the event into a parable of a people's betrayal of their sovereign. This interrelationship between the figures of Charles II and Moteuczoma II is also suggested by a telling passage in Solís's *Historia,* in which the author's treatment of the Aztec king's death seems almost a veiled description of Carreño de Miranda's portraits of Charles II: "[Moteuczoma] had himself adorned with his royal robes and he called for his crown and cloak, forgetting neither the jewels he wore for public events, nor any other formalities. All of this exposed his diffidence, making it appear that he stood in need of exterior show to gain respect and that the assistance of purple and gold was necessary to cover and conceal his interior weakness of Majesty" (Solís 1684:II, Bk. 4, ch. 14).

The Kislak paintings and other visual images of the Conquest of Mexico produced in late-seventeenth-century New Spain document the embrace of a particular version of the Conquest narrative by a sector of New Spanish society at a time of political, economic, and military crisis. The version of the narrative recounted in the imagery stresses ideas of kingly strength and imperial expansion, issues that were under siege on a variety of fronts in the late-seventeenth-century Hispanic world. That version of the narrative, however, was one of a number of competing Conquest narratives that populated the historiographic landscape in early modernity. Indeed, Solís, in the introduction to his *Historia,* critiqued the content of other seventeenth-century Conquest accounts, alleging that he found in the works of other authors "[g]reat daring and no less maliciousness in inventing whatever they wished against the Spaniards, spending entire volumes citing the errors committed by some in order to discredit the achievements of all; and we find in the accounts of Spanish writers little uniformity or agreement, the diversity of information revealing a common danger: that the truth is often disfigured when it comes from afar, the distance from its source degrading its truthfulness" (Solís 1684:I, Bk. 1, ch. 1).[24]

As Royal Chronicler of the Indies, Solís was bothered in particular by the form of Antonio de Herrera's (1601–1615) *Historia general de los hechos de los castellanos* (*General History of the Deeds of the Castilians*), which he saw as flawed in its failure to consider the Conquest of Mexico as a discrete historical event. He was also troubled by the Conquest history by Bernal Díaz del Castillo (1632), which was, in his view, plagued by its numerous and unwarranted "complaints against Hernán Cortés, the famous hero of this story" (Solís 1684:I, Bk. 1, ch. 2).[25] It is perhaps understandable that the account of Solís, written by a man who had served as Royal Chronicler of the Indies under both Philip IV and Charles II (Serralta 1986), would acknowledge the founder of that dynasty as a driving force in the expansion of Spain's empire into the Americas. But it may come as more of a surprise that so laudatory a mode of historiography should emerge as well in late-seventeenth-century New Spain, in the medium of painting and from the hands of those working in less direct and less official relationships to the king. Indeed, the visual images of the Conquest of Mexico produced in late-seventeenth-century New Spain establish a dialogue with Solís's historiographic concerns as stated in his *Historia*. Like that account, the visual images, with their liberal use of texts to aid in the interpretation of their imagery, attempt to exert control over the narrative and guide the viewer's interpretation of it, forcefully asserting that even though they "come from afar," their versions of the story are neither "daring" nor "malicious" nor "disfigured." As objects displayed in domestic interiors of the Spanish and New Spanish elite, the paintings' embrace of an official, imperial version of the Conquest visibly proclaimed their patrons' allegiance to the king at a time when that history and, indeed, the power of the Crown were being contested on a variety of fronts.

NOTES

1. One of the four is in a private collection in Madrid. Three others are in Mexico City collections: one in the Franz Mayer Museum, another in the National Museum of History in Mexico City, and the third in a private collection. These screens are identified as a corpus in Castelló Yturbide and Martínez del Río de Redo (1970:31–37); Cuadriello (1999:65–71). The two other Conquest *biombos* do not juxtapose their representation of that event with a view of Mexico City. Both are in the collection of the Banco Nacional de México, and one of them bears an allegorical representation of the Four Parts of the World on its reverse. I am grateful to Arthur Dunkelman, the participants in the Invasion and Transformation symposium, and the editors of this volume for their insightful comments and critiques of this chapter.

2. Casa y balcon dond. dieron la pedrada a Mocthza. The translations of this and all other texts in this chapter are by the author. Whenever possible, I have attempted to adhere to the orthography as it appears on the paintings and in the printed sources.

3. Cue q. estaba en la plaza d. Mexco. dond. oi esta Palacio.

4. Cue q. estaba en S.tiago Tlatiloco. dond. esta. oi la Ygla.

5. Calzada de Guadalupe por donde entraron los Españoles y los indios e Tlaxcala en su fabor.

6. Llegaron brevemente a las islas de América las influencias del Nuevo rey, obrando en ellas su nombre tanto como en España su presencia. Dispusiéronse los ánimos a mayors empresas, creció el esfuerzo en los soldados, y se puso la mano en las primeras operaciones

que precedieron a la conquista de Nueva España, cuyo imperio tenía el cielo destinado para engrandecer los principios de este agusto monarca.

7. The screen in the Madrid private collection was formerly in the collection of the Dukes of Almodóvar del Valle, who are said to have acquired it in Mexico in 1894 (Artiñano y de Galdácano and Navarro 1930:n.p.; Castelló Yturbide and Martínez del Río 1970:31). The screen in the collection of the National Museum of History in Mexico City is said to have been acquired in Madrid from an undisclosed source for the Instituto Nacional de Antorpología e Historia by the historian Artemio del Valle Arizpe and is anecdotally associated with the Counts of Moteuczoma (De la Maza 1968:13; Castelló Yturbide and Martínez del Río 1970:35). Kagan (2000:217n5) suggests that the Countess of Moteuczoma may have commissioned it. He also indicates (2000:217n11) that the screen in the Museo Franz Mayer in Mexico City was acquired in Europe by José Fernando Ramírez in 1859 and suggests that it, too, had been in the collection of the Counts of Moteuczoma. A fourth screen in a private collection in Mexico City may possibly be the one Castelló Yturbide and Martínez del Río (1970:36) described as having belonged to the collection of the Marquis Gianori-Lisci in Milan and, later, that of Francisco González de la Fuente.

8. On the Madrid series, see Toussaint (1952); García Saíz (1980:19–69, 1992:105–116, 1999a, 1999b); Dujovne (1984:174–200); Vargas Lugo (1994:119–123). On the Buenos Aires series, see Dujovne (1972, 1984:117–169, 1998); García Saíz (1999a).

9. Travaxan en Fabricar la Villa Rica los Soldados del Capitan Cortes, í les ayudan los yndios totonaques.

10. Manda el Capitan general Cortes Redocar [sic?] los Ydolos que estavan En el Pueblo de Zenpoal.

11. Dan la obediencia al Rey de España los de Cholula.

12. Da el emperador Moctesuma la obediensia A su Magestad. Other loyalty scenes appear on the fifth and twenty-fourth panels of the Buenos Aires series.

13. García Saíz (1999a:134) suggests the involvement of Siguenza y Gongora in the design and/or production of the Conquest *enconchados.*

14. 24 tablas que pueden servir de respando o biombo bajo de estrado de charol embutido de nácares.

15. Another set of twenty-four Conquest *enconchados* was until recent years in the collection of the Dukes of Moteuczoma, the descendants of José Sarmiento de Valladares, the thirty-second viceroy to New Spain (ruled 1696–1701) and the last such appointee to serve under the Spanish Habsburgs. This provenance, together with the coincidence of the period of his rule with the date of 1698 that appears on the Museo de América series, suggests that the viceroy or someone in his administration was involved in the production and circulation of those two sets of panels. On this hypothesis, see García Saíz (1999a:113–114).

16. On the economy of the gift and the counter-gift more generally, see Mauss (1990).

17. Gana Pedro de Alvarado el alto cu de guichilobos, y pone las banderas de Su Majestad.

18. Solís 1684:I, Bk. I, ch. 5.

19. Ibid., Bk. 5, ch. 25.

20. De la Maza (1968:13) dated the Conquest screen currently in the collection of the Museo Nacional de Historia in Mexico City to 1695. Kagan (2000:153, 217n12) dated the Conquest screen in the collection of the Franz Mayer Museum to ca. 1690–1692. As for the Conquest *enconchados,* the suite of twenty-four panels in the collections of the Museo de América bears the date 1698 and is documented as having been in the collections of Charles II by 1700. See García Saíz (1999a:109–114). The Kislak series is dated to the 1660s in Ángeles et al. (2005).

21. Kamen (1980:21) cites Gabriel Maura Gamayo, *Vida y reinado de Carlos II* (Madrid: Aguila, 1990), on these matters.

22. On Carreño's portraits of Charles II, see also Orso (1986:42–43, 181).

23. Un indio le tiro una pedrada y los demas indios lan[z]an unas flechasos de q[ue] m[urió?]

24. Grande osadía y no menor malignidad para inventar lo que quisieron contra nuesta nación, gastando libros enteros en culpar lo que erraron algunos para deslucir lo que acertaron todos; y en los naturales poca uniformidad y concordia en la narración de los sucesos: conocindose en esta diversidad de noticias aquel peligro ordinario de la verdad, que suele desfigurarse cuando viene de lejos, degenerando de su ingenuidad todo aquello que se aparta de su origen.

25. Quejas contra Hernán Cortés, principal héroe de esta historia.

7

Painting a New Era

Conquest, Prophecy, and the World to Come

Diana Magaloni-Kerpel

The Conquest of Mexico, the encounter and confrontation of two civilizations, and the beginning of a New World were events of momentous historical importance.[1] Beginning in the sixteenth century and continuing to the present, Western accounts have tended to create what Matthew Restall has called "a mythic narrative of Conquest" (Restall 2003:18, Chapter 5, this volume). According to this narrative, elements and events are set up so that they lead inexorably to European victory, giving "an explanation that ultimately testifies to the civilizational superiority of the Spaniards, a glorification of Cortés and an endorsement of the myth that a few great and exceptional men made the Conquest possible" (Restall 2003:18). The power and pervasiveness of this mythic narrative have tended to obscure our understanding and appreciation of indigenous views of the Conquest, such as those present in the works created by the Nahua of central Mexico, who wrote extensively on this subject (León-Portilla 1962; Lockhart

1993).[2] With the European invasion, the Nahua experienced a true apocalypse: war, famine, and disease, followed by the imposition of a new social system that featured forced labor, abuse, and an insulting misunderstanding of their culture. In the face of these enormous challenges, the Nahua painter-writers (*tlacuilome*), in their role as preservers of knowledge and tradition (*tlamatinime*), created their own histories of the Conquest. One of the most important works in this tradition is "The Book of the Conquest of Mexico," preserved in Book 12 of Bernardino de Sahagún's sixteenth-century *Historia General de las Cosas de la Nueva España,* also known as the *Florentine Codex.*[3]

This chapter focuses on "The Book of the Conquest of Mexico," an outstanding work bearing the voices of "the people who fought the war." This Nahua narrative, first collected and transcribed around 1555 by Friar Bernardino de Sahagún, was reviewed and interpreted by Nahua-Christian intellectuals between 1576 and 1578, resulting in the creation of Book 12 of the *Historia General.* Book 12 also includes the Spanish translation or paraphrase by Sahagún of the Nahuatl text, which also dates to ca. 1576–1578 (Sahagún 1950–1982:Bk. 1, 101; De'Olwer and Cline 1973:13, 201–202). To show the complexity of this work, which deserves profound and attentive study, I will focus on the eight famous omens listed at the beginning of the narrative, which are said to have predicted the Conquest. In this chapter I will demonstrate how, by means of the eight omens, the *tlacuilome* of Book 12 were able to explain the Conquest as an event of cosmic consequences: the omens helped them compose a work that literally recorded the end of the Aztec era and the beginning of the Christian period in Mesoamerica. By replicating ancient Nahua rituals and myths, the eight omens constitute symbolic stages that established the conditions necessary for human existence to continue into the new Nahua-Christian era.

BOOK 12, THE BOOK OF THE CONQUEST OF MEXICO IN THE *HISTORIA GENERAL*

Book 12 is bound together with the other eleven books comprising the *Historia General,* which resembles a medieval encyclopedia (Robertson 1994:170). It is divided into forty-one chapters ordered chronologically. The reader moves forward in the story by turning the pages, as in any other Western book. It bears two columns of handwritten texts: one in Nahuatl, the language spoken by the indigenous peoples of central Mexico, and the other in Spanish, which is a paraphrase of the original text. Placed within the Spanish column is a series of framed ink drawings created in a painterly, naturalistic style reminiscent of medieval and Renaissance woodcuts. The familiar and seemingly Western European appearance of this work has helped create a false idea about its nature and identity;

it has obstructed inquiries about its Nahua facture and its relationship to the Mesoamerican practice of painting-writing history, which is neither linear nor self-evident. The so-called Europeanized style of the ink drawings in Book 12 (Robertson 1994:178) has caused many scholars to deny the possibility that these images could be as "original" as the written Nahuatl text. Thus characterized, the images have received little attention because they were thought to lack important messages to be decoded (cf. Lockhart 1993:11, 13).

In opposition to this interpretation, I see the images as important, with their origins in the ancient painting-writing tradition. The ancestors of the sixteenth-century Christian-Nahua *tlacuilome* who created Book 12 had bequeathed to them a tradition that recorded events through a system of conventionalized images. Writing, in the Western sense of the word—meaning the symbolic representation of speech—was introduced to central Mexico by the Europeans. Previous to that time, the Aztecs had mastered a sophisticated technique of inscribing knowledge metaphorically, called *in tlilli in tlapalli*, or black ink/red ink, in which the noble scribe-painters, *tlacuilome*, drew and painted on the surface of extended cotton cloth and bark-paper or deer-hide books folded in an accordion fashion (Townsend 1992:160). To decode the images, the initiated reader, *tlamatini* (he who knows something), uttered words preserved in oral tradition, including dates, names, and place names. The images served as symbolic and mnemonic devices to recall a sophisticated oral tradition that preserved the myths of the creation of the earth, humankind, and time. Images were both windows into the time of creation and precedents that could be used to interpret the present. As documents of history, they further represented historic events as the materializations of patterns established in the time of creation.

Book 12 is radically different from, and much more complex than, most sixteenth-century Western books, producing three versions of the Conquest on each page. First, in the right-hand column of the page is the early transcription (ca. 1555) from alphabetical Nahuatl of the story as preserved in the oral tradition, originally composed by the people who took part in the war (Sahagún 1950–1982:Bk. 1, 101). In the left-hand column is a free translation or paraphrase of this story into Spanish made by Sahagún in the years 1578–1579 (Cline 1973:13, 201–202). And most important for this chapter, there are 161 images also made in the late 1570s by the *tlacuilome*, which are framed in sets of single, double, or triple rectangles between the Spanish columns. All of these "texts" are in dialogue with each other and comprise a multicultural and multitextual work on the Conquest (Magaloni-Kerpel 2004b). In the rest of this chapter I will explore the complexity of this work by focusing on the eight omens and their relationship to the images.

THE EIGHT OMENS IN BOOK 12 OF THE *HISTORIA GENERAL*

The first chapter in Book 12 starts by listing the portents that occurred a full decade before the war of Conquest: (1) a huge pyre of fire appeared at midnight, (2) the temple of Huitzilopochtli (Hummingbird of the Left) burned, (3) the temple of Xiuhtecuhtli (Turquoise Lord) burned, (4) a comet crossed the sky, (5) the waters of the lake seemed to boil, (6) a weeping woman appeared at night calling for the end of time, (7) a crane with a magic mirror was captured, and (8) groups of two-headed men were seen in Tenochtitlan. Although modern scholars have fully acknowledged the symbolic nature of the eight omens at the beginning of chapter 1 in Book 12, the specific meaning of each of these omens and their relevance as devices to encode the Nahua interpretation of the Conquest have not been recognized (Carrasco 1982; Tomicki 1986; Martínez Baracs 1998; Fernández-Armesto 1992; Rozat 1993; Graulich 1994). Although recorded as an independent and succinct list of strange occurrences in the first chapter of Book 12 and never mentioned again throughout the following forty chapters, I contend that the eight omens prefigure specific historical passages along the narrative. That is, the forty chapters of the story of the Conquest can be divided into eight sections, each introduced and symbolically denoted by an omen. In this manner, the eight omens can be understood as a device invented by the Nahua creators of Book 12 to provide the Book of the Conquest with both an underlying cyclical structure (the eight symbolic sections into which the forty chapters can be divided) and meaning that goes beyond the actual events; through the omens, they linked history to the patterns of mythic, cosmic time (Magaloni-Kerpel 2004a, 2004b).

In this regard, it is highly significant that there are eight omens and not four or five (also important symbolic numbers in Mesoamerica). Eight is the number of partitions in the time-space unity that gave a geometric shape to the universe and was also the structure of the ancient calendar, which ordered the recording of knowledge and history (Freidel, Schele, and Parker 1993:71). The concept of space-time unity in the form of a cosmogram, or calendar, is masterfully rendered on the first page of *Codex Fejérváry-Mayer* (Figure 7.1).

This frontispiece presents the surface of the earth, with its five regions, as a Maltese cross. The East at the top has a sun disk rising from a temple. West is below with the head of a *tzitzimime*, a skeletal-goddess, depicted hanging upside-down. North is at the right of the sun, and South is at its left. Eight lords, two at each cosmic region, revolve around Xiuhtecutli, the god of time, who stands at the center, the fifth direction. The four rounded diagonal petals between the trapezoidal arms of the Maltese cross represent the houses of the sun in the sky: two in the East, two in the West. These are the solstices in the western and eastern

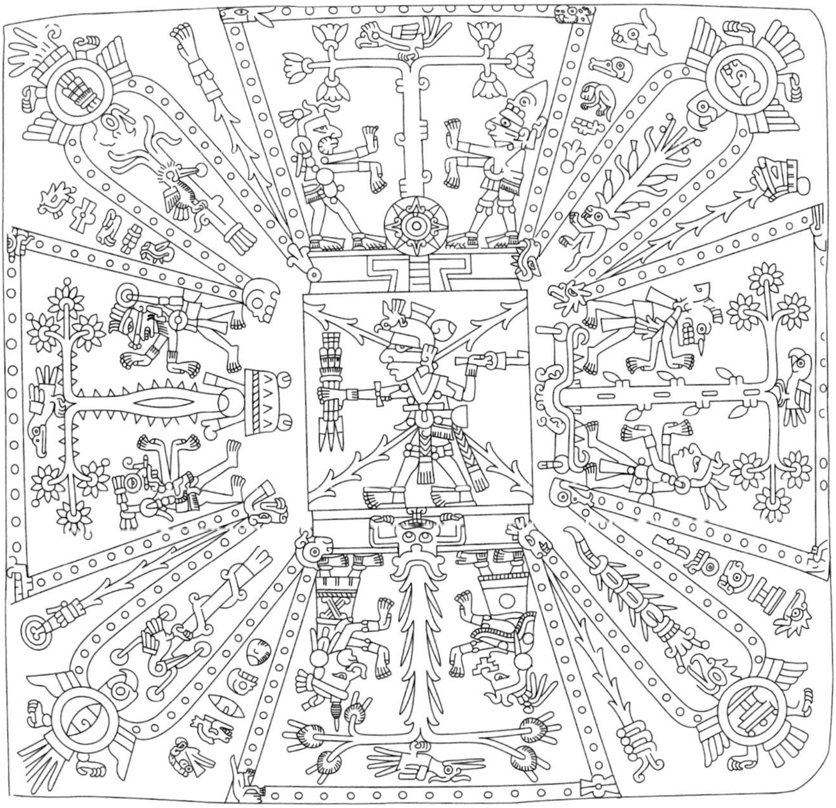

Figure 7.1. Frontispiece, *Codex Fejérváry-Mayer*. Drawing by Citlali Coronel Sánchez.

horizons, and therefore they signal the yearly calendar (Aveni 2001:150–151). As Alfredo López Austin has explained, time was the consequence of the movement of divine influences through the surface of the earth (1989:80). The cosmic trees at each cardinal direction, as seen in the frontispiece, served as paths through which different sacred forces, coming from the heavens and the underworld, traveled to the surface of the earth and influenced human destiny. The gods that inhabited each region, called year bearers, took turns carrying the sun along their journey. This division gave rise to the days and years of the East, named with the sign Acatl (Reed); of the North, Tecpatl (Flint); of the West, Calli (House); and of the South, Tochtli (Rabbit)—in short, to the calendar (Soustelle 1996:144–165). These year signs are placed on top of each of the four petals representing the solstices in the *Fejérváry-Mayer* frontispiece.

In the recording of history, the Nahua followed the pattern provided by this structure. Their *xiuhtlapohualli,* or history annals, are composed by relating the historic events to a ribbon of alternating dates placed to represent world directions. The dates run 1 Tochtli (South), 2 Acatl (East), 3 Tecpatl (North), 4 Calli (West), 5 Tochtli (South), and so on. Each year will bear the count thirteen years to conclude a cycle of fifty-two years, and then the cycle will start all over again. As Michel Graulich has pointed out, the history of a people, of the universe, of a year, of an era could be always compared with or equated to this cosmic pattern (1994:228–234).

Using the *Fejérváry-Mayer* representation of the time-space unity as a template, a particular position can be attributed to each of the eight omens. In this representation (Figure 7.2), we have a hypothetical reconstruction of the sequence the omens could assume according to the order in which they appeared. Beginning with East at the top, the omens can be placed counterclockwise in this template: omens 1 and 2 belong to the East, 3 and 4 to the North, 5 and 6 to the West, 7 and 8 to the South. Thus, the omens at the beginning of Book 12 comprise the structure of a cosmogram, that is, a complete cycle of time, and provide the narrative with the same practical and symbolic structure as the ancient calendar. This has important implications because each omen represents a place in space and a stage in the creation of a new world.

As in any cycle of time, the eight omens comprise two opposing forces. The first four omens relate to fire, while the next four relate to water. In this manner, the omens tell the story of a sacred conflagration *in atl in tlachinolli* (water-fire) of the Conquest. The sacred conflagration recalls the pact of blood established on the eve of creation, in which men were required to feed the earth and the sun with the blood and hearts obtained through sacrifice and war (Graulich 1994:228–234). The polarity of water and fire (*atl tlachinolli*) implied in the eight omens refers to the confrontation between the two creative forces that propelled a new time.

This polarity also has Christian significance. According to St. John the Baptist, a substantial change in Christianity was to be achieved, first through a baptism with water performed by him and second through a baptism with fire given by Jesus (Matthew 3:11).[4] The eight omens of the Conquest relate how Christ became the new sun in Mesoamerica (Burkhart 1988; Bricker 1989; López-Austin 1990; Lara 1999). Their significance, therefore, has to be seen within the multivalent context of the Christianized Nahua of colonial times. The eight omens symbolically represent the cosmic union of two peoples in conflict, the ancient Nahua and the Christian newcomers (Graulich 1994:228–234). This is the reason the drawings and metaphors of the omens incorporate influences from both cultures. In the following sections I analyze in greater detail the first cycle of four omens of fire and briefly mention three other omens related to water and the eighth and last omen representing the union of both cycles.

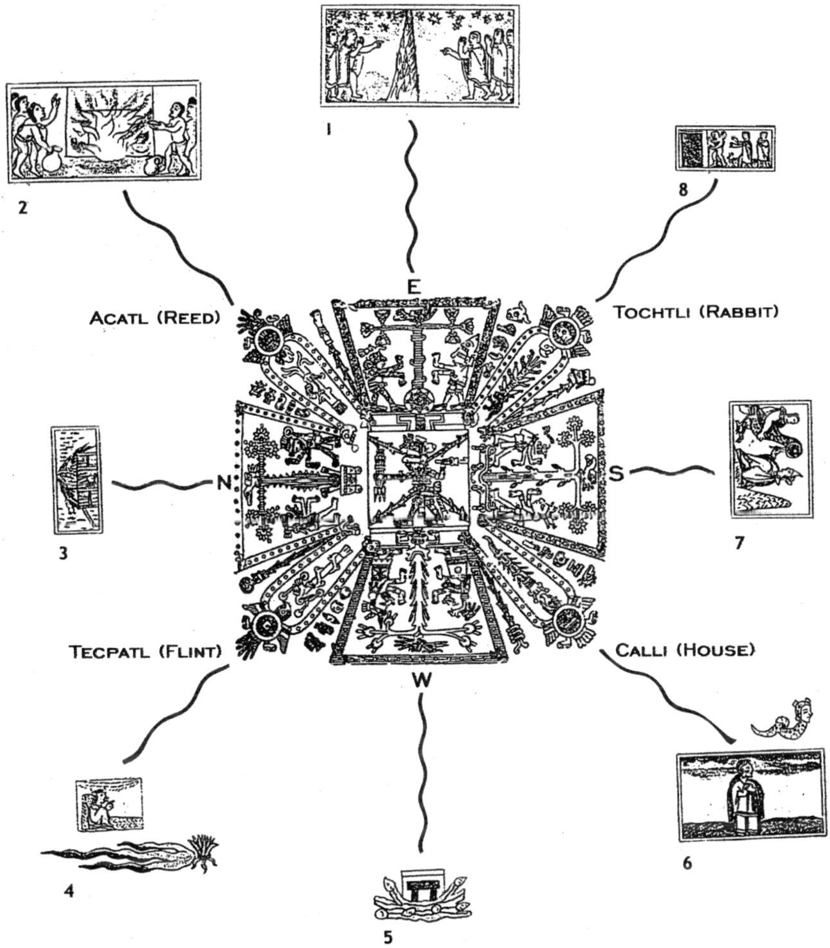

Figure 7.2. The Eight Omens as a Cycle of Time, using the *Codex Fejérváry-Mayer* as a template. Drawing by Diana Magaloni-Kerpel and Ricardo Alvarado.

THE FIRST OMEN: VISIONS OF THE NEW SKY

"Ten years before the Spaniards arrived here an omen of evil first appeared in the heavens. It was like a tongue of fire, like a flame . . . piercing the heavens." It was wide at its base, it was pointed at the head. It appeared in the eastern horizon at midnight, and "it looked as if the day had dawned. People saw this for a whole year it was the year 12 house" (Sahagún 1950–1982:Bk. 12, 1).

The first omen is not related to any specific passage of the narrative, but it works as a cosmic overture announcing the end of an era (Figure 2.1; see omen 1 in Figure 7.2). It is highly significant that the huge tongues of fire formed a structure "wide at its base and pointed at its head," which, like a pyramid, established a link among the vertical realms of heaven, the underworld, and the surface of the earth, becoming an *axis mundi*. Yet through fire, this pyramid radically changed the ordered structure of the universe, making dawn break at midnight.

Pyres of fire are the material of transformation and transfiguration in Nahua mythology. The Nahua epic of creation culminates when the gods decided to create a new sun to light the earth and the people who inhabited it. They gathered at the ancient city of Teotihuacan, the symbol of a glorious previous era, and prepared a huge *teotexcalli,* sacrificial hearth, where through the transforming effects of fire Nanauatzin (the sun) and Tecuciztecatl (the moon) were changed into celestial bodies. The sacrifice of these two gods took place at midnight, the same time the pyramid of fire is said to have appeared in the first omen. Furthermore, both fires came into view at the dawning of a new era: the fire that created the dawn of the Aztec era was set at Teotihuacan; the fire signaling the Christian time emerged at Mexico-Tenochtitlan (Sahagún 1950–1982:Bk. 7, 5–6). In addition, both fires are said to have risen in the East. Thus, the pyramid of fire, as a *teotexcalli*, represents the creative energy for the dawning of a new sun: Jesus.

However, the image of the perforated sky was also a sign of doom, war, and destruction. A poem preserved in *Anales de Tlatelolco*, in which the Mexica recall the war against the Tepaneca at Chapultepec, illustrates this point: "The margins of the earth were broken. Omens of evil came down upon us. The sky was broken, divided, upon us. . . . They say with good reason that the Mexica do not exist anymore. That nowhere can the origins (the root) of their heaven can be found" (Berlin and Barlow 1948:286). Both the first omen and the poetic metaphor of a broken sky are reflected in the collapse of the sun and the destruction of the world in the four previous cosmic eras, as represented in the *Codex Ríos*. From an opening in the sky a deity, the sun of that time, descends upon humanity, destroying and transforming everything.

According to the first omen's text, this phenomenon appeared in the eastern horizon, thus signaling a specific direction from which to start ordering the eight omens in the space-time unity. The sun begins its daily and yearly journeys in the East, so it is logical that this cosmic cataclysm would have appeared at this point. The omen also describes how tongues of fire pierced the heart of the sky at midnight. Midnight for the Nahua was the moment at which the sun reached its nadir, at the lower point in the vertical axis of the world, considered to be the North. The North was believed to be the place of death, of transformation and regeneration (Carrasco 1979:53; Brotherston 1992:82–96; Graulich 1997:274; Milbrath 1989:106; Broda 2003:147, 154).[5] Moreover, the omen also states that the phenomena lasted for the year sign 12 House, and, as we know, House is the year bearer of the West (see Figure 7.1). In this manner, the first omen describes the direction in which the cosmic transformation of the sun and of time proceeded: from east to north and from north to west. The first omen provides important information about the direction in which the omens should be placed in the space-time unity. This first half-cycle, from east to north to west, corresponds to the first four omens related to the transmuting power of fire. The order of the omens in the cosmogram can be seen in this illustration (Figure 7.2). Beginning with the East, at top, the viewer can make the correlation by analyzing the image in counterclockwise sequence.

THE SECOND OMEN: THE ENDING OF THE MEXICA TIME

The second omen signals the beginning of "human time" of history and confirms the conflagration announced by the first omen. It describes how the temple of Huitzilopochtli burned "[o]f its own accord" and how "[f]rom within emerged the flame, the tongue of fire, the blaze." The narrative continues: "Thereupon there was an outcry [the priests] said: Oh Mexicans! Hasten here let the fire be put out! Bring your water jars! But when they cast water upon it . . . all the more did it flare up. It could not be put out, it all burned" (Sahagún 1950–1982:Bk. 12, 2).

The image of the burning temple is a visual metaphor widely used by Mesoamerican peoples to express the capture of a city. A burning temple is pictured in the mural paintings of Cacaxtla, Tlaxcala, ca. A.D. 600, and can also be seen in the sixteenth-century *Codex Mendoza*'s frontispiece (Figure 2.1; see omen 2 in Figure 7.2). Accordingly, the image of the burning of Huitzilopochtli's temple signaled the capture of the religious center of Mexico-Tenochtitlan. However, as I have argued elsewhere, the second omen, as a prophecy, is only fully unveiled by the narrative and drawings in Book 12 (Magaloni-Kerpel 2003).

Chapters 19 and 20 describe how the war between the Mexica and the Spaniards started with the massacre at the Templo Mayor when the Mexica were celebrating Huitzilopochtli's feast in the month of Toxcatl. The Spaniards, commanded by Pedro de Alvarado, were invited to witness the celebration; they were inside the sacred precinct with the unarmed Mexica warriors who were performing dances for their patron deity. This fact is illustrated in a symbolic manner in both Diego Durán's sixteenth-century *Historia de las indias de la Nueva España islax de la tierra firme* and *Codex Aubin,* where the massacre is portrayed as the actual capture of the *axis mundi* of the Mexica, the Templo Mayor (Magaloni-Kerpel 2003). The image in *Codex Aubin* reiterates the mythic, dreadful consequences of this battle. The historic events were as follows: Cortés left the city to fight against the men Diego Velázquez had sent to apprehend him. The Mexica asked Pedro de Alvarado, second in command, if they could celebrate the feast of their god. Alvarado accepted and even showed interest in the celebration. When all the Mexica priests and warriors were reunited inside the courtyard, Alvarado attacked and slaughtered most of the people inside the plaza.

The image in *Codex Aubin* represents this tragic moment. The painter, however, does not represent the massacre and its bloody chaos but rather presents Templo Mayor as the orderly image of the cosmos, where the four sides of the plaza are equivalent to the four regions of the cosmos, with the Templo Mayor standing at the center of time and space. This representation is equivalent to the metaphor in the omen: "From within the tongues of fire, the flames came forth." The second omen and the image of the burning temple in Book 12 should be understood as a symbolic representation of the massacre of the people inside the great plaza at Huitzilopochtli's feast. From the narrative, it is clear that Alvarado started an unexpected war while the Mexican warriors were completely unprepared; they were unarmed, singing, and dancing for Huitzilopochtli. Thus, a war was started without being announced or even expected. The ritualized procedure through which a war was waged in ancient Mexico had been violated; thus, a fire, *in tlachinolli*, had started "of its own accord" and "it had flared greatly."

THE THIRD OMEN: MOTEUCZOMA'S JOURNEY INTO THE UNDERWORLD

The third omen describes how the temple of Xiuhtecuhtli, at Tzonmolco, was inexplicably struck by a thunderbolt while it was only drizzling and how it burned and was destroyed, which metaphorically prefigures Moteuczoma's death (Sahagún 1950–1982:Bk. 12, 2) (Figure 2.2; see omen 3 in Figure 7.2).

The narrative in chapter 23 relates that after the massacre in the central plaza announced by the second omen, Moteuczoma's dead body was found at the edge of the water (Figure 7.3). Like the metaphor of the soundless thunder that struck Xiuhtecuhtli's temple while it was only drizzling, Moteuczoma inexplicably died in silence. Xiuhtecuhtli, Turquoise Lord and the Lord of Time, represented the "foundation of the city," its center (Carrasco 1982:189). Book 1 of the *Florentine Codex* states that Xiuhtecuhtli was especially honored every four years when "Moteuczoma danced a princely dance before his temple at a place called *Tzonmolco*" (Sahagún 1950–1982:Bk. 1, 26–30). Thus, Moteuczoma dancing at Tzonmolco as the impersonator of Xiuhtecuhtli represented the foundation of the city. Consequently, the third omen relates, as prophetic history, to Moteuczoma's actual death during the Conquest. By referring to Moteuczoma's death as the portentous burning of Xihutecuhtli's temple at Tzonmolco, the omen is implying that his death was considered a cosmic event of dreadful consequences. The drawings illustrating this passage in the narrative help us understand the depth of this cosmic transformation.

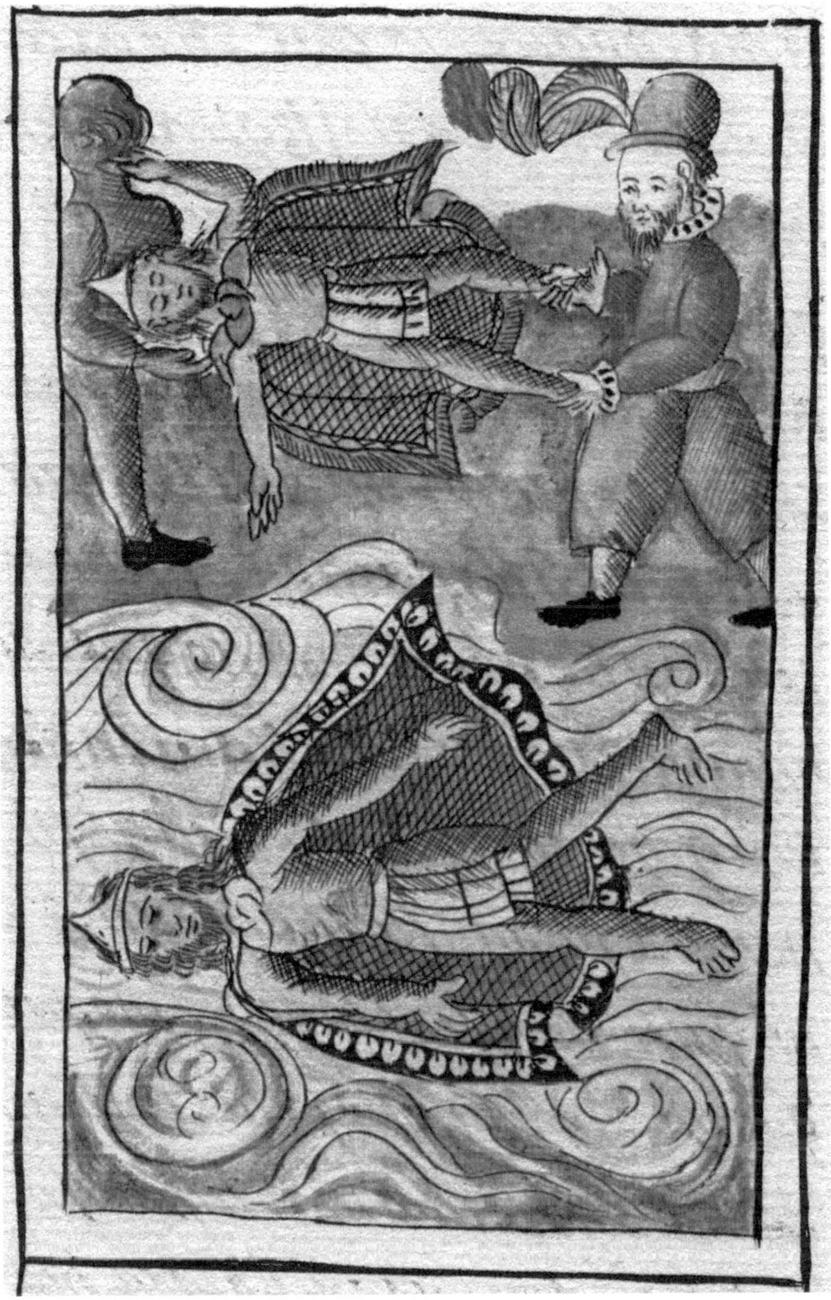

Figure 7.3. *Moteuczoma and Itzquauhtzin Dead at the Edge of the Water,* in Friar Bernardino de Sahagún, the *Florentine Codex* (Book 12). Courtesy, Biblioteca Medicea Laurenziana, Florence.

The text states that when the people found the dead bodies of Moteuczoma and Itzquauhtzin, Lord of Tlatelolco, at the edge of the water, they "quickly took Moteuczoma in their arms, they carried him to a place called Copulco, they placed him in a pile of wood and set fire to it." Copulco was the place where, in the New Fire ceremony, two priests set the first fire of the year in the open chest of a sacrificial victim (Sahagún 1950–1982:Bk. 7, 26). Thus, Copulco in the text suggests that the fire in which Moteuczoma was burned was equivalent to the first light of the world in the New Fire ceremony. That is, his immolation was necessary for the alternation of world eras.

The mythical patterning the painted story of the Conquest has undergone can be further illuminated when comparing the representation of Moteuczoma and Itzquauhtzin being thrown into the water with the depiction of Moteuczoma's recovery from the water by the Nahua and his immolation at Copulco (Figure 7.4). Both these images form part of a single unit divided into two frames. That is, the painters made these three scenes into a single unit, intending them to be seen together.

In the first scene, two Spaniards deliver the former Mexica and Tlatelolca rulers into the water. They hold their bodies by the legs and shoulders, as if both dead men were sacrificial victims. Although Moteuczoma's lifeless body is floating, it does not seem to respond to the pressure and movement of the water around it. His corporal position and rigid style of representation recall pre-Hispanic artistic conventions. Furthermore, this image is completely colored, as the traditional *amoxtli* were. The whole representation recalls the depictions of the Mexica era. In contrast, the image just below this, which represents both the recovery of Moteuczoma from the water and his immolation, is an ink drawing with absolutely no coloring. Both drawings imitate the line and style of Christian religious woodcuts. Moteuczoma's body is carried by two Nahua men. His loincloth-clad body, the manner in which the two men hold his emaciated and stiff form by the shoulders and knees, his bearded countenance, and his peaceful expression all call upon the traditional iconography of Christ's deposition from the cross, as seen in this contemporary mural from Hidalgo (Figure 7.5). Thus, when recovered from the edge of the water, Moteuczoma is transformed into the image of the dead Christ (Magaloni-Kerpel 2003:209–213).

Accordingly, the painters used images to symbolize the passage from the old Mexica era to the new Christian time. The images representing the painting style of each world era were juxtaposed to create contrast. By the same token, the painter signaled that Moteuczoma's role during the Conquest was to serve as a mediator between world eras. Jacques Soustelle considers sacrifice by fire a condition for the sun's resurrection: this is the cosmic transformation announced by the third omen (1996:108–109).

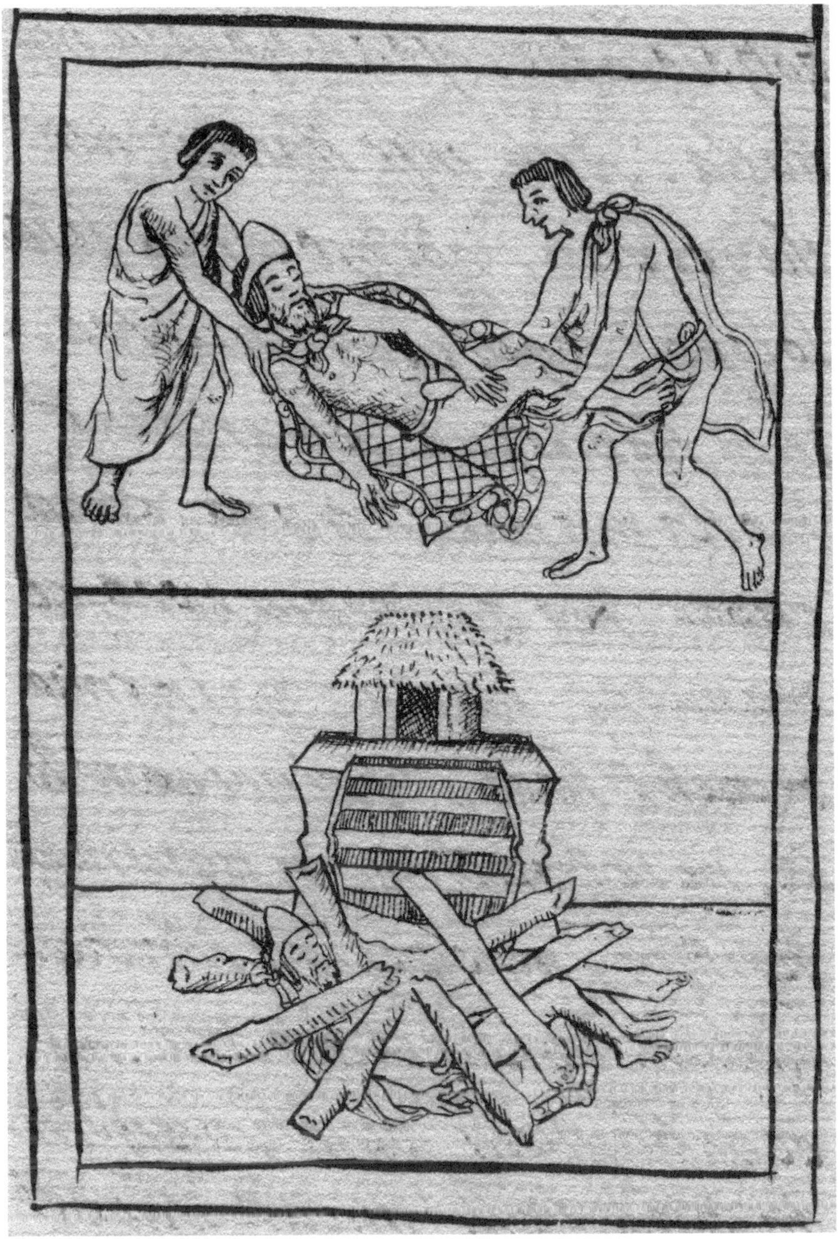

Figure 7.4. *The Recovery of Moteuczoma's Body from the Water by Two Nahua and His Immolation at Copulco*, in Friar Bernardino de Sahagún, the *Florentine Codex* (Book 12). Courtesy, Biblioteca Medicea Laurenziana, Florence.

The third omen of fire, following the order suggested by the first omen, has to be placed at the North in the space-time unity. North is the place of death and regeneration, equated to midnight (Figure 7.1). Moteuczoma, the symbolic sun of his community, descended to Mictlan, the place of death and transformation. The cosmic cataclysm announced by the first omen is confirmed by the second and third omens. The conflagration begins at the heart of Mexico-Tenochtitlan, in Templo Mayor. The Aztec *tlatoani* (ruler) is inexplicably killed. Thus, the heart of the sky was pierced at midnight, making it look as if day had dawned, announcing a new day, a new era—that of Jesus.

THE FOURTH OMEN: HERALDING A NEW TIME

The illustrations of the omen of the comet in both Book 12 (Figure 2.2; see omen 4 in Figures 7.2, 7.6) and Diego Durán's *Historia* (Figure 7.7) show the comet being observed by Moteuczoma. In both paintings the Aztec ruler points to the star with one arm (Durán 1984:2, fig. 48). It is significant that the painter of Book 12 represented the tail of the comet with three parallel lines and left the star implied outside the visual frame. The artist linked in a subtle but precise manner the three-part tail of the comet mentioned in the omen to the Aztec *tlatoani*, even though its presence is not mentioned in the text.

This is not a completely strange association, however. Comets, or, more precisely, *citlalin popoca*, smoking stars, according to Sahagún's collaborators, were "said to be an omen for the ruler. Because of it a ruler was to perish" (Sahagún 1950–1982:Bk. 7, 13). In this regard, the fourth omen, the last augury of fire, is the culmination of the third. The burning of Xiuhtecuhtli's temple prefigures the death of Moteuczoma. The burning of his body at Copulco, as in the ancient Nahua creation myths and the New Fire ceremonies, allows for both his transfiguration into a celestial body and the continuation of a new cycle of time.

The nature of the next cycle of time is also present in the drawing, as well as the interpretation of the fourth omen. On one hand, Christ's birth was announced to the Magi by the appearance of a brilliant star seen in the East (Matthew 2:2), creating an association between Christ and the star of Bethlehem in Christian theology. On the other hand, we have the codified notation in Book 12: "There was yet sun when a comet fell. It became *three parts* [emphasis added]." That is to say, the sun, the *tlatoani*, was thought to be alive; unexpectedly, he died. The *tlatoani* therefore became a smoking, wounded star. The smoking star, however, meaning the dead ruler, became *three parts* and traveled from west to east. Catholic theology teaches that God is the Father, the Son, and the Holy Ghost. He is, like the comet's tail, three in one.

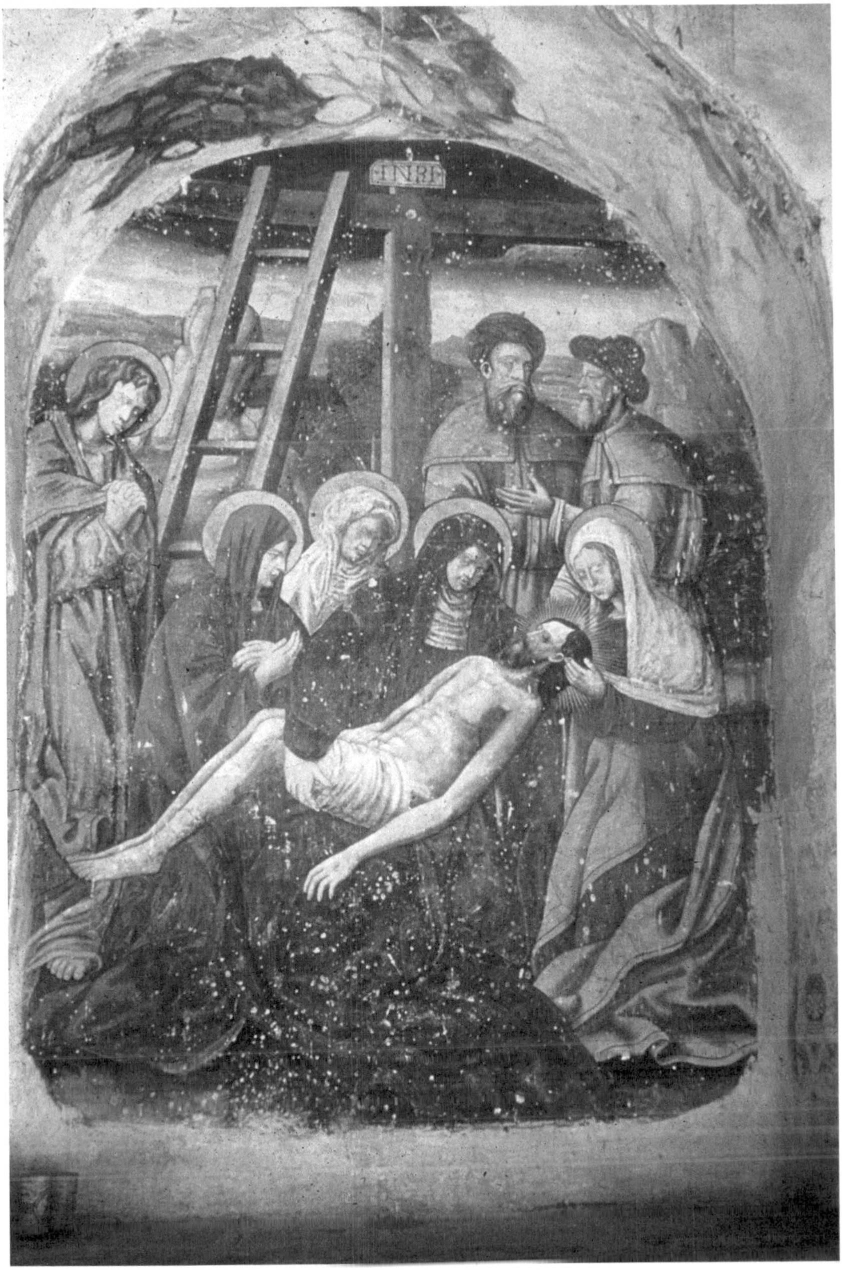

Figure 7.5. *Deposition from the Cross,* mural, sixteenth century, Augustinian monastery of Epazoyucan, Hidalgo. Photo by Diana Magaloni-Kerpel.

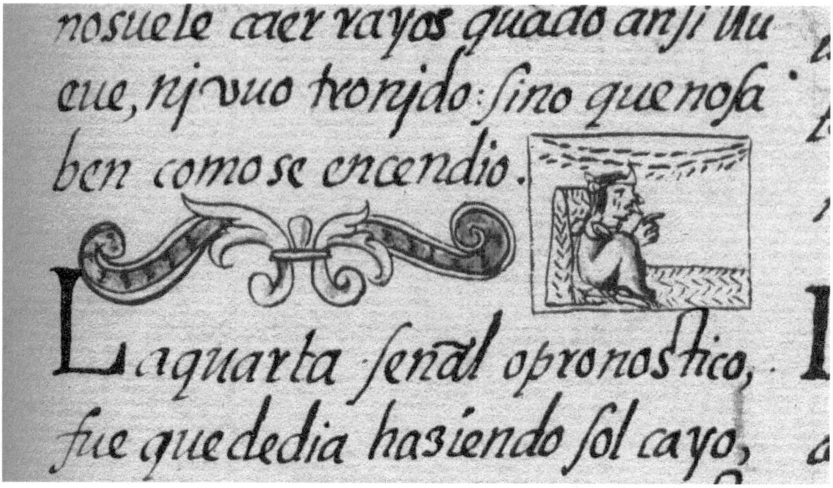

Figure 7.6. *Omen 4*, in Friar Bernardino de Sahagún, the *Florentine Codex* (Book 12). Courtesy, Biblioteca Medicea Laurenziana, Florence.

The fourth omen corresponds to the north-west intercardinal point in the space-time unity (Figure 7.1). This location is consistent with the nature of the revelation, for the smoking star represents the transformation of the death of Moteuczoma (at the North, the place of regeneration), into a smoking star, which traveled "from west to east." The fourth omen points to the direction from which the next four omens have to be placed within the space-time unity of the calendar, moving counterclockwise from west to south to east.

The direction in which the star is said to have traveled also recalls Quetzalcoatl's journey from Tollan in the West to Tlillan Tlapallan in the East, where he immolated himself and was resurrected as the Morning Star. The drawing of this same omen in Book 8 of the *Florentine Codex* shows Moteuczoma not in a representational manner but rather in a conceptual one (Figure 7.8). The omen of the comet in Book 8 is drawn as a yellow star with a bundle of quetzal feathers attached to one side. This bundle of quetzal feathers recalls what Susan Gillespie (1989:125–127) has identified as the *quetzalmachoncatl*. This device, according to sixteenth-century indigenous representations of Aztec kings, was only worn by the two rulers named Moteuczoma the Elder and Moteuczoma the Younger. The device differentiated the two Moteuczomas from the other seven Aztec *tlaltoque* (rulers). As Gillespie has remarked, both *tlatoque* named Moteuczoma structurally served the same function; they were conceived as boundary markers between cycles of time (1989:125). Moteuczoma the Elder ended the first cycle in the Aztec dynastic history, whereas Moteuczoma the Younger marked the end of the

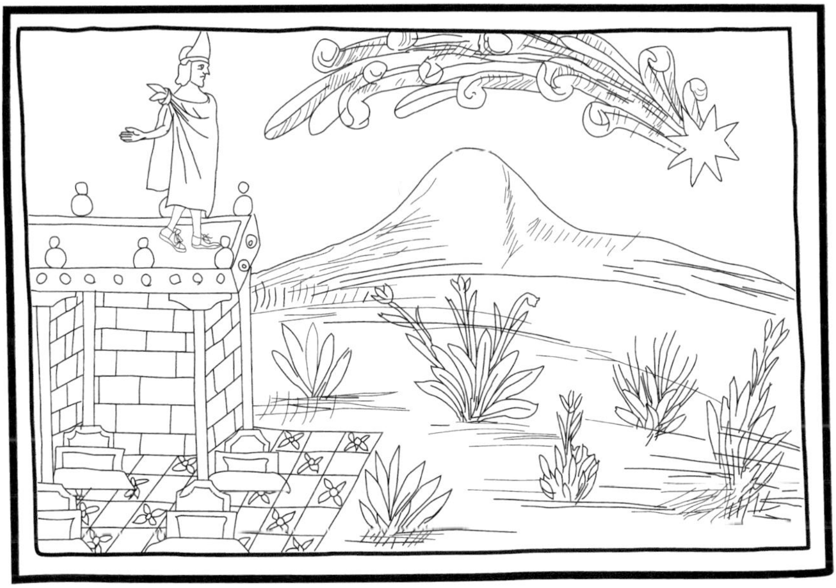

Figure 7.7. *Omen 4* (The Comet Seen by Moteuczoma), in Diego Durán, *Historia de las Indias de la Nueva España*. Drawing by Citlali Coronel Sánchez.

Aztec time and the beginning of the Christian era. Both Moteuczomas were also related to the legendary Toltec ruler Topiltzin Quetzalcoatl.

Quetzalcoatl, says Gillespie "appears in different texts as the first or the last ruler, or both of the Toltecs" (1989:136). This apparent contradiction between sources, Gillespie remarks, is now attributed to the Mesoamerican cyclical concept of history. To bound different cycles of time, the ending of one cycle has to coincide with the beginning of the next. As Gillespie has argued, "If Topiltzin Quetzalcoatl is associated with the end of Tollan he has to be simultaneously linked to its rise" (1989:136). Topiltzin Quetzalcoatl is the boundary marker of the Tollan cycle, while Moteuczoma is the boundary marker of the Aztec cycle. As confirmed by the fourth omen, Moteuczoma had to be linked to both Quetzalcoatl and Christ to be consistent with the end of the past cycle and the beginning of the present cycle of time. The fourth omen thus represents this linkage between world eras. Moteuczoma's death and resurrection into a smoking star (the same symbolic function as Venus) will allow the new sun, Christ, to rise. As Louise Burkhart (1992) observed, Quetzalcoatl was also equated to Jesus. *Anales de Cuahutitlan*, redacted by a Christian Nahua author in 1570, tells the story of how Quetzalcoatl lay in a stone coffer for four days before departing from Tollan to Tlillan Tlapallan. The god immolated himself and went to the underworld for

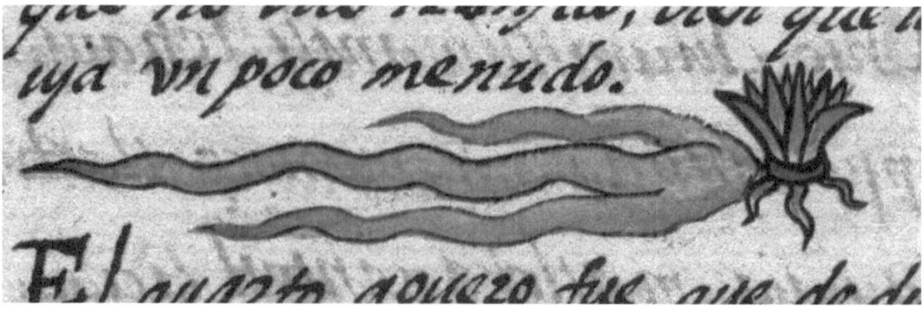

Figure 7.8. *Omen 4*, in Friar Bernardino de Sahagún, the *Florentine Codex* (Book 8). Courtesy, Biblioteca Medicea Laurenziana, Florence.

four days, at the end of which he rose into the sky in the form of a quetzal bird's heart as a symbol of Venus (Burkhart 1992:355). The drawing of the fourth omen in Book 8 seems to be representing this same metaphor of rebirth.

THE FIFTH OMEN: A NEW TIME IS CRADLE IN THE WATER

The fifth omen describes how the "lake water foamed up," how it seemed "to boil and rose upward" until it flooded the bases of the houses and made them crumble (Sahagún 1950–1982:Bk. 12, 2). This fifth omen is the first omen in the series of portents related to water and marks the starting point of the next cycle of omens (Figure 2.3; see omen 5 in Figure 7.2).

The description of the boiling water actually prefigures the final battle between the Spaniards and the Mexica when Cortés attacked the island by water with the twelve brigantines built at Texcoco. Two years had passed since the massacre during Toxcatl at Templo Mayor and the death of Moteuczoma. The scenes of this last battle are portrayed in chapter 30 of Book 12. They are spectacular aerial views of the brigantines shooting their cannons. One can imagine that the cannonballs created a large splash in the water, and this is perhaps the original image of "the boiling water of the lake." The narrative describes how the cannonballs struck the Mexican boats and destroyed them. The Mexican warriors were faced with such a weapon for the first time, and they must have been terrified.

This omen corresponds to the West in the space-time unity (Figure 7.2). It is known that the West is the place of women, where the sun sets and dies. It is also associated to rain, water, and fertility. It is the place where Tamoanchan, the creative foggy paradise, resides (Soustelle 1996:144–145). All these symbolic associations are implied in the omen. The lake was conceived as a feminine deity, the goddess Chalchihuitlicue (She of the jade skirt). Moreover, before the major attack by water, the Spaniards sent two boats to test the depth of the canals that crossed the island-city. These two boats arrived at Ilyacac, an island north from Tlacopan, the western part of Tenochtitlan. From the northwest, the enemy army arrived at the heart of the city, Quauquiyauac (the Eagle Gate), within three days and burned the Great Temple once again (Sahagún 1950–1982:Bk. 12, 83–89).

In both the narrative and the drawings of Book 12, the artists described in great detail the way the Spaniards disembarked from two exploratory boats and the manner in which the soldiers marched slowly in war array. A leading soldier carried a large cotton banner. He was followed by a group that went on "beating the drums and blowing [trumpets] and wooden flutes" (Sahagún 1950–1982:Bk. 12, 85). In fact, the illustration of the drummer and flutist in Book 12 (Figure 7.9) was modeled on a woodcut from the *Nuremberg Chronicle* (Figure 7.10) (Schedel 2001:fol. CLXXXVIIr). Today there are extant copies of the *Nuremberg Chronicle* in Mexican collections, which were imported during the sixteenth century by the missionaries. It is therefore likely that the painters of the *Florentine Codex* knew this book and its images (Careño Velázquez 2000:153–156). This drawing in the *Nuremberg Chronicle* forms part of the set of events and auguries that prophesized the end of the sixth world era, the last era before the millennium promised in the Apocalypse. The use of the *Nuremberg*'s woodcut is not coincidental. The painters consciously introduced elements of Christian prophetic tradition into the omens, in particular the knowledge of the end of time that Saint John had opened with his book of Revelation (Magaloni-Kerpel 2004b:196–221).

The indigenous painters and writers of Book 12 used a particular image as a template to link the Conquest of Mexico with the end of the sixth Christian era. Fernando Cervantes (1994:63) has pointed out that the Franciscan missionary "had identified Saint Francis with the angel of the Apocalypse who would unlock the seal of the sixth age and inaugurate the age of the Holy Spirit." This fifth omen, the first in the cycle of three omens associated with water, earth, and femininity, also establishes a connection with Christian eschatology; as a place of creation in the West, it unites the former Aztec world with the apocalyptic "world to come."

THE SIXTH OMEN: THE APOCALYPTIC CIHUACOATL

The sixth omen reads: "[O]ften was heard a woman weeping at night . . . she went about saying 'oh my beloved sons, now we are about to go . . . whither am I to take you?'" (Sahagún 1950–1982:Bk. 12, 2). This sixth omen represents the very end of the Aztec era. This woman, as León-Portilla pointed out, is Cihuacoatl,

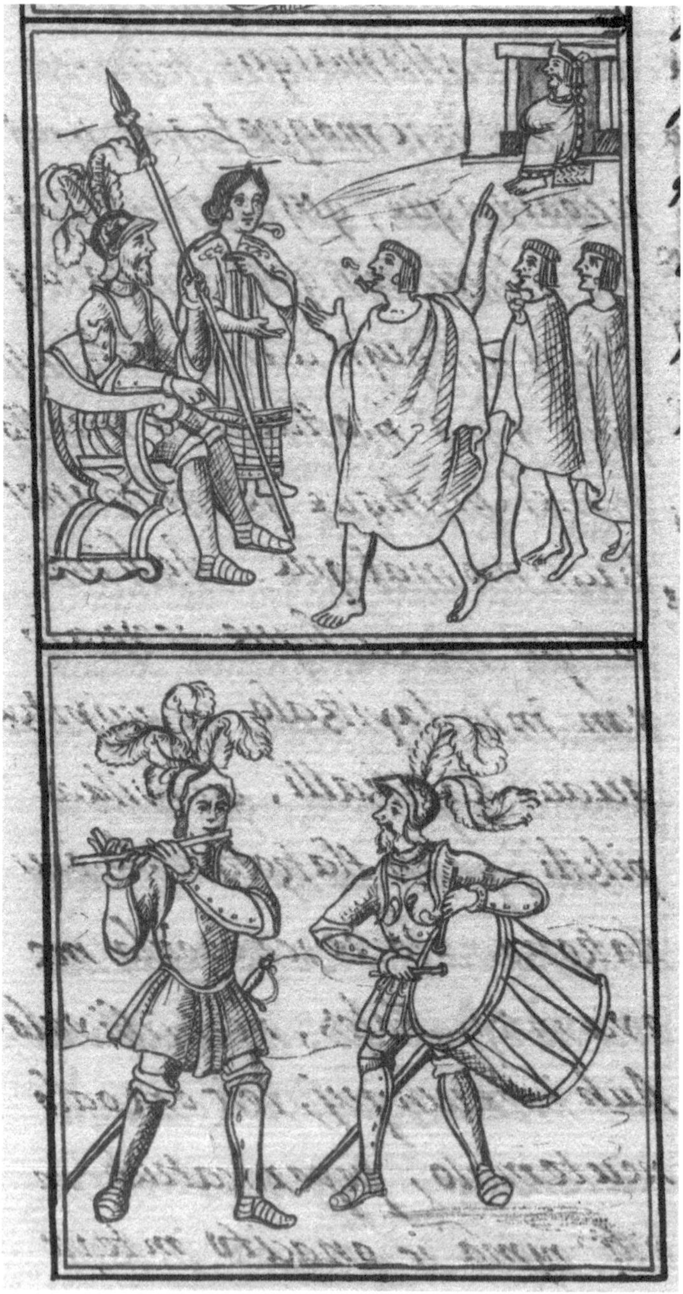

Figure 7.9. *A Flutist and a Drummer Announce the Final Attack on Tenochtitlan*, in Friar Bernardino de Sahagún, the *Florentine Codex* (Book 12). Courtesy, Biblioteca Medicea Laurenziana, Florence.

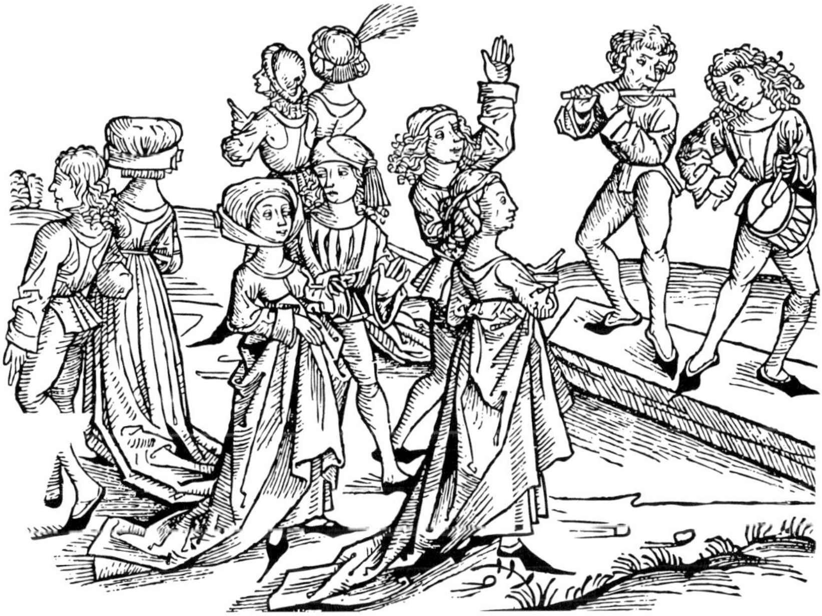

Figure 7.10. *A Flutist and a Drummer Announce as Symbols of Decay*, in Hartmann Schedel, *Liber chronicarum (1493),* fol. CLXXXVIIr. Drawing by Citlali Coronel Sánchez.

"Snake-woman, the earth goddess declaring that time has reached its end" León-Portilla 1964:31). In fact, a Cihuacoatl illustrates this omen in Book 8 of the *Florentine Codex*. The omen corresponds to the west-south intercardinal point where the year bearer Calli, or House, resides (Figure 2.3; see omen 6 in Figure 7.2). In this manner, this date confirms the prophetic date given by the first omen: 12 House. In fact, the war ended, according to the narrative in Book 12, in the year 3 House (Sahagún 1950–1982:Bk. 12, 122). There are many other implications of Cihuacoatl's presence in the Book of the Conquest; however, the fact that Cihuacoatl appears at the end of the war, during the siege of the city, has a self-evident purpose: to mark the end.

THE SEVENTH OMEN: TEZCATLIPOCA'S MIRROR

The seventh omen tells how fishermen caught a huge brown crane (Figure 2.4; see omen 7 in Figure 7.2). Because of its rarity, the bird was taken to Moteuczoma. "When the fishermen [went to see him] at the Tlillan Calmecatl it was past noon, still early," refers the omen. Moteuczoma held the bird and saw on its head "a mirror, round, circular. There appeared the heavens, the stars—the fire drill (constellation)." Then he looked into the mirror a second time "[a]nd saw a little beyond, what was like people coming massed, coming as conquerors, coming girt in war array. Deer bore them upon their backs." Moteuczoma asked the soothsayers if they could see through the mirror, but when they looked the image vanished (Sahagún 1950–1982:Bk. 12, 3). If we accept that the sixth omen, the weeping woman, is Cihuacoatl and that her presence marks the end of the Mexica time, then the seventh omen has to be understood as the prolegomena of the new, Christian era. I believe the archetypal role Moteuczoma has played in this prophetic and symbolic story of the Conquest is key to interpret the seventh omen.

The seventh omen in the cosmogram (Figure 7.2) belongs in the South, and it is directly opposite the third omen, in the North. The third omen, as discussed earlier, symbolizes Moteuczoma's death during the Conquest and the beginning of his mythic journey through the underworld. Thus, the third and the seventh omens, as opposites, represent the beginning and ending of Moteuczoma's astral journey. While the third omen symbolizes Moteuczoma's contact with Mictlan in the North, the heart of the night, the seventh omen represents Moteuczoma's emergence from the womb of Ciuhuacoatl in the sixth omen. In the seventh omen, Moteuczoma emerges as the "first light of the world"; he acts, like Venus, as the Morning Star, heralding the emergence of the sun—the new Christian sun (see Figures 2.1–2.2, omens 3–7).

Moteuczoma's underworld journey through omens 3, 4, 5, and 6, and finally his emergence at the seventh omen, follows a pattern established in the Nahua myths of creation of the earth and humankind (Magaloni-Kerpel 2004b:224). In fact, the emergence of Moteuczoma at the South and his bird-mirror oracle are reminiscent of the creation of human beings and the beginning of time in the myth of Tamoanchan. The story tells that the gods dwelled in a primeval paradise. As in the seventh omen, the Nahua myth also involves Tezcatlipoca, "Smoking Mirror," disguised as a fantastic bird. In the myth Tezcatlipoca seduced the young earth goddess Xochiquetzal. From this union Centeotl was born. The birth of Centeotl, described as the first light of the world in the painted manuscripts, also caused the beginning of time and the birth of the first human being (Graulich 1994:52–59). Thus, Moteuczoma, as Centeotl or Quetzalcoatl, is the seventh omen. He looks into the bird-mirror oracle, that is, Tezcatlipoca's mirror, and foresees Chrstianity coming into his land. He acts as Centeotl, a harbinger of the sun, in this case the Christian sun or era.

When Moteuczoma looked into the "bird-mirror oracle" he saw the stars, that is, the mythical realm of time. He tried it again and "saw a little beyond (the future): people coming as conquerors, coming girt in war array." In fact, the description of the men in war garments riding deer-like beasts is fairly similar to the description in Durán's passage of the Conquest. Quilaztli showed Moteuczoma an old book containing images of the conquerors: "White and bearded men, dressed in different colors . . . riding deer-like beasts and flying eagles" (Durán 1984:2, 515). The description of the seventh omen, as well as Quilaztli's paintings, recalls, in turn, a passage in Saint John's book of Revelation. "Now in my vision . . . I saw the horses and their riders. They wore red, blue and yellow breastplates" (that is, different colors, as did the men shown to the Tlatoani by the mirror and by Quilaztli). "Out of their mouths came fire, smoke and sulfur. By these three plagues of fire, smoke and sulfur a third of the human race was killed" (Revelation 10:17–20). This passage is illustrated by Albrecht Dürer's well-known woodcut, *Four Riders of the Apocalypse* (ca. 1496). The four riders appear galloping in the heavens, just as in Moteuczoma's vision of the conquerors through the magic mirror. Moreover, the four riders, through sickness and hunger, killed "a third of the human race," just as the riders seen by Moteuczoma disseminated epidemics that killed almost 85 percent of the indigenous population.[6] The conquerors, as the riders of the Apocalypse, inflicted a siege upon the city, closing all roads into Tenochtitlan.

The fact that Moteuczoma is the only one who can see through the mirror has several connotations. In the first place, to him alone is granted the revelation of the conquerors riding their deer against a starry sky. This revelation, as can be proven by the similarities between the woodcut of the *Four Riders of the Apocalypse* and the *tlatoani's* vision, has biblical overtones. In this sense Moteuczoma alone can participate in Christianity and the world to come—his "soothsayers" cannot. The seventh omen thus confirms Moteuczoma's role as a boundary marker between two world eras. It also reveals that the Conquest was equated to the Apocalypse. This relation has to be understood in the context of the utopian ideas of the Franciscans, who viewed simultaneously the Garden of Eden and the heavenly Jerusalem in the New World. This interpretation, as noted by John Phelan (1956:25), was based in Joachim of Fiore, who had predicted that when all the Jews and Gentiles were converted, a millennium dominated by the religious orders would follow. Hence, Moteuczoma sees a revelation similar to that of Saint John at Patmos: the end of the world brought by the Riders of the Apocalypse.

In this seventh omen, the Nahua painters express that the Conquest was the consummation of a prophecy inscribed in both the Nahua myth of the world eras and the book of Revelation. As Graulich observed (1997:187), the Nahua myth of the world eras, which tells the story of how the world had been destroyed and recreated anew four times before the Fifth Sun, was in reality the "story of a people." In this sense, Moteuczoma's revelation of the Conquest is a combination of both the pre-Hispanic and Christian prophetic traditions. It represents the advent of the new group of people that was to dominate a cycle of time.

Moteuczoma could see into the future and thus knew that the world was coming to an end because it was through his sacrifice that Jesus would be sent as a new sun. Moteuczoma's sacrifice thus opened the door to the next cycle of time. This new time, according to the book of Revelation, was the time of the New Jerusalem, which in the Franciscan view was the Indian Church of New Spain.

THE EIGHTH OMEN: THE RENEWAL OF HUMANKIND

"Often were discovered men—thistle-men having two heads but only one body. They took them there to the Tlillan Calmecatl. There they showed them to Moteuczoma. When he had beheld them they vanished" (Sahagún 1950–1982: Bk. 12, 2).

Omens 7 and 8 conclude the epic story of the Conquest. Paradoxically, as they are related to the final chapters describing the devastating final battles of Tenochtitlan, they also transform these horrible events into the story of the creation of a new time and a new group of people: the mestizo of New Spain. While omen 7 recasts the creation myth at Tamoanchan and transforms Moteuczoma into a Centeotl-like figure, the harbinger of the Christian sun, omen 8 closes the creation story, uniting the first four omens as the cycle of fire and the last three omens as the cycle of water (Figure 2.4). Following the pattern established by the myth of Tamoanchan, omen 8 thus symbolizes the creation of the new earth and the birth of the first new human beings. The monstrous double-headed men, having two heads and one body, are the mestizo of New Spain. Significantly, omen 8 is located in the cosmogram (see Figure 7.1) at the place where the winter solstice is and the year bearer Tochtli resides. The date 1 Tochtli signals the date-birth of the earth. Cihuacoatl, woman of the Apocalypse, represented in the sixth omen, has given birth to Centeotl-Moteuczoma, who looks into Tezcatlipoca's mirror, a harbinger of Christianity. His light, as that of Venus in the beginning of time, also causes the new human beings to be born: the thistle-headed men of the new era, representing the suffering and uncertainty of change and transformation, the basic condition of the Nahua people's life in the New World.

FINAL THOUGHTS

I have shown that the eight omens preceding the history of the Conquest in the *Florentine Codex* are ordered as a complete cycle of time according to the space-time unity of the calendar. The omens are the means to transform the chronicle of the Conquest into a prophetic sacred book based in the black ink/red ink tradition of painting-writing history. I have shown that it is through the omens and drawings that a Nahua-Christian prophetic history of the Conquest was created.

In fact, the eight omens and the drawings illustrating the historic passages in the chronicle are the means to structure the narrative as prophetic history according to the ancient Nahua calendar. However, I have also shown that the drawings and omens in Book 12 are a recasting of history, for they incorporate Christian precepts and a new visual text into their meanings. These drawings were an act of neither surrender nor nostalgia but instead represented a vision that, paradoxically, altered the past to help the vanquished conquer the future. According to this Nahua-Christian prophetic history of the Conquest, therefore, the old book of paintings owned by Quilaztli and seen by Moteuczoma was, in fact, an illustrated Bible.

NOTES

1. This work is part of my doctoral dissertation, "Images of the Beginning: The Painted Story of the Conquest of Mexico in Book XII of the *Florentine Codex,*" Department of Art History, Yale University, 2004.

2. The Nahuas, as defined by James Lockhart (1992:1), are the peoples of central Mexico who by the time of the Conquest were united by a shared culture and language called Nahuatl. This term is preferred to Aztecs or Mexica in this chapter because at the time the works about the Conquest were written, the Aztec polity no longer existed.

3. The *Historia General,* or *Florentine Codex,* is a twelve-volume sixteenth-century encyclopedia about the life and culture of ancient Mexico written by the Franciscan Bernardino de Sahagún with the aid of Nahua collaborators.

4. I owe this observation to Eric Velázquez (personal communication, May 2003).

5. We do not have original documents that discuss the relationship between cosmic directions and stages of the day. It is clear, however, that both the vertical and horizontal structures of the world had associations with darkness and light. While the surface of the earth was imagined as a flat disk floating in waters divided into four regions and the center, the universe was thought of as a structure with three layers. Above, the upperworld, the heavens, was a luminous space where the sun dwelled. The underworld was watery and dark; it was thought of as the starry night sky and the ocean. The North, called Mictlalpan in Nahuatl, "Towards the Place of the Dead," was related to darkness and the night in the vertical axis of the world. North was thus considered the direction of the ancestral dead, a place of regeneration and transformation. In the horizontal axis, however, as noted by Pedro Carrasco (1979) and Gordon Brotherson (1992), the North in the horizontal axis is related to daytime, while the South is related to midnight.

6. The most serious and widespread of these plagues occurred in the years 1545–1548, 1576–1581, 1629–1631, 1692–1697, and 1736–1739. In 1532 there were perhaps 16 million Indians in the entire central Mexico area. In 1570 the number was 2.6 million (Gerhard 1972:44).

PART III

EFFECTS OF INVASION

Death and Conquest

8

Indian Autopsy and Epidemic Disease in Early Colonial Mexico

Martha Few

Epidemic diseases introduced during the Spanish Conquest and colonization of Mexico and the Americas have long been acknowledged as key features that helped shape European expansion into the Americas (see Chávez Balderas, Chapter 9, this volume).[1] One of the most devastating and enigmatic of these diseases was *cocoliztli*. Beginning in 1575, a *cocoliztli* epidemic swept through Mexico City and the surrounding region, leaving many dead in its wake. *Cocoliztli* is associated with a wide array of symptoms, including hemorrhagic bleeding, gangrene, jaundice, delirium, convulsions, and dysentery. According to various eyewitness accounts, the indigenous population was particularly hard-hit, dying in alarming numbers. In response to the death toll, the viceroy of New Spain ordered Francisco Hernández, a Spanish physician in Mexico on a Crown-sponsored visit, and Alonso López de Hinojosos, a barber-surgeon at the Royal Indian Hospital in Mexico City, to conduct a series of Indian autopsies and report on the results in the hopes of finding a cure.

In this context, colonial officials hoped the autopsies would provide a standardized system with which to evaluate and represent the biological effects of a devastating epidemic disease on the human body. In this case, however, the physicians conducted autopsies solely on Indian bodies, despite the fact that the epidemic afflicted all ethnic groups in colonial New Spain. And so, in early colonial Mexico, as the autopsies worked to promote and standardize human biology, the reports also represented and emphasized the strangeness and extreme effects of the disease on the bodies of native peoples, even to the point of monstrosity. Colonial physicians attributed *cocoliztli*'s dramatic effects on native peoples to, among other things, what they considered their inappropriate diet. Medical practices and discourses developed by the formal medical community, such as the Indian autopsies conducted in the wake of the late-sixteenth-century *cocoliztli* epidemic considered here, utilized representational practices that aided in the construction of ethnic differences between colonizers and colonized and interacted with and helped legitimize colonial social hierarchies in New Spain (Kleinman 1980; Kleinman, Das, and Lock 1997; Farmer 1999).[2]

This study suggests a new area of investigation into the history of epidemics in early colonial Spanish America by analyzing Indian autopsies as evidence of how medical and biological discourses and representations contributed to the construction of ethnic differences between Spanish and indigenous peoples. Much of the historiography of epidemic disease in early colonial Latin America has focused on three areas. The first is demographic studies—documenting, quantifying, and periodizing indigenous population loss and how it varied regionally (Cook and Borah 1960, 1963; Borah 1964; Deneven 1992). Other scholars working on epidemic diseases have attempted to accurately identify the diseases and cures according to contemporary scientific criteria from evidence found in colonial-era travel narratives, contemporary histories, and other firsthand accounts (Prem 1992; Ortiz de Montellano 1990). A third group of scholars has examined biological and environmental changes as one part of assessing the impact of European Conquest colonization of the Americas (Crosby 1972, 1986). A key example is Alfred Crosby's (1972) Columbian exchange model, which broadened Conquest-era history beyond its military and religious aspects to consider the biological, environmental, and social consequences on New World peoples and the landscape.

The sources for this chapter include two sixteenth-century autopsy reports written by Spanish physicians on orders from the viceroy to search for a way to halt the *cocoliztli* epidemic. Francisco Hernández's autopsy report is found in his essay "On the Illness in New Spain in the Year 1576 Called Cocoliztli by the Indians."[3] Alonso López de Hinojosos's autopsy findings are included in the last section of his larger work on surgery published in Mexico in 1578.[4] Together, these sources provide findings from autopsies conducted on Indian bodies as the *cocoliztli* epidemic raged through the capital and contain information on the city-wide strategies used by both the political and religious arms of the colonial state through their most important representatives: the viceroy and the archbishop. These strategies included religious processions, consultations with indigenous leaders, and the distribution of food and clothing—public responses designed to calm the rattled capital.

MEDICINE, AUTOPSY, AND EPIDEMIC DISEASE IN SPAIN AND NEW SPAIN

The practice of human dissection began in the Iberian Peninsula in the kingdom of Aragón circa 1340, a result of the Crown of Aragón's ties to important Italian universities of the era.[5] Beginning in the fifteenth century the universities in Barcelona (1402) and Valencia (1477) also practiced human dissection. Only in the sixteenth century, however, did human dissection become regularly used across the Iberian kingdoms, the result, in part, of the University of Valencia's promotion of the work of the Flemish anatomist Andreas Vesalius (1514–1564). Vesalius outlined a systematic framework for human dissection, which came to be known as Vesalian anatomy, in his work *Fabrica,* published in 1543. As a result of the adoption and promotion of Vesalian anatomy in Spanish universities, human dissections became popularized in medical education, undertaken to describe both normal and pathological anatomies. Beginning in the 1560s, autopsies to determine cause of death became frequently practiced in Spain, especially during outbreaks of epidemic disease (Risse 1987:22–23).

In Spanish colonial Mexico, institutions and bureaucracies dealing with health and healing were established almost immediately after the military defeat of the Mexica at Tenochtitlan. In 1521 Hernán Cortés founded and endowed the first general hospital in New Spain, called the Hospital de la Concepción de Nuestra Señora (Risse 1987:38). The Franciscans established the first exclusively Indian hospital in Mexico in the 1530s, called the Hospital Real de San José de los Naturales. This hospital was expanded and rebuilt in 1555–1556 and contained eight wards and 200 beds, staffed with two physicians and two surgeons (Risse 1987:39; Muriel 1956–1960:1, 36–48). Formal medical education in colonial Mexico began at the University of Mexico, established in Mexico City in 1551. In 1553 Juan de Alcazár de la Fuente held the first medical chair (Risse 1987:34). Medical authorities in Mexico City and elsewhere in colonial Latin America conducted autopsies in city hospitals for public health reasons (such as epidemics), as they had in Spain (Risse 1987:39).[6] In 1525 the Spanish Crown established the *Protomedicato* in New Spain, a bureaucracy designed to regulate official medical practice there and directed by the *protomédico* (chief medical officer).

Francisco Hernández and Alonso López de Hinojosos, who conducted the autopsies, were both Spanish medical practitioners, but they came from very different training backgrounds. Hernández attended medical school in Spain and rose through the ranks to become one of Spain's most important physicians in the sixteenth century. He served as the official physician to the king of Spain, Phillip II. In a 1570 royal edict, the king appointed Hernández *protomédico* of the Indies and sent him to the Americas to study indigenous medicine and *materia medica* (substances used in the practice of medicine) for both scientific and economic reasons (Varey 2000:46–47). Part of the edict instructed Hernández to experiment with illness and healing herbs and plants in New Spain, and the autopsies he conducted with López de Hinojosos formed a part of this process (Varey 2000:46): "[Y]ou shall experience and test at first hand all the above-mentioned [herbs and plants] if you can . . . [and] you shall cause to be sent here all the medicines or herbs and such like that you may see in those parts, provided that they are noteworthy in your judgment and do not already grow in these realms."

At the time of the arrival of the Spanish, the Nahua had a well-developed system of medicine that included a wide range of medical specialists, along with botanical gardens to grow and test medicinal plants and herbs (Ortiz de Montellano 1990). Hernán Cortés, in a letter to Charles V in 1521, made a point to describe Mexica herb sellers and their medicines at the giant Tlateloco market: "[T]here are streets of herbalists where all the medicinal herbs and roots found in the land are sold. There are shops like apothecaries', where they sell ready-made medicines as well as liquid ointments and plasters."[7]

Once in Mexico, Hernández wrote a series of letters to King Phillip II reporting on his progress.[8] In 1574, for example, he visited the Hospital de Santa Cruz in Huaxtepec, about fifty miles outside Mexico City. This hospital was located on a site that had been a retreat for Mexica rulers, and it included a botanical garden that emphasized medicinal plants important to pre-Hispanic healing strategies (Risse 1987:40). Hernández conducted a study of this *materia medica* and classified his findings according to Hippocratic and Galenic models of illness and healing. As part of this process of classification, Hernández tested many of the plants and herbs on himself, which often made him ill (Risse 1987:44). After he finished his work at the Hospital de Santa Cruz, Hernández moved to the Indian Hospital in Mexico City (Hospital Real de los Naturales) and worked with López, with whom he later conducted the *cocoliztli* autopsies.

Alonso López de Hinojosos (ca. 1534–1597) was not a university-trained physician but an apprentice who became a barber-surgeon and phlebotomist. He first practiced healing in his native Spain, then emigrated to Mexico in 1567, where he worked at the Indian Hospital and the Hospital de la Concepción de Nuestra Señora, both in Mexico City. He gained much clinical experience there and developed an excellent reputation among both Spaniards and Indians. Some sources suggest that López actually conducted the 1576 autopsies under the supervision of Hernández (Fernández del Castillo 1936; Risse 1987:46–47). In 1585 López joined the Jesuits and became the *portero* (gatekeeper) for the Colegio Mayor de San Pedro y San Pablo, also in Mexico City. He continued to treat patients until his death.

EPIDEMIC DISEASE AND INDIGENOUS PEOPLES IN NEW SPAIN

The 1576 *cocoliztli* epidemic was only one of a series of epidemics that swept through Mexico during the sixteenth century. In 1520–1521 a smallpox epidemic decimated the Mexica population of Tenochtitlan during Cortés's siege of the capital. Another smallpox epidemic (possibly combined with measles) lasted from 1531 to 1532. The first *cocoliztli* epidemic raged from 1545 to 1548 and caused widespread regional depopulation, beginning first in central Mexico and then spreading southward into Guatemala (Risse 1987:51).

One scholar has characterized the 1576 *cocoliztli* epidemic as the "most significant in the history of Mexico" because of the high death toll compared with other epidemics (Prem 1992:38). Spanish eyewitness accounts in particular tended to emphasize the large numbers of indigenous dead as a result of the epidemic, even though Spanish and black populations suffered as well (Malvido and Viesca 1985:29). Death toll counts ranged from 100,000 reported by the archbishop of Mexico to 2 million reported by Juan de Torquemada (Torquemada 1723; Prem 1992:41). In contrast, indigenous accounts tended to focus more on the horrific symptoms of the disease, especially the hemorrhagic bleeding (*flujo de sangre,* literally "bloody flux") from the eyes, ears, anus, nose, and mouth (Prem 1992:38; Malvido and Viesca 1985:28).

Contemporary scholars continue to debate the exact medical identification of *cocoliztli,* with no clear resolution. The term *cocoliztli* is the Nahua word for "sickness" or "pestilence." Two major outbreaks of this disease occurred in early Mexico, first in 1545 and again in 1576 (Malvido and Viesca 1985:27). *Cocoliztli* continued to flare in 1579 and 1588 and again in 1601–1602 (Gibson 1964:449; Malvido and Viesca 1985:31; Cook 1998). Reports of *cocoliztli* can be found in mid-sixteenth-century Guatemala as well, where the disease was called *k'ucumatz* in K'iche' Maya and by the variation *gucumatz* (MacLeod 1973:19; Lovell 1991:71–72). Some scholars suggest that the illness was a kind of typhus that included high fevers; others argue that the disease was the plague.[9] Scholars studying colonial Guatemala suggest that *cocoliztli* was pneumonic plague, which "develops when bubonic plague attacks the lungs and respiratory system" (MacLeod 1973:19).[10]

Whatever its exact classification, *cocoliztli* was a horrifying illness, in terms of both the way the disease destroyed the human body and the number of deaths it caused. Juan Bautista de Pomar, a chronicler in Mexico in the 1580s, wrote that indigenous peoples of Tetzcoco in central Mexico called the epidemic *cocoliztli ezahualhuacque*, meaning "pestilence of gloomy and brown colored fury," and continued that "most who died expelled from their mouth a humor like petrified blood" (cited in Cook 1998:101–102). Francisco Hernández wrote of *cocoliztli* that "the fevers were contagious, burning, and continuous, entirely pestilential, and in a great many cases, lethal" (Varey 2000:83).

AUTOPSIES AND REPRESENTATIONS OF THE INDIAN BODY

The viceregal order for Hernández and López to conduct the autopsies to search for a cure formed part of an overall plan that drew on scientific, religious, and public health strategies to counteract the epidemic's further spread.[11] It appears that these were among the earliest autopsies performed in the Americas.[12] Hinojosos wrote that the viceroy chose the Indian hospital in Mexico City as the site to conduct the autopsies because of its excellent reputation in caring for Indians and because the hospital "had the most coolness in all of New Spain," which prolonged preservation of the bodies (López de Hinojosos:209). In their reports, neither Hernández nor López made drawings or illustrations to represent their autopsy findings. Instead, they relied on vivid pictorial descriptions to represent the afflicted Indian bodies, a strategy they may have employed to make their work more accessible to others conducting similar autopsies. Both men made strong use of graphic colors in their descriptions of the effects of *cocoliztli*.[13] This is especially the case for Hernández, whose autopsy account focused in particular on the corporeal outcomes of the disease. Hernández carefully described the colors on the outside of the body: the eyes and the entire body were yellow, and the tongue was "dried out and black" (cited in Varey 2000:84). He also noted in detail the varying colors of the urine: "sea green urine or vegetable green and black, but from time to time the color would change from deep green to pale" (cited in Varey 2000:83). López also described yellow bodies and urine that was "dark-colored, like wine" (López de Hinojosos 1977:210). The opening of the Indian body in the process of autopsy also revealed a wide array of colors, presenting an interior transformed by the disease. Hernández described a swollen liver, a dry stomach, a blackened heart "emitting pale yellow liquid and later black blood," black bile in the blood vessels, and "green or very pale" blood, which he obtained by vivisection (cited in Varey 2000:84). The lungs, however, were blue and dry (López de Hinojosos 1977).

In addition to the consistent emphasis on color in describing their findings, both men described Indian bodies as literally rotting from the inside out. During the height of the epidemic, in September and October 1576, López conducted bloodletting as part of his healing strategy, and he noted that the blood taken from the sick "did not have any wateriness; instead it was clumpy matter" matter (López de Hinojosos 1977:210). Hernández noted blood running from the noses and ears of the afflicted and the emergence of abscesses behind the ears. When these abscesses burst, either spontaneously or after the recommended application of a "red-hot iron," they drained noxious pus. He also described how gangrene accompanied the disease in some patients, which "invaded the lips, pudenda and other putrefied parts of the body" (cited in Varey 2000:83).

The opened Indian body also provided more images of the body breaking down from the inside out, to the point of monstrousness. The autopsies revealed "black and semi-putrefied spleen and lungs" (Varey 2000:84). According to López, the disease so transformed the liver "that it appeared to be [the size of] a bull's liver," and when he raised the ribs while performing the autopsy, "one could see that it [the disease] made the chest very deformed, [and] because of its huge size and misshapenness it became a monstrosity" (López de Hinojosos 1977:209–210).

Both men were struck by the large number of indigenous deaths and conducted the autopsies on the orders of colonial officials as one way to search for a cure. At the same time, however, they both used certain kinds of language strategies in their reports, which had larger implications for creating biological divisions between the colonizers and the colonized in the process of establishing and maintaining colonial rule. My concern here is to highlight the ways visual representations of the sick and their bodies can legitimate colonial medical knowledge claims, in this case words and images that characterized afflicted Indian bodies as pestilential and rotting, with monstrously transformed organs and bodies. Early efforts at representing biological differences between the Spanish and indigenous peoples with regard to disease effects, here through state-sanctioned autopsies, formed one part of ideological efforts to construct and legitimate the ethnic hierarchies that underpinned Spanish colonial rule in the Americas.

MEDICINE, ETHNICITY, AND THE SPANISH COLONIAL PROJECT

It is important to restate that the autopsies were performed only on Indians who died from *cocoliztli,* even though they were not the only social group affected. Both Hernández and López described the disease as affecting not only indigenous populations but also blacks and Spaniards. Hernández wrote that the *cocoliztli* epidemic "infected different areas in turn, beginning with those occupied by Indian tribes, then places where Indians and Africans lived, then those with a mixed population of Indian and Spanish, and later still, those areas where Africans lived, and now finally it is attacking the Spanish" (cited in Varey 2000:84). López noted that "at this time many Blacks and Chichimeca Indians have died leaving Mexico, and the mines, and all of New Spain almost without labor" (López de Hinojosos 1977:210).

Despite this, colonial authorities perceived and represented *cocoliztli* as primarily an Indian illness. This can be seen not only in the decision to conduct the autopsies exclusively on Indian bodies but also in the way the viceroy and the archbishop formulated a general policy to combat the illness and deal with the public's fear in the capital city. Viceroy Enríquez sent for the city's Indian *gobernadores* (governors) and *alcaldes* (mayors), along with an interpreter, to meet with him to discuss the epidemic. The indigenous officials brought López with them, probably because of his position as head of the Indian hospital. Native peoples in the *barrios* of Santa María and Santiago were particularly hard-hit by the epidemic, and López noted that in one day alone they visited more than 100 of the sick. Priests concentrated on ministering to the Indians in these neighborhoods, going house to house to clean up after the sick to prevent further spread of the epidemic and to provide clean clothes and food to the afflicted and their families. The archbishop ordered the city's priests to go house to house to hear the confessions of the dying. "And so went th[ose] anxious for the health of humankind among the sick," wrote López, "not fleeing from the danger even though it was grave and contagious, but plunging into it, caring more for the salvation of souls of the Indians than for their own health" (López de Hinojosos 1977:207).

The representation of *cocoliztli* as primarily an Indian disease can also be seen in the explicit link Hernández made between those afflicted by *cocoliztli* and indigenous culture and behavior in general. Hernández pointed to what he described as the Indians' extreme fondness for alcohol and their inappropriate diets as central reasons for their susceptibility to *cocoliztli.* "The Indians were great lovers of wine," Hernández wrote, "and indiscriminately ingested chile and corn—which generated profuse bile [and] blood—as well as other substances, [they consumed] not just bad coarse juices but also the most sordid food" (cited in Varey 2000:84). This kind of knowledge claim, legitimized by the language and practice of colonial medicine, reinforced ethnic difference in colonial society by marking indigenous peoples as both different from the Spanish and also culturally responsible for their susceptibility to the disease because of their inappropriate diets. In this sense, colonial medicine produced causal frameworks for illness that interacted with ideologies of Spanish imperialism, which included representations of indigenous peoples as uncivilized heathens and also as having diseased and susceptible bodies.[14]

A key part of this process was the effort to "Europeanize" illness as part of the Spanish colonial attempt to tame and cure *cocoliztli* and other diseases, as the effort to define and maintain order under Spanish colonial rule included not only social order but biological and bodily order as well.[15] Physicians such as Hernández and López had to adapt and recreate European medical explanatory frameworks to new bodily contexts and illnesses found in colonial Mexico. Sixteenth-century medical practices in this new setting proved flexible and innovative in this regard.[16] With *cocoliztli,* Hernández and López experimented by opening Indian bodies through state-sanctioned medical autopsies and presented their findings in official reports and books—analyzing the effects of *cocoliztli* on Indian bodies and at the same time making broader claims and generalizations about indigenous culture, representing native peoples as biologically different from other groups in their susceptibility to the disease.

Moreover, both men worked to fit *cocoliztli* into European medical explanatory frameworks to create an official healing strategy specifically targeting the disease. Hernández's and López's understandings of *cocoliztli* were framed by Galenism, which combined humoral theory and bloodletting with other extractive and purgative therapies to restore humoral balance (Lindemann 1999). These ideas formed the core of Spanish medical theory and practice throughout the seventeenth century. For years, Avicenna's *Canon of Medicine*, based on Galenism, was one of the most popular texts used in Spanish universities (Risse 1987:21). Once the medical practitioner determined what kind of humor had caused the illness, the practice was then to somehow expel it from the body using bloodletting, purging, sweating, or vomiting (Risse 1987:23; Lindemann 1999:66–77).

Because part of the goal of the autopsies was to find a treatment and cure for *cocoliztli*, Hernández and López had to classify the disease within the humoral framework. Hernández argued that *cocoliztli* was caused by venom and should be classified as "hot." He then prescribed various therapies that had the goal of expelling the offending material from the body. These therapies used purgatives, including one made from a combination of tamarind, rhubarb, and senna (a yellow-flowered plant used as a laxative). Together, this concoction purged "bilious and atrabilious humors, provoked urine, and counteracted the toxin" (Varey 2000:84). Poultices and ointments worked to release the offending material through the skin. Additionally, Hernández recommended an ointment made from the New World plants *cococtlacol chipaoac* and *atochietl*, which were to be rubbed over the sick person's chest "to open all the orifices through which the poison, which was also evacuated by urine, could be expelled" (in Varey 2000:84). Doctored broths and food, such as ones that included cabbage, were also fed to the patient in the hope that they would encourage the sick person to "expel decayed matter"(in Varey 2000:84).

Based on Hernández's classification of *cocoliztli* as venom, López fashioned a comprehensive four-part treatment strategy for healers to follow depending on the centrality and severity of the wide array of bodily symptoms *cocoliztli* presented. For those who had *flujo de sangre*, he prescribed bloodletting with a cupping glass applied beneath the breasts and at the nape of the neck. If that appeared to have no effect, the sick person was bled next above the liver and spleen. If male, the testicles were to be washed with cold water and a wet handkerchief suddenly placed on the nape of the neck "so the sick person becomes frightened." This process was followed by a series of purges.

Hernández complained that other, undefined healers—probably indigenous, mixed-race, and female healers—were applying "everything that came to hand," alluding to a sense of desperateness that must have accompanied the epidemic (in Varey 2000:84). He continued that "there was no shortage of people who, to the great detriment of the sufferers, washed their bodies with cold water and rubbed their foreheads with the juice of cooked *coatli* [literally "water snake" in Nahuatl] [and also gave] them juice of *iztacpali* [a type of plant used in Nahua healing] to drink." Hernández countered his descriptions of healing disorders in the capital with a portrayal of López and himself as following an orderly process of experimentation to search for a cure: "But for our part the medications that we have said were most useful, we tried to test by proper experiment and administered them with the result of enormous improvement in health and the happiest outcome. We made this clear to others, so that they in turn could apply these remedies against this most terrible of plagues" (in Varey 2000:84).

While ultimately Hernández and López did not find a cure for *cocoliztli,* the appearance of biological order in colonial medical practice proved just as crucial. By conducting autopsies and advocating a uniform therapeutic strategy to follow in efforts to slow or counteract the illness, colonial physicians helped to reinforce the social order the rattled Mexico City needed in times of epidemic disease outbreaks.

CONCLUSION

As the dramatic symptoms and horrifying death counts of the *cocoliztli* epidemic plagued Mexico City, colonial physicians such as Hernández and López, in conjunction with city political and religious officials, worked to reestablish biological and social order through the practice and knowledge claims of colonial medicine. Formal medical activities, such as the autopsy considered here, suggest that colonial physicians and scientists also worked to create clear distinctions between

Spanish and indigenous bodies and between official and popular medical practice in ways that represented and reinforced the ethnic distinctions between colonizer and colonized that structured hierarchies of Spanish colonial rule. While more research on this topic is needed to outline the scope of this process and to historicize it, the use of Indian autopsies as diagnostic tools in early colonial Mexico provides evidence of how the construction of such differences took place beyond the realms of biology and ideology. The visual and representational realm proved equally critical for the Spanish imperial project—in this case, the ways colonial medical practice constructed and depicted diseased Indian bodies within the context of epidemic outbreaks.

Despite Hernández's claims of having the right remedies and López's detailed healing strategy for *cocoliztli,* epidemic diseases and other illnesses continued to affect colonial peoples of all social and economic groups. This revealed the limits of the power of colonial medicine and its attempts to "Europeanize" illness and establish biological order in ways that mirrored the colonial state's efforts to create social order, leaving open possibilities for competing local cultures of healing in colonial New Spain.

NOTES

1. For the historiography of epidemic disease in early colonial Latin America, see Cook (1998, esp. 1–14). Previous versions of this chapter were presented at the annual meeting of the Rocky Mountain Council for Latin American Studies, Phoenix, February 2003, and at the symposium Invasion and Transformation: Interdisciplinary Perspectives on Images of the Conquest of Mexico, University of Miami, March 2003. Thanks to Marten Brienen, Susan Deeds, Lina Del Castillo, N. David Cook, Sasha Cook, Kevin Gosner, and Tracy Brandenburg Kazaz for their comments on earlier versions of this essay.

2. This chapter uses the case study of the 1575 *cocoliztli* autopsy to explore how formal medical activities, in addition to other colonial processes including religious conversion, forced labor policies, and the like, created clear distinctions between Spaniards and indigenous peoples by using scientific and biologically based arguments. These issues are explored in more detail in my book manuscript in progress, *Colonial Medicine and Atlantic World Healing Cultures in Guatemala, 1680–1830.* For more on gender, healing, and magical illness in late-seventeenth-century Guatemala as viewed through Inquisition trials, see Few (2002), especially chapter 4, "Illness, Healing, and the Supernatural World." For a related topic of colonial medical and scientific writings that focus on sexual difference and its connections to gender and racial hierarchies in Enlightenment Guatemala, see Few (2005).

3. Hernández originally wrote this report in Latin. Germán Somolinos D'Ardois published a Spanish translation of the text in his article "Hallazgo del manuscrito sobre el cocoliztli, original del Dr. Francisco Hernández" (1956). The direct quotes in this chapter are from an English translation, published in Varey (2000:83–84).

4. López de Hinojosos (1977, esp. tratado 7, "De pestilencia, el cual tiene cuatro párrafos," 207–213).

5. Katharine Park has written that Italian medical practices of opening the body occurred in three contexts: public anatomical dissections for teaching purposes, private autopsies requested by elite families, and postmortem autopsies conducted by public health officials in Italian cities beginning at least in the thirteenth century. For more on autopsy in Italian medical practices, see Park (1995).

6. George Cheever Shattuck mentioned an epidemic that swept through Santiago de Guatemala, capital city of colonial Central America, in the late seventeenth century, during which autopsies were performed: "Some of them [the victims] died suddenly; others expired under the most acute pains in the head, breast and bowels. No remedy was discovered that could check this progress, although many of the deceased were opened, to endeavor, by that means, to come at the cause of the disorder." He gives no citation for this statement. See Shattuck (1938:41).

7. This description is found in Cortés's "Second Letter," in Pagden (1986:103).

8. These are transcribed and translated in Varey (2000).

9. Cook (1998: 100–101). Typhus and the fevers associated with it, however, are usually classified in colonial sources as *tabardillo*. Malvido and Viesca (1985) argue that *cocoliztli* is the plague.

10. Sandra de Orellana (1987:269) agreed with MacLeod and defined *k'ucumatz* as a kind of plague, deeming it pneumonic plague. The definition of pulmonary plague is found in Lovell (1991:72).

11. Fernández del Castillo (1936:6) noted that Doctor Juan de la Fuente was also involved in the *cocoliztli* autopsies. Malvido and Viesca (1985:31) only mentioned Hernández and López by name in their work. D'Ardois (in Malvido and Viesca 1985:35–36) noted that three "others," whom he did not name, also participated in the autopsies.

12. Fernández del Castillo (1936:6) argued that these were indeed the earliest autopsies performed in the Americas. Somolinos D'Ardois stated that he is convinced these were *not* the first autopsies performed in New Spain but did not provide evidence of earlier autopsies (in Malvido and Viesca 1985:36).

13. I cannot tell if this is a new technique of description, a strategy used in the absence of illustrations, or if *cocoliztli* was an illness that presented its symptoms in color in ways other illnesses did not.

14. See Comaroff and Comaroff (1992:216), who observe that European imperial expansion in Africa and nineteenth-century medicine "each played off the other within the unfolding of a particular historical process—that they were in fact cut from the same cultural cloth."

15. Ibid. Comaroff and Comaroff identify the use of social images to mediate physical realities: "Thus not withstanding its status as an emerging science, medicine drew upon social images to mediate physical realities, giving colonial power relations an alibi in the ailing human body. And colonial regimes, in turn, drew upon medical icons and practices to impose their domination upon subjects and collectivities everywhere" (1992:216).

16. For example, European adoption of New World herbs, plants, and roots into remedies in early colonial medicine is well documented. Risse (1987:50) calls this process

"reverse acculturation." See also Quezada (1978:51–68); Comas (1954). Hernández's use of New World plants and herbs in healing strategies is discussed in more detail in Malvido and Viesca (1985). Hernández and López built on Nahua medical knowledge regarding local plants and their medicinal properties. Both recommended local healing plants and herbs such as the *coanepelli* root to help cure *cocoliztli,* a plant well-known in pre-Hispanic healing practices for its coagulent properties and its ability to reduce fever and prevent spasms.

9

Death during the Conquest Era

Ximena Chávez Balderas

The way the dead are buried reflects their social condition and identity. Funeral rites can proclaim the manner of a person's death, the social level he or she occupied, and society's ideas about the afterlife. Although ancient Mesoamerica was characterized by an enormous variety of funeral patterns, a great deal of what is known is based on Spanish chroniclers' accounts, which tend to focus on the Mexica—also known as the Nahua or Aztecs—whose empire flourished between the fourteenth and sixteenth centuries. The manner in which the Mexica disposed of their dead took into account both the identity of the deceased and the way he or she had died; these aspects, in turn, determined the funeral geography or the place to which the person's soul was believed to travel after death. These practices and beliefs took place within the framework of a religion that regarded death as the main creator of life.

The Conquest and the years that immediately followed it were marked by rapid and violent social change. Spanish ideology and social practice had an immediate impact on the indigenous view of life and death. The destruction caused by the war led to a vast number of deaths on the battlefields, and the Spanish also introduced new diseases to the indigenous population, resulting in even more deaths. The imposition of the Christian tradition led to many changes in how these dead were treated, and funerary practices in the colonial era developed new forms and meanings. Through a comparison of the religious beliefs and rituals of both the conquered and the conquerors—as evident in archaeological, historical, and osteological data—this chapter examines the nature of the conflict between the Spanish and the Mexica. By addressing changes in funeral rituals before, during, and after the Conquest, this study sheds light on the Conquest's ideological impact on the native population.

THE NATURE OF SOCIAL CHANGE BETWEEN TWO CULTURAL TRADITIONS

Spanish colonial rule and the way it affected the natives' thinking are discussed by Alfredo López Austin in his book *Cuerpo humano e ideología* (1989). According to the author, colonial domination must be understood as the clashing of two distinctive cultural traditions, where one subordinates the other. According to this view, the subordinated people (the Mexica in the case discussed here) established a precarious congruence between two types of world perceptions: their own and the dominant one, which was not completely understood. The Spaniards considered indigenous belief systems culturally retarded and ignominious (López Austin 1989:25–26), although as the centuries passed resistance gave way to syncretism and new ways of thinking. As argued by Clinton Bennet (1996), when two cultural traditions—each with very different religious systems—come into contact, it is feasible to register several phenomena: acculturation, continuity, change, and either unity or diversity. Or, to follow the title of the present book, invasion and transformation. Generally speaking, political systems are the most sensitive to transformation, with changes readily observable in the short term. In contrast, changes in the magical system take much longer to manifest themselves (López Austin 1989:19–20). As a result, historical and archaeological evidence often seems to portray different rhythms of transformation for the religious, political, and ideological planes. The former may nonetheless be considered the agent causing changes in ideology.

To understand the changes in indigenous ritual forms within the context of the Conquest, it is necessary to emphasize certain issues. It is feasible to consider ritual evidence an indicator of social change only after a thorough analysis of archaeological contexts and written records. In this sense, it is important to bear in mind that although the social change is total, it may be considered heuristically as disentangled from its political, religious, and economic dimensions to facilitate its understanding. The magnitude of the transformation that occurred during the Conquest was so immense that it was manifested clearly in everyday life as well as in ritual practices such as funerals. Although the latter convey perceptions of the world, death, and afterlife, they must first be evaluated as the immediate reflection of a change in history and, therefore, of the everyday life of individuals.

At the beginning of the Conquest, the manner in which the dead were buried varied but did not necessarily imply a transformation of religious beliefs. On the other hand, the changes in funerary practice during the colonial period implied a radical transformation of death and afterlife conceptions. Thus, burials during the first period of contact underwent an immediate modification as a result of the invasion and political changes. This predated the radical transformation regarding the perception of the world that would take place in subsequent centuries.

DYING BEFORE THE CONQUEST: GEOGRAPHIES AND FUNERAL RITUALS

Despite the wide range of Mexica funeral practices, the rituals were unified by a religion that regarded death as the principal generator of life rather than a symbol of annihilation. In fact, according to Mexica mythology, mankind was created thanks to death. Within this belief system, symbols of death were usually linked to the most important aspects of the culture and society: the calendar, sowing time, maize, birth, myths, poetry, and language. Images of death were incorporated into architecture, sculpture, ceramics, painting, and other forms of artistic expressions. When Eduardo Matos refers to the obsessive way death was represented by the Mexica, he adds that it should be regarded as "the worship of life through death" (1986:16). As with other religions, one finds what appear to be contradictions in the Nahua view of death. On the one hand, Nahua poetry states that man only lives once on earth, although there is evidence that the Mexica also thought it was possible that some of the dead could be transformed into another type of being when they died (Matos 1986:89). Rather than a source of contradiction, scholars now feel this type of inconsistency instead reflects the extraordinary richness and polysemy usually found in belief systems.

Historical sources have enriched our knowledge of Mexica ritual life, particularly with respect to the funerals of important persons. One of the most widely consulted works is *La Historia General de las Cosas de la Nueva España* by Friar Bernardino de Sahagún (ca. 1578–1580), a Franciscan priest who spent decades compiling information from native informants about the land and people of New Spain. Significant differences exist, however, between Sahagún's book and the records of other chroniclers. For example, Sahagún (1997:207) mentions that those who died of a common illness or old age (the majority of the population) were cremated and their *teyolía*, a sort of soul located in the heart, would travel to Mictlan, the Nahua underworld or place of the dead. Mictlan, which Sahagún compared to hell, was a dark place without windows, ruled by a death deity named Mictlantecuhtli and his wife, Mictecacíhuatl. Sahagún is insistent that dead people who traveled there were cremated regardless of whether the person was a "nobleman or low-class," a claim in opposition to both the archaeological evidence found to date and the accounts of other chroniclers. In the discussion that follows, which uses Sahagún as one of its main sources, it is nonetheless clear that the place and the way the dead were buried were neither coincidental nor accidental. On the contrary, these things reflected the social condition and identity of individuals and even their manner of death (Figure 9.1).

When individuals met their deaths as a result of water-related causes, they were buried in direct contact with the earth, and it was thought that their souls traveled to Tlalocan, a mountain paradise presided over by Tlaloc, the deity of rain and agricultural fertility. Sahagún (1997:207–208) compared Tlalocan to the Judeo-Christian idea of paradise, a place of abundance and year-round "verdure and summer." The offerings given to those who had died this way consisted of seeds and food, although the quantity and quality depended on the individual's social position.

If a person died in battle and his body could be recovered, he was cremated and his soul was thought to travel to the Tonatiuh Ilhuícatl, or Solar Heaven. There dead warriors had a cosmic mission: they were to help preserve the universe by transporting the sun from its lowest point at dawn to its midday zenith (Sahagún 1997:208, 301–304). Evidence indicates, however, that bodies were rarely recovered from the battlefield; warriors remained where they had met their deaths. In Tenochtitlan relatives therefore made a bundle from branches to represent their loved one. This enabled them to socialize the loss through the elaboration of a funeral. The sumptuous funeral rites described by Friar Diego Durán in *Historia de las Indias de la Nueva España e Islas de tierra firme*, an important sixteenth-century Spanish source (1579–1581) (1995 I:204–205, 343), appear to be descriptions of the effigy bundles of warriors slain in combat.

Like warriors, women who died during childbirth were also believed to travel to the Solar Heaven after death. There they also became participants in the mission of keeping the sun in motion: they received it at its zenith and handed it over to the inhabitants of the underworld at nightfall. Unlike the warriors, however, these women were not cremated; rather, they were buried in a temple specially designated for this purpose. After burial, relatives removed the bodies to protect them from thieves because many attributed special powers to the body parts of such women. Relatives consoled themselves about their loss by thinking that

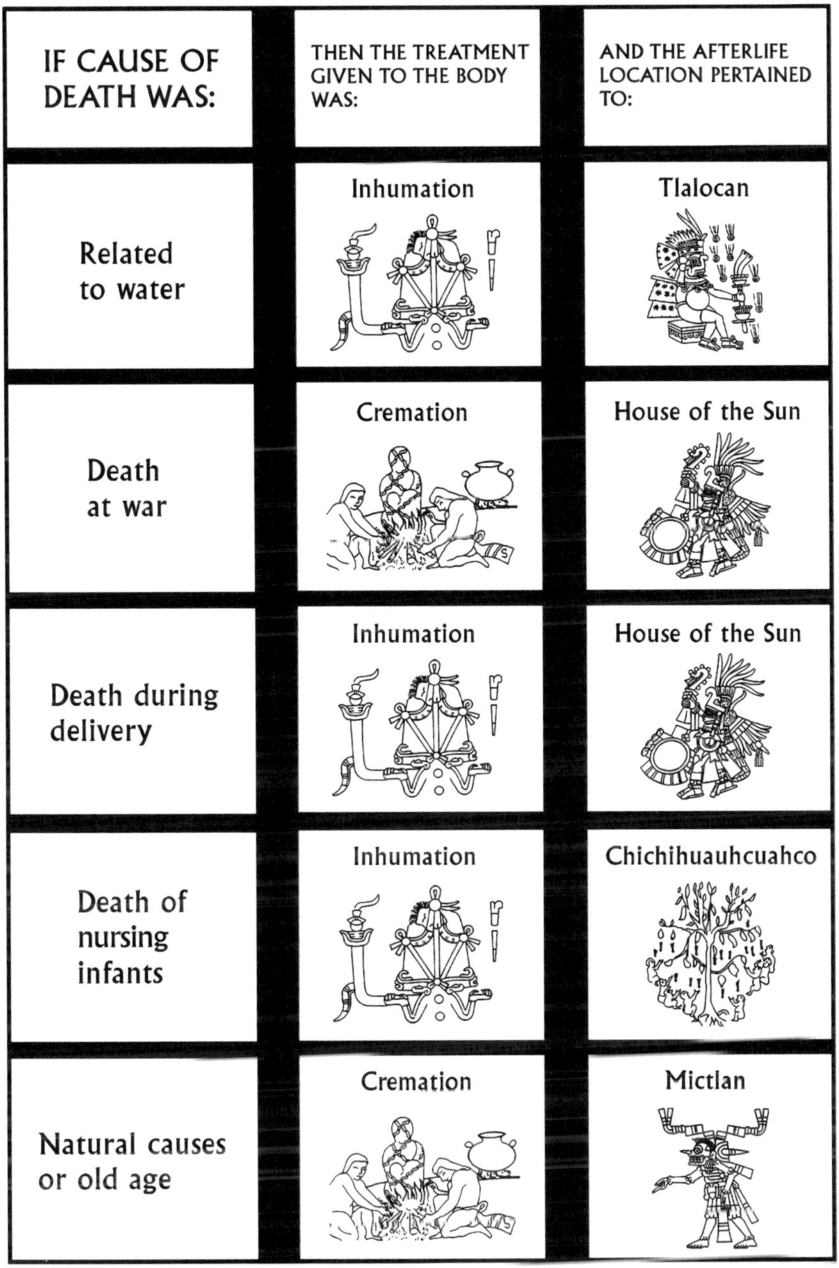

Figure 9.1. Chart showing correspondence among cause of death, geography, and funeral practice. Graphics by Luz Maria Muñóz. Courtesy, Proyecto Templo Mayor/INAH.

the women had met a glorious death: the dead women were regarded as equal to goddesses, who could return to earth and had the capacity to cause harm. This is why, in addition to celebrations held for them in the temples, women who died in childbirth were also invoked at crossroads, where bread, tamales, and toasted maize offerings were left for them (Sahagún 1997:25, 34–35). Different practices were adopted for unweaned babies. Upon their deaths, they were buried and their souls were thought to travel to a region known as Chichiuauhcuahco, believed to have been located in the Tlalocan paradise. There, a life-giving tree would continue to suckle them (López Austin 1989 1:384–385).

Sahagún's descriptions have been interpreted as proof of a linear correspondence among cause of death, position of the body, and funeral geography. There are, however, elements that suggest that the link among these three aspects is more complex and that many other factors also came into play. To prove this, it is essential to talk about the funerals linked to Mictlan through death by common illness or old age, in other words, the most common causes of death. According to Toribio Benavente, also known as Motolinía, a sixteenth-century priest in New Spain who wrote *Memoriales* (ca. 1536–1543; Benavente 1971:304–305), the dead person's body was wrapped in cloth and a green stone placed in his or her mouth as a symbol of the heart. A lock of hair was cut from the top of his or her head because it was believed this was the place that contained "the memory of his [or her] soul and the day of his death." This hair was placed in a painted box next to another lock of hair that had been cut off on the day of the person's birth. The funeral parcel was adorned with the insignia of the main god of the town, in whose temple or patio the burial was to be held. The death was announced, and all those who attended the funeral took offerings with them. Sahagún (1997:206) states that water was poured onto the dead person's head while those present declared: "This is the water you enjoyed when you were alive." A jug of water was then placed on the shroud, and the corpse was handed a series of pieces of paper, while those present told the corpse the route it should take to Mictlan and the dangers it would face on the journey. The rites carried out in the presence of the body lasted until the fourth day, at the end of which it was cremated. A reddish-colored dog was placed on the funeral pyre next to the body because it was believed it would serve as a guide to the dead during the day (Sahagún 1997:206). The ashes, bones, and charcoal were collected and buried in the place set aside for this purpose: the exact location depended on the status of the dead individual (Figure 9.2).

Other chroniclers suggest that the individual's social position determined not only the place of the burial but also the practices adopted for the funeral. Friar Juan Torquemada, who wrote *Monarquía Indiana* in 1615 (1977:4, 306–308), for example, agrees that those who died a natural death were cremated. He

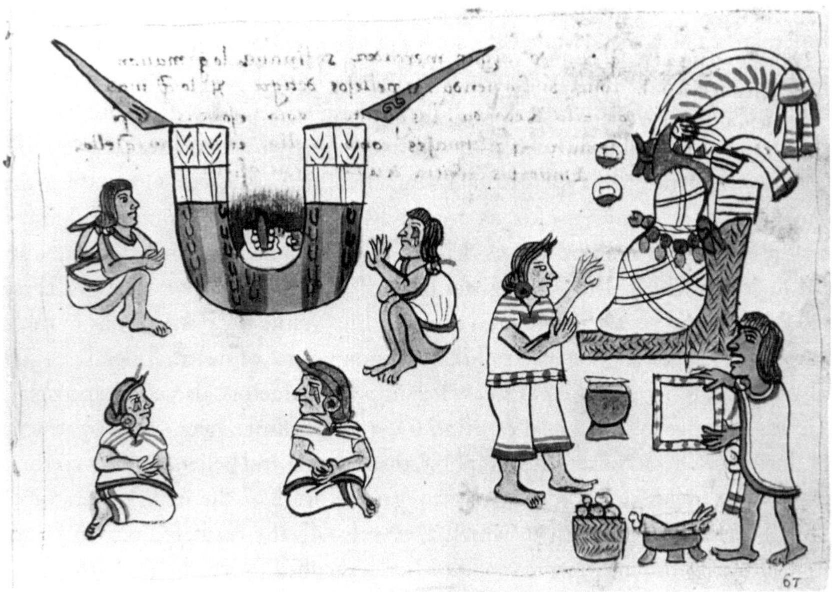

Figure 9.2. *Rites in the Presence of the Body and Burial*, from *Codex Magliabechi* (1996:67r). Photograph by Germán Zúñiga. Courtesy, Proyecto Templo Mayor/INAH.

points out, however, that this description refers "to the burials of kings and highly-respected lords in the kingdoms and republics." In *Historia Eclesiástica Indiana,* Friar Jerónimo Mendieta (ca. 1571–1596; 1945:180) agrees with Sahagún's version but similarly notes that "[t]his was how the great lords were buried and less ceremony was involved in the burial of other personages, in accordance with their quality and status and even less in that of the common people." Benavente (1971:307) is far more specific, stating that unmarried people were buried rather than cremated and that this means of "burying the dead was the most common and widespread practice among the Nahual." Another extremely detailed anonymous document, "Costumbres, Fiestas, Enterramientos" (ca. 1553; 1945:57–58), states that cremation was a treatment given only to the bodies of the great lords. It goes on to say that lords with the lowest status were buried in the patios of their homes. They were wrapped in coarse cotton cloth and feathers and given offerings of food; these lords were also buried with their servants so the latter could continue their service in the next world. The use of cremation as a funeral practice exclusive to the pre-Hispanic elite is consistent for other Mesoamerican groups of this period, such as the Tarascans, the Tlaxcaltecans, and the Maya (Alcalá 1980:276–277; Muñoz Camargo 1991:562; Landa 1938:139).

Among the Spanish chroniclers were also those who felt cremation was a funeral practice typical of the elite, such as Francisco López de Gómara (1941:2, 230), who states that "poor people were usually buried . . . while lords and rich men were burnt and then buried." Indeed, the best descriptions of funerals are those of kings and lords, which probably explains why cremation is the most commonly mentioned type of funeral practice in the sources. Conversely, the funeral rites of common citizens are rarely mentioned. "Costumbres, Fiestas, Enterramientos" (1945:58) states that dead commoners were shrouded and buried in cotton cloth. They were given food offerings, since it was thought these would be useful to sustain them in the next life. While the descriptions in these chronicles suggest some correspondence among cause of death, funeral geography, and treatment of the corpse, other important factors also come into play, such as occupation and social position. Despite the differences in the treatment of the deceased and funeral geographies, these rituals and beliefs were given their framework by Mexica religion, which regarded death as the main generator of life, as related in the myth in which Quetzalcoatl, the feathered serpent hero, went down to the underworld to ask Mictlantecuhtli for the bones with which he would create mankind (Figure 9.3).

EVIDENCE IN THE GREAT TEMPLE: FUNERALS OF MEXICA DIGNITARIES BEFORE THE CONQUEST

The excavations of the Templo Mayor (Great Temple) in Mexico City, directed by Eduardo Matos, have been a particularly rich source for archaeological evidence on Mexica funeral rituals. Seven graves have been found in the southern half of the building, which was dedicated to the main god of the Mexica, Huitzilopochtli. An earlier research project (Chávez 2002) characterized three different types of funeral practices associated with the Templo Mayor burials. The first, represented by Offerings 10 and 14 (Stage IVb, 1469–1481 A.C.), consisted of cremating a corpse at low temperatures or for a short time and then carefully separating the bones by hand. The bones were then deposited in an urn that was buried outside the temple at the foot of the staircase. A second type of ritual, Offering 3 (Stage IVb, 1469–1481 A.C.), consisted of cremating a body at high temperatures, with several offerings, and then separating the bones while they were still hot. The remains were divided and taken to various destinations, one of which was outside the temple at the foot of the staircase. The other locations are still unknown. The third type of funerary treatment is associated with the inside of the temple, the most sacred area. This involved the manual, yet highly selective, collection of bones, which aimed at representing the whole of the skeleton through a small quantity of bony remains. This third type of funeral ritual, rep-

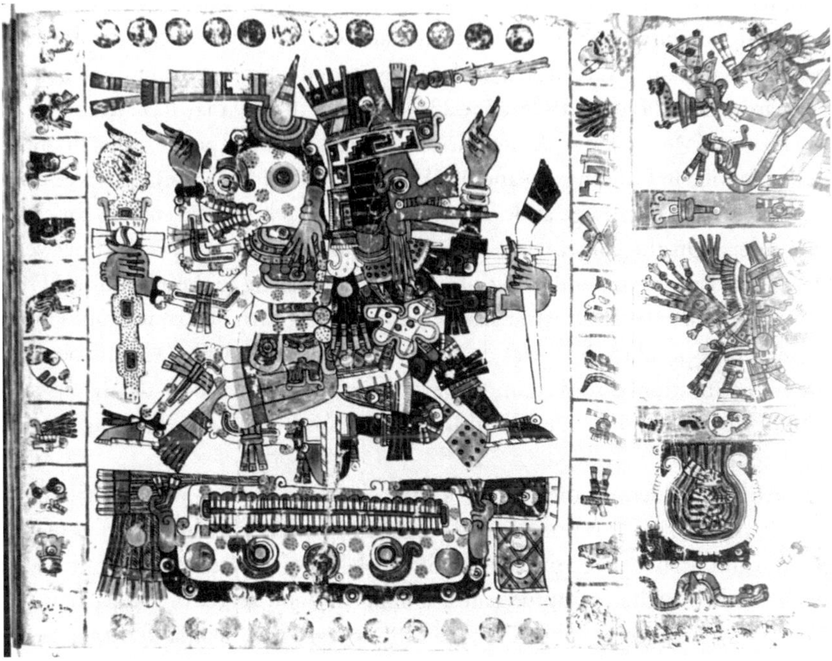

Figure 9.3. *Mictlantecuhtli and Quetzalcoatl*, from *Codex Borgia* (1993:56). Photograph by Germán Zúñiga. Courtesy, Proyecto Templo Mayor/INAH.

resented by Offerings 34–39 and 37–44 (Stage II, 1375–1427 A.C.), used very small urns; the amount of bones deposited in them accounted for less than 20 percent of each individual, as though each bone was a sort of relic. The rest of the skeleton might have been buried in an important place, a possibility suggested by the apparently contradictory testimonies of the chroniclers, which state that the Mexica kings were buried in a building named *cuahxicalli,* the royal palace, inside the temples and at the feet of the effigy of the god Huitzilopochtli (Alvarado Tezozomoc 1944:242; Durán 1995 I:303, 357, 455; Alva Ixtlilxóchitl 1952:2, 328; Cortés 1994:64). Unfortunately, the sources contain insufficient information to confirm any of these assertions.

The identity of the individuals whose graves were found in the Templo Mayor has been the subject of much scholarly debate; it has even been suggested that they were certain Mexica rulers (Umberger 1987; López Luján 1993). Nonetheless, analysis suggests that the only grave that might be that of a ruler is the one represented by two funeral urns (Offerings 34 and 39), which contain the bony remains of one individual. Both urns were located in the temple dedicated to Huitzilopochtli, at the foot of the pedestal holding the image of the god, regarded as the most sacred place in Tenochtitlan. This is the spot where, according to Durán (1995 I:357), the remains of the Mexica *tlatoque* (or at least part of his remains) were buried. If this does indeed represent the grave of a ruler, Leonardo López Luján (1993:235–236) suggests that he may have been one of the first two Mexica kings, Acamapichtli or Huitzilíhuitl. The age at death of the person buried in Offerings 34 and 39 (Stage II, 1375–1427 A.C.), however, does not correspond to the age at death quoted by several historical sources for these two rulers. On the contrary, the individual buried at the temple died between the ages of twenty-one and twenty-four, which according to the accounts of Friar Diego Durán, Hernando Alvarado Tezozómoc, and Juan de Tovar, would more closely correspond to the age at death of the third Mexica ruler, Chimalpopoca. This identification is uncertain, however, since Chimalpopoca's death was surrounded by political intrigue, resulting in some historical sources stating he died at a later date.

Although identifications with a high degree of accuracy are problematic among the Mexica, it is nonetheless possible to analyze the various types of cremation and propose a reconstruction of rituals. Pre-Conquest Mexica burials are distinguished by their sumptuousness, complexity, and degree of social participation. As we shall see later, however, after the arrival of the Spaniards, funeral rituals in the context of war were transformed, together with the country's history (Figure 9.4).

DYING IN LIGHT OF THE CONQUEST: FUNERAL GEOGRAPHIES AND RITUALS

The period following the arrival of the Spaniards in the early sixteenth century was marked by turbulence. In a state of war, it was not always possible to bury the dead according to the usual customs. This does not mean, however, that it was not important to the Mexica to preserve the basic form of the rites; rather, they were more concerned with life. Also, as mentioned earlier, the political system is one of the most sensitive to transformations, and its repercussions are readily observable in the short term, whereas changes in the magical system are evident at a longer interval (López Austin 1989:20). This period saw the emergence of a new way of looking at life and with it new ideas about death, funeral geographies, and rituals. To understand the impact of the clash between the Catholicism of the Spanish and the Nahua religion of the Mexica over indigenous funerary practices, it is necessary to review certain aspects of these two traditions of thought.

Unlike many other religions, which seem to regard death as a generating factor, Catholicism, generally speaking, appears to classify death as an element of

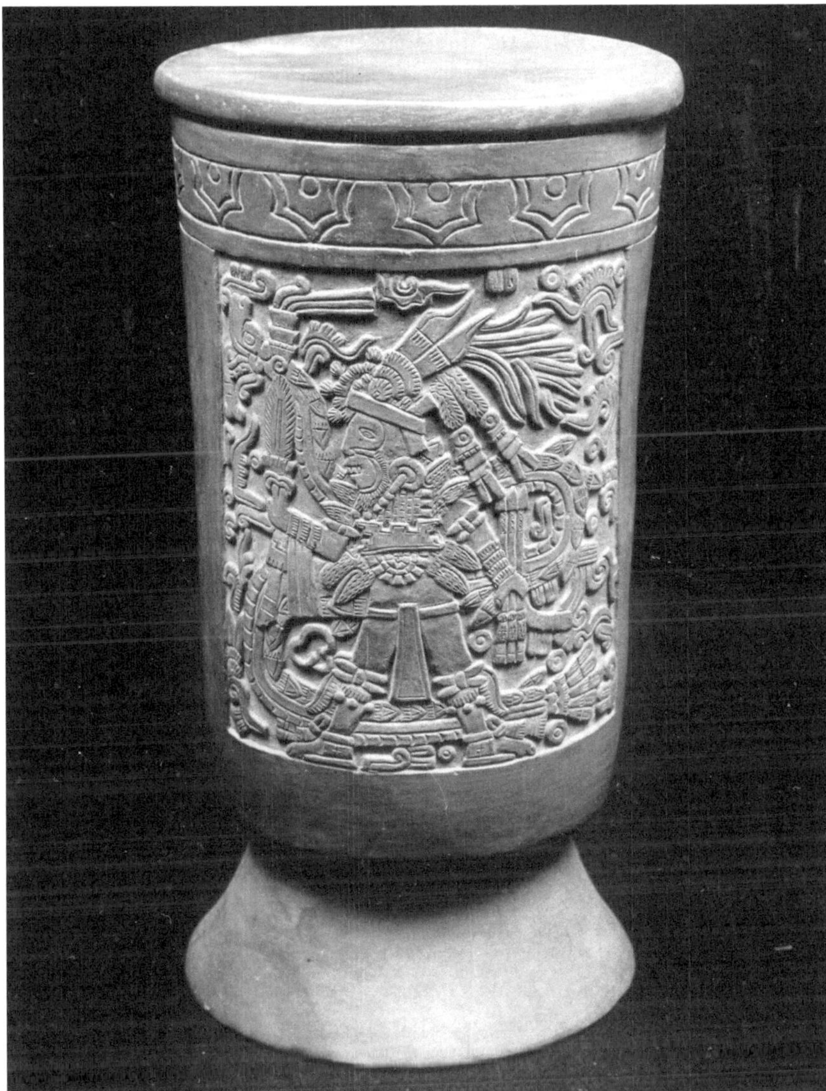

Figure 9.4. Funeral Urn. Photograph by Germán Zúñiga. Courtesy, Proyecto Templo Mayor/INAH.

annihilation. According to Edgar Morín (1979:269), obsession with and horror concerning death never penetrated the heart of life, as seen in accounts of the Apocalypse, which will end death and therefore pain. In keeping with this idea, Helmut Thielicke (1984:154, 162) adds that death is the queen of terror in Christianity. He also points out that the biblical message of death is not constant but rather a polyphonic chorus, resulting from a historical process ranging from resignation to the hope of resurrection; it magnifies the incorruptibility of bodies while proclaiming the maxim "ashes to ashes, dust to dust."

Within these apparent contradictions, Louis-Vincent Thomas (1995:216–217) distinguishes three fundamental connotations of death within Catholicism: (1) death as the separation of the spiritual soul and the corruptible body; (2) death as annihilation, resulting from sin; and (3) death as transformation, linked to resurrection, in which the corrupt will become incorrupt and the mortal will become immortal. Within this body-soul dualism, the former remains on earth while the latter travels to another plane. The location of funeral geographies within Catholicism is not conditioned by the type of death but rather by the actions taken during one's life. Unlike pre-Hispanic religion, these worlds of the dead are conceived in terms of good and bad, punishment and reward. It is possible to have movement from one to another, thanks to the notion of repentance. Both religions have the concept of an underworld, yet Mictlan and hell are not the same. Since they share certain features, Sahagún (1997:205–207) compared them with Nahua funeral geographies, although they have a completely different meaning. Mictlan is not the home of Satan and the damned, as in the Christian hell; Mictlan may be dark, but it is not a place of punishment.

Other funerary geographies in Roman Catholic doctrine include Limbo, which is inhabited by those souls who could not be baptized: they could not be linked to Christ through this rite of incorporation. While they experience no suffering there, they are unable to experience God. Purgatory is the geographic destination of sinners' souls, the place where they suffer for the acts they committed while alive. Nonetheless, sins are unimportant: they can be paid for, thereby satisfying divine justice. Suffering and repentance for one's sins contribute to salvation: the soul's period in purgatory is a time of change during which salvation and condemnation are in the balance (Thomas 1995:220–222). Conversely, suffering in hell never ends: the sin was mortal, the offense infinite, and it must therefore be paid for forever. The opposite case is paradise, where, thanks to one's blameless conduct on earth, one's soul will obtain everlasting happiness in the presence of God (Basave 1983:130–131).

In Catholicism, one's behavior on earth determines where one's soul will travel after death and whether one will achieve happiness or suffering. Conversely, in the Nahua belief system, in the world of the dead a person does not obtain a reward or punishment but instead is given a duty of cosmic importance, such as assisting the daily journey of the sun. Another significant difference between the two traditions is that in Catholicism there is, generally speaking, just one funeral practice, regardless of the world of the dead one will inhabit. To fully understand the way the body is arranged, it is essential to discuss a central Catholic concept:

resurrection. One's immortality belongs to his or her total being, body and soul; it therefore demands the resurrection of the body, as with the resurrection of Jesus. The glorious, resurrected body of Christ, the loveliest of all images, is the example to be followed (Thomas 1983:243–245, 310). Considering this belief in the resurrection, bodies must be buried as Jesus was buried. Tradition requires washing the body and dressing it in a white shroud, with the connotation that the soul must be whitened and cleansed of all sin. Dressing the body in a shroud and placing it in a set position in a coffin evokes Christ's death (Malvido 1999:47).

The arrival of this Catholic belief system in Tenochtitlan in the sixteenth century did not translate into an immediate imposition of Christian funeral rituals. There was an initial phase during which change reflected extraordinary circumstances within the context of the war, during which death became a part of everyday life. The gravity of the changes and their consequences did not go unnoticed by certain chroniclers because dying became a common and expensive event in light of the Conquest.

Some accounts are dramatic. Benavente (1971:14, 97), for example, mentions having heard that when a person died after having been in bed for several days, the spouse had to gather up his or her assets to pay for the medicine and the doctor's fees, which meant that very little remained to pay for the burial. Given this situation, the chronicler recounts that he heard a wise married man say that when one's spouse fell ill, the best thing for the healthy person to do was to kill the spouse and bury him or her in any cemetery. The survivor would thus avoid incurring debts, since people could not afford to pay for a long illness. Likewise, epidemics changed the outlook for funeral rituals. The first documented epidemic took place in 1520, and the friar relates that it was impossible to bury all the dead. In some cases, all the members of a household died. To remove the smell of decomposing bodies, neighbors preferred to knock down people's dwellings, which then housed them in death as they had in life. Epidemics proved a vital ally in the Spaniards' domination of the local population (Muriel 1956–1960 I:288).

EVIDENCE IN THE GREAT TEMPLE: FUNERALS OF MEXICA DIGNITARIES DURING THE CONQUEST

Of the few funerals of dignitaries during this period discussed in historical sources, the descriptions of Moteuczoma II's are the most polemical. Moteuczoma II was, of course, the ill-fated ruler seated at the head of the Aztec Triple Alliance at the moment of European contact. After a series of political intrigues and having been held in custody by the Spanish invaders, Moteuczoma II was eventually assassinated in 1520 under unusual circumstances.

Versions of his death are contradictory: in some accounts the Mexica are said to have stoned him to death, while according to other versions the Spaniards murdered him. The first explanation is so implausible that not even the Spanish friars seem to have believed it; several include contradictory evidence in their accounts. This was the case with Sahagún (1997:456, 783), who in Book 8 of the *Florentine Codex* first records that the *tlatoani* was stoned by his vassals. Later, in Book 12, he nonetheless states that the Spaniards threw the lifeless bodies of Moteuczoma and the *tlatoani* of Tlatelolco "onto the banks of the lake" in a place called Teoáyac. When the Mexica recognized the bodies, they took them to a place called Copulco, where they built a wooden pyre and burned them (Figure 9.5).

Although seventeenth-century author Fernando Alva Ixtlilxóchitl (ca. 1600–1640; 1997:828) accepts the official version of Moteuczoma II's death, he also mentions that the Spaniards killed the Mexica leader by sticking several swords into him. Durán (1995 I:630) states more pointedly that the version of the stoning is patently untrue. Instead, he describes how the Mexica found him chained up and dying from five dagger wounds in his chest. The friar reports that Moteuczoma II's body was burned and turned into dust, with no pomp or ceremony.

Accounts of the final destination of his body are as contradictory as those of his death. "Costumbres, Fiestas, Enterramientos" (1945:57) states that his body was taken to a ruined temple that was in flames. After his body had been burned, his remains were consumed by the other famous persons there. If this version is true, it did not follow the usual funeral pattern but rather was an exceptional situation in the context of the turbulent period of the Conquest. Another version recorded in the *Codex Ramírez*, attributed to Juan de Tovar (1583–1587; 1975:100), relates that after Moteuczoma II's murder, the people did not want to give him a funeral. One of his servants, therefore, cremated him and buried his ashes in a pot in an unknown place. Torquemada (1975:2, 214) mentions yet another version: the king was buried in Chapultepec, a location near the area of Tenochtitlan. The manner of Moteuczoma II's burial and the rituals performed upon him thus remain unknown, and there is insufficient evidence to favor any particular version. The various procedures recorded by the chroniclers regarding the way his body was arranged, however, do not follow the established pattern of the pre-Hispanic era but instead suggest the exceptional and turbulent period in which he lived and died.

In keeping with the conquistadors' interests, the official version of stoning was supported by figures such as Díaz del Castillo (1979 I:274), who says he saw stones thrown at Moteuczoma II—one at his leg, another at his arm, and a third at his head, the last of which killed him. The painting *The Death of Moteuczoma at the Hands of His Own People,* formerly owned by the Jay I. Kislak Foundation

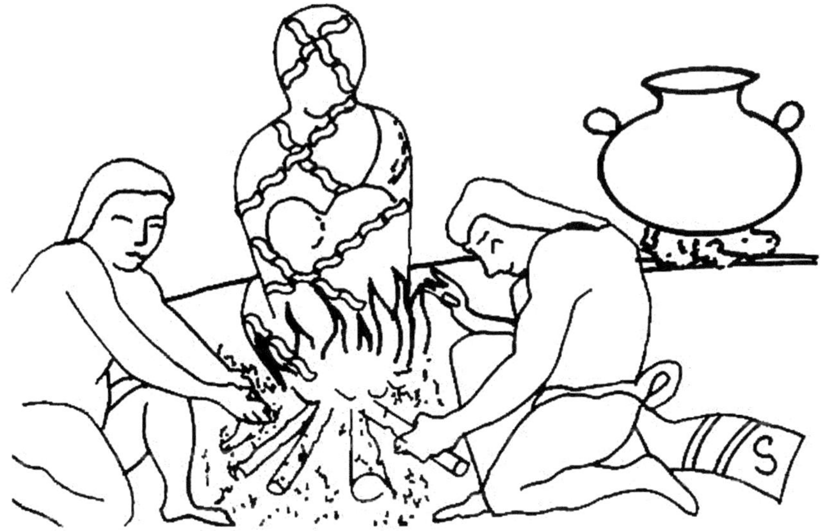

Figure 9.5. *The Cremation of Itzcuauhtzin, the Tlatoani of Tlatelolco,* in Friar Bernardino de Sahagún, the *Florentine Codex* (Book 12). Courtesy, Proyecto Templo Mayor/INAH. Drawing after original.

and now in the collection of the Library of Congress, is fascinating, since it is based on accounts of the official version (Plate 4). Likewise, an anonymous seventeenth-century screen in the Franz Mayer Museum Collection in Mexico City also shows scenes from the conquistadors' version (Figures 6.1–6.2). Screens such as this are discussed in detail by Michael Schreffler (Chapter 6, this volume).

The emperor's death was an event of great importance, given the political and economic interests that surrounded it. In the Kislak canvas (Plate 4), the official version of the ruler's assassination is conveniently portrayed. The corpses of powerful persons were thought to be as politically dangerous as the persons were when they were alive (Nigel Barley 1995:148). Following this interpretation, the burial of figures such as Moteuczoma II occupied a special place in the political struggle. As a paradox of death, funerals transformed the defeat into triumph by transfiguring the dead into martyrs, trophies of the cause, and manifestations of strength. In the atmosphere surrounding a burial service, they turned pain into political frenzy. Besides being a part of the political drama, the funeral of a ruler could be transformed into a cosmological event, unleashing an episode relevant for the history of that people: the succession (Huntington and Metcalf 1979:122). It is most likely, as the friars' comments show, that the official version recorded by the conquistadors was a dissimulation for the benefit of the Spanish Crown.

DYING IN THE COLONIAL ERA: INSTITUTIONS AND NEW RITUAL FORMS

The diseases the Spanish introduced from the Old World, in addition to other acute changes in environmental conditions, are some of the factors that adversely affected the indigenous people's health during this period and caused many deaths (see Martha Few, Chapter 8, this volume). Lourdes Márquez (1984) has shown, for example, that hydraulic works, such as aqueducts and irrigation canals, changed from systems that permitted farming and the production of food to sources of infection. Health problems increased as a result of the destruction of the water-works, overflowing canals, flooding, and even the drying up of lakes. Thus, water changed from a symbol of life to an agent of death and disease. According to Josefina Muriel (1956–1960 I), the indigenous population was struck by seven epidemics; during the 1576 epidemic so many people died that their bodies were thrown into ditches, which contributed to the spread of disease. In this context of war and disease, elaborate and sumptuous funeral rites became a thing of the past.

As Elsa Malvido has noted (1999:47), because of the enormous range of funeral practices among the native population, one of the most serious problems involved unifying burial procedures according to the canons established by the recently arrived Catholic religion, which ordered that people had to be buried in church floors and atriums or adjacent to the church on holy ground. Cremation, a popular funeral practice during pre-Hispanic times, was not permitted by the Roman Catholic Church during the early modern period because it brought about the destruction of the material body, rendering it incapable of resurrection. The colonial era led to a rupture, which converted the variability of burial practices into a standardized practice.

To understand the changes that took place with respect to funerary rituals during the colonial era, it is important to mention the emergence of essential institutions that influenced the concept of death and the way in which bodies were disposed. These institutions were established as a result of the fact that the indigenous population was suddenly exposed to serious health problems, while the magnitude of events meant traditional medicine was seen as less effective than it had been. This period saw the emergence of an important phenomenon: the establishment of hospitals. These institutions were linked to the Christian tradition through the ideals of charity and hospitality toward pilgrims, neither of which had parallels in pre-Hispanic life. The institutions were relatively small, such as the Hospital de la Concepción de Nuestra Señora, which was the first to open, probably between 1521 and 1524 (Muriel 1956). The hospitals, such as the Hospital Real de San José de los Naturales, were founded to care for the indigenous populations, which suffered from the violent effects of the Conquest. The Hospital Real de San José attended both the local population and outsiders, meaning that during the most severe epidemics it found it extremely difficult to cope with all those who were ill, and many people died.

A patient admitted to this hospital, which cared for indigenous people of all social strata, must have immediately noticed the vast differences in technique between traditional and Spanish medicine. This was probably offset in part by the fact that the hospital staff provided medical services by incorporating certain local customs and speaking indigenous languages. Despite this, admission to the hospital could easily have involved a clash between the two belief systems because the sick were sent directly to a Catholic priest and subsequently attended by a physician. In contrast, during the pre-Hispanic era, illnesses were attributed as much to nature as to the supernatural world, meaning remedies needed to be aimed at both areas, which implied performing certain rituals (López Austin 1989). Death within a hospital context was something new for the indigenous population, even though the Spanish concept of a hospital was founded on the Christian idea of charity.

The Hospital Real de San José de los Naturales had a cemetery and a church. Excavations conducted between 1992 and 1993 in the hospital's first cemetery yielded valuable information. Archaeologists José Cabrera Torres and María de los Ángeles García Martínez Mayo (1998) recovered the remains of 430 individuals, the bones of which had been placed directly in the ground accompanied by a very small number of objects, such as crosses, necklaces, and beads. The type of offerings included in these burials has led researchers to conclude that this cemetery held the bodies of the very poor, a hypothesis confirmed by the historical record. Nonetheless, some of the early graves, dating from the beginning of the sixteenth century, still have pre-Hispanic features. This is true of one individual, whose remains were apparently placed in a pot in a fetal position. Another was found making an offering consisting of a spindle, two zoomorphic figurines, and a ceramic figurine of a woman with a headdress shown in a kneeling position. These last cases demonstrate the existence of a somewhat hybrid treatment of the dead, which place pre-Hispanic funerary forms and rituals within the framework of Spanish and Catholic institutions.

The contrast between the two funeral systems is highlighted in a study by Márquez (1984:44–47), which undertakes an intriguing comparison of peninsular, colonial, and pre-Hispanic practices. Regarding the former, Márquez distinguishes a homogeneity that contrasts with Mexica diversity. He focuses on a key aspect of peninsular customs: burial inside the church or in a place adjacent to it. These locations were also favored in the colonial era. In general, funerals organized during the sixteenth–eighteenth centuries displayed these features: the corpse was arranged for the funeral wake, adorned with jewelry, and placed in a wooden coffin, the quality of which was determined by his or her relatives' financial status. Conversely, a Mexica wake lasted four days, during which offerings were brought and speeches delivered to the dead person. This contrasts with the Catholic tradition, which does not favor long periods of ritual in the presence of the corpse. To return to Márquez's work, he mentions one of the most important stages in burying someone during the colonial era: paying the parish dues, which were extremely costly. Dying became an expensive business. Previously, money and other valuables had not been given to the parish priest but had been offered to the gods or to the dead person, which is why precious materials and offerings were buried along with a person's mortal remains. They were for the next world, not for this earth.

Conversely, Malvido (1999:49) states that the poor and members of the indigenous population were wrapped in straw mats and buried in atriums, the open ground in front of the church entrance. If the dead person was extremely poor, his or her body was arranged in the shape of a cross and left in the Plaza del Volador, in the center of Mexico City. Passersby left alms to pay for the tariffs and provide the person with a decent burial. The viceroy could also intercede with the parish priest to avoid the need to pay alms and remove bodies in an advanced state of decomposition. The high cost of obtaining a Christian burial was gradually reduced, first through the Bourbon reforms in the eighteenth century, which urged that the dead be buried on the outskirts of cities rather than in churches. Civil graveyards were subsequently created during the administration of Benito Juárez, and as a result of the Law of Internment (1859), burials became nonreligious and free (Malvido 1999:51).

FINAL CONSIDERATIONS

With the introduction and imposition of Catholic beliefs and funerary practices, the Mexica clearly had to give up the variety of rituals and practices they had traditionally used in burying their dead. The adoption of Catholic forms and acceptance of an annihilating view of death, in place of the life-giving principle of death in the Nahua religion, did not take place overnight but instead was the result of a lengthy process. This change should not be regarded as the blind acquisition of the rites and beliefs of the Spanish conquistadors. Within the context of the colonial era, new institutions, forms, and meanings emerged that demonstrate the unmistakable influence of the customs and habits of the native population. This period of confrontation and change is crucial to the study of current society, since it created certain notions and established the bases for the development of new practices. Over time, these practices have been transformed and combined with new ritual forms, thereby contributing to the cultural richness of contemporary Mexico. In the words of Thomas (1995:217), "[R]ather than technical changes, what affects practices is their change of meaning."

PART IV

CONQUEST OF MEXICO PAINTINGS

The Kislak Collection, Library of Congress

10

The Kislak Paintings and the Conquest of Mexico

Rebecca P. Brienen and Margaret A. Jackson

Events from the Conquest of Mexico were not unusual subjects for works of art produced in colonial Mexico in the late seventeenth and eighteenth centuries, despite the fact that the majority of visual production was given over to religious representation.[1] Drawing on published histories, such as Antonio de Solís's 1684 *Historia de la conquista de Mejico* and Bernal Díaz del Castillo's *Historia verdadera de la conquista de la Nueva España* (1632), workshops produced individual representations, series of paintings, and especially folding screens (*biombos*) depicting events from the Conquest. The Conquest of Mexico paintings in the Kislak Collection at the Library of Congress are outstanding examples in this genre of history painting because of their early date, fine condition, and the skill of the artists involved. Painted in Mexico during the second half of the seventeenth century, the Kislak series is considered the earliest of the three complete cycles of paintings of the Conquest that still exist.[2] Beginning with *The Entrance of Hernán Cortés into Tabasco* (Plate 1), these images highlight the battles between the Spanish and Mexica of the Aztec Empire. The series ends with the dramatic *Conquest of Tenochtitlan* (Plate 7) and *The Capture of Cuauhtemoc* (Plate 8), the last Aztec king. These works are also distinctive for their ethnographic detail, especially the attention they pay to the costumes and other finery worn by the Mexica.

The dark, rich reds, dramatic compositions, and crowded atmosphere of these paintings owe much to the Baroque vocabulary found in contemporary works of art created in Italy and Spain. Paintings of successful battles, often including the surrender of the defeated party, were common in European art in the early modern period. In particular, they formed an essential part of princely self-fashioning, with military victories proclaiming the strength, the authority, and even the moral superiority of the ruler. The Kislak Conquest of Mexico paintings follow the traditional formula for seventeenth-century Spanish battle paintings in which large figures, often on horseback, are highlighted in the foreground, with fighting and other types of activities occurring in the middle and backgrounds. A well-known example of this type of image is Diego Velázquez's *Surrender of Breda* (1635), which decorated the Hall of Realms in the Buen Retiro Palace of King Philip IV (1605–1665) (Brown 1986:107–123). As is typical of such works, this painting is not limited to one moment from the narrative. Rather, a series of events is compressed onto a single canvas.

Determining an exact date for the creation of these works has proven difficult given the anecdotal nature of the evidence; it nonetheless seems clear that they were acquired by the Chomley family in Britian sometime around the end of the seventeenth century.[3] Although these eight paintings ended up in British hands, they may have been painted with a Spanish destination in mind, perhaps even the royal collection of King Charles II (1661–1700). Inventories made following the king's death in 1700 record his interest in paintings of this subject. Works of art displaying scenes from the Conquest were also in the collections of high-ranking Spanish officials during this period, who may have wanted to claim a piece of the glory for themselves. It is nonetheless important to note that in these works of art, it is not simply Cortés, the great leader, who is responsible for the ultimate victory over the Aztecs; he shares this honor with his captains, who are prominent figures within the narrative as it unfolds on the canvases. Unlike the Buen Retiro battle paintings created for Philip IV, for later audiences in Spain and Mexico the Conquest was not a contemporary event, and images of it could not portray the brilliance of Charles II and his armies. Had the Kislak series joined the royal collection, as perhaps originally intended, the paintings would have contributed to the mythology surrounding the Spanish triumph in the New World and offered a strategic distraction from the less than impressive leadership of Charles II (see Schreffler, Chapter 6, this volume).

During most of the seventeenth century, however, the subject of the Conquest seems to have held relatively little interest for artists and writers in Spain and its colonies. This changed with the 1684 publication of Solís's *Historia de la conquista de Mexico,* which reproduced the narrative in "the form of a heroic drama" (Keen 1971:176). Solís was the official chronicler of the king and a noted playwright, and the elegance of his work stimulated a new interest in the Conquest. Written over 150 years after the Conquest began, Solís's chronicle draws heavily on letters of Cortés, Díaz's eyewitness account, as well as other works by Francisco López de Gómara and Antonio de Herrera. The popularity of Solís's book is testified to by the numerous Spanish editions published into the eighteenth century. Translators throughout Western Europe were also eager to make the great actions of Cortés and the elegant pen of Solís available to the widest possible audience, and his work also appeared in multiple English, French, and Italian editions. Although the artists who created the Kislak Conquest of Mexico paintings clearly used Díaz's book as one of their primary sources and included his image in two of the paintings, in their theatrical style and high Baroque drama these works of art are closest to the refined language of Solís (Cuadriello 1999; García Sáiz 1999a; Jackson and Brienen 2003).

It seems probable that a member of New Spain's Creole population, which included people of "pure" Spanish ancestry as well as those of mixed Spanish and indigenous descent, commissioned this series of paintings, perhaps intending them as a present for the king of Spain. For Creoles in Mexico at the end of the seventeenth century, both the Spanish and the Mexica of the Aztec Empire had already become part of their ancestral mythology, so it was imperative to portray both groups with dignity. Scholarship remains divided as to whether these works of art could have served the cause of Creole nationalism in Mexico or if their message is less ambiguously a celebration of the Spanish Empire and its illustrious past (Restall, Chapter 5; Cortez, Chapter 4; Schreffler, Chapter 6, this volume).

The Kislak Conquest of Mexico paintings have been a point of departure and an oft-cited reference for the chapters in this volume. Although the volume's central goal has been to nuance understanding and create broader awareness of the multiplicity of effects and transformations brought about by the Conquest of Mexico, the Kislak paintings follow the traditional historical narrative, which we have provided here as a reference for understanding the paintings. We emphasize, though, that the history of the Conquest as presented by the paintings is limited, highly biased, based on Spanish sources, and presented in such a way that Spanish victory was both inevitable and sanctioned by God (see Restall, Chapter 5, this volume).

NOTE ON INSCRIPTIONS AND NUMBERS

The paintings in this cycle include inscriptions and a numbering system designed to explain to viewers both who and what they are looking at. Over the last three centuries, these texts and numbers have been worn away and are now very difficult to read. In these entries on the paintings, we gratefully acknowledge the assistance of Dr. Michael Schreffler and Dr. John Beusterien in making transcriptions of the Spanish texts on the paintings. We have attempted to preserve as much as possible the spelling and wording of the original captions, which are written in the Spanish of a semiliterate person in Mexico in the second half of the seventeenth century.[4]

The quotes from Solís in the catalog descriptions that follow are drawn from Thomas Townsend's 1724 translation of this work into English.

Painting 1 (Plate 1)

The Entrance of Cortés into Tabasco / La Entrada de Cortés en Tabasco

Second half of the seventeenth century

Mexico

Oil on canvas, 48" × 78"

Kislak Collection, Library of Congress No. N8214.5.A45 C65 1750. 0001

N° 1

Entran en Tabasco las nuestros por la punta de los palmares guiados de geronimo de Aguilar q[ue] hullaron entre los Indios, los quales dieron sobre los españoles. [H]acen pazes y son los primeros cristianos desta Nueva España.

Fernando Cortes–1

Bautisase D. Marina y otras cinco–2

Casiques de Tabasco–3

Ciudad de Tabasco–4

Gonzalo de Sandoval–5

Cristobal de Oli[d]–6

Jeronimo de Aguilar–7

Pedro de Albarado–8

No. 1

Our entry into Tabasco through the point of the palms [a geographic location marked by palm trees, depicted in the middle ground on the left], led by Jerónimo de Aguilar, whom they found among the Indians that surrendered to the Spanish. They [the people of Tabasco] make peace and are the first Christians of New Spain.

Hernán Cortés–1

The Baptism of Dona Marina and five others–2

Caciques (leaders) of Tabasco–3

City of Tabasco–4

Gonzalo de Sandoval–5

Cristobal de Olid–6

Jerónimo de Aguilar–7

Pedro de Alvarado–8

Because earlier exploratory voyages by Europeans to Mexico were small and had relatively little impact, the official beginning of the Conquest dates to February 1519, when Cortés departed from Havana for the Gulf of Mexico with eleven ships and over 500 men. Although their relationship soured shortly thereafter, in late 1518 the governor of Cuba, Diego Velázquez, appointed Cortés commander of a new expedition to further investigate the region's natural resources and indigenous groups, including the great Aztec Empire of the interior. The primary desire of all involved was to discover new sources of wealth. The fact that the Spanish ships carried cannon, artillery, guns, and horses demonstrates that the conquistadors were prepared from the very beginning to take what they wanted by force.

Hernán Cortés and his men first sailed to the island of Cozumel, a few miles off the eastern coast of the Yucatán Peninsula, where they had a friendly encounter with a local Maya settlement. The Maya were an important indigenous group in Yucatán and Central America and remained independent from the Aztec Empire of the Mexica. After learning of the existence of Europeans among an inland Maya group, Cortés sent men to find them. As a result, the Spaniard Jerónimo de Aguilar joined Cortés and his men. Having spent years living among the Maya, Aguilar spoke their language, a talent that would prove very useful as the Spanish made their way inland. Cortés's first major conflict with indigenous Mexicans occurred as the Spanish traveled toward the city of Tabasco, located on the mainland of Mexico. Although the Spanish captured the city, the conflict continued. The Spanish were outnumbered, but Cortés apparently used cannon and men on horseback to great effect and eventually won the battle. According to Spanish sources, the *caciques,* or indigenous leaders, of Tabasco begged Cortés for forgiveness. More important, they gave Cortés and his men twenty women, one of whom was Malinche, also known as Doña Marina or Malintzín. She spoke both Nahautl, the primary language of the Aztec Empire, and Maya. The presence of Malinche and Aguilar allowed the Spaniards to gather information and communicate with local populations as they journeyed through the Mexican interior on their way into the heart of the Aztec Empire. Having good translators proved an extraordinary tactical advantage for Cortés and his men because it allowed them to enlist thousands of indigenous allies for their later siege of Tenochtitlan.

In the painting, the Spanish troops, most in full armor and on horseback, are engaged in a furious battle with the inhabitants of Tabasco. In contrast to the metal armor and rapiers of the Spanish, the native Mexicans wear elaborate and colorful feathered costumes and carry spears and *maquilhuitl,* wooden clubs inset with black, razor-sharp pieces of obsidian. Although Solís describes Cortés as leading the battle on horseback, the most prominent figure in the foreground is Cristóbal de Olid, one of Cortés's captains. Mounted on a pale horse, he rises above the confusion of the battle with his rapier held high, about to deliver a deadly blow to the Indian leader threatening him. Other members of Cortés's senior staff depicted here include Pedro de Alvarado and Gonzalo de Sandoval. In the background of the painting we see the baptism of Malinche and five other indigenous women in a small grove of trees. Cortés appears here as a witness to this event, not as a main figure in the battle. As described by Solís, among the women the Spaniards received was "one principal *Indian*, well made, and of more than ordinary beauty, who was afterwards baptized, and received the name *Marina*, and proved very useful to the Conquest" (Bk. 1:65). Baptisms were a common subject in colonial painting because Europeans typically equated conversion to Christianity with the acceptance of colonial rule. The European-looking fortress in the deep background represents Tabasco, described in contemporary accounts as a heavily fortified city.

Painting 2 (Plate 2)

The Arrival of Cortés at Veracruz and the Reception by Moteuczoma's Ambassadors / La llegada de Cortés a Veracruz y la recepción de los embajadores de Moteuczoma

Second half of the seventeenth century
Mexico
Oil on canvas, 48" × 78"
Kislak Collection, Library of Congress No. N8214.5.A45 C65 1750. 0002

Veracruz N° 2

Llega Cortes a la veracruz da fondo en veracruz . . . ban los casiques con Enbaxuda de parte del enperador Montesuma i lleban presentes de oro y mantas. Cortes los recibe desp[ues] . . . por medio de los interpretes Marina y aguilar. Come con ellos y despues les hizo correr los cavallos y. . . .

Cortes–1
Vernal–2
Caciques de pre–3
Mensajeros[?]–4
Los q[ue] corri[eron]–5
La artilleria–6
Marina–7
La demas gente–8

Veracruz No. 2

Cortés arrives and anchors in Veracruz . . . the caciques and their entourage go forth on behalf of the emperor, carrying gifts of gold and textiles. Cortés receives them [the gifts] after . . . by means of the interpreters Marina and Aguilar. He [Cortés] eats with them after . . . he made the horses run and . . .

Cortés–1
Bernal Diáz–2
Caciques–3
Messengers–4

Those that ran–5
The artillery–6
Marina–7
The rest of the people–8

Note: The small cartouche to the left is of an unknown date and includes most of the same information.

Hernán Cortés and his army began their march inland toward the Aztec capital of Tenochtitlan from the coastal city of Veracruz, which Cortés founded in July 1519. Shortly after Cortés and his men arrived in the Yucatán, the emperor Moteuczoma began to receive reports about them through a well-organized system for relaying information throughout the empire. In response to the Spanish presence, Moteuczoma sent a group of ambassadors with elaborate presents for Cortés and his men, just as he might have sent gifts to any visiting dignitary. Gift exchange was part of the proper political and social etiquette. Moteuczoma's extraordinary gifts, which are described in detail by Díaz and Sahagún, included foodstuffs, fine cloth, elaborate featherwork, and beautifully made gold objects (Plate 2). The objects chosen by Moteuczoma carried encoded signals about Aztec power, but the subtleties of the messages were lost on the foreigners. Although Moteuczoma may have intended his gifts to encourage the Spanish to leave Mexico, the gold only increased their desire to travel to Tenochtitlan.

Most of this painting depicts the show of military strength and prowess Cortés ordered to impress the Mexica ambassadors. These activities take place in the middle of the painting, which is filled with galloping horses, cannon fire, and Spanish soldiers in full armor. The effect of this display of military force and European technology is demonstrated by a group of indigenous men armed with bows and arrows on the right, who prostrate themselves. The massive ships docked in the harbor are decorated with red and white imperial flags, demonstrating a powerful Spanish presence. The gift exchange is depicted on the left of the painting, where elaborately dressed Mexica ambassadors bring gifts to Cortés, who is seated with Malinche and others around a banquet table. Unfortunately, most of Cortés's figure, which was originally seated at the head of the table on the left, has been cut off of the painting. All that remains are his hands and his armor-clad knee. This painting is one of only two in the series to list Bernal Díaz del Castillo (1495–1583) among those present, although he is not pictured. (For reasons that are not entirely clear, the large rock directly off the coast is labeled "vernal" or Bernal.) Díaz was a solider on Cortés's Mexican expedition, an eyewitness to the events depicted in the paintings. His history of the Conquest, *Historia verdadera de la conquista de la Nueva España* (The True History of the Conquest of New Spain), was written to counteract what he considered the overvalorization of Cortés by other authors, although it was not published until 1632.

Certainly, the clear emphasis in the paintings on the achievements of Cortés and his men reflects this point of view. Díaz was used as a source by Solís, who stated: "It cannot be denied but that he was a valient Solider and the style of his History shews, that he understood a Sword better than a pen" (Bk. 1:56).

Painting 3 (Plate 3)

The Meeting of Cortés and Moteuczoma / El encuentro de Cortés y Moteuczoma
Second half of the seventeenth century
Mexico
Oil on canvas, 48" × 78"
Kislak Collection, Library of Congress No. N8214.5.A45 C65 1750. 0003

Bolcan de Mexico N° 3

Sale Cortes para [syle?] de iztapalapa donde descubre villas y ciudades en el agua y la calsada [derecha?] sale de Mexico Moctezuma arrecirle y le present[a] una cadena que traia al cuello. Cortes le ba a echar los brasos y le detiene por no usarse entre ellos [. . . hacer?] las andas 4 Reyes q[ue] lo trae[n] en [h]ombros.

Cortes–1
Moctesuma–2
Marina–3
Pedro de alvaro–4
Xpal de Olid–5
Andas de Moct.[ezuma]–6

Volcano of Mexico No. 3

Cortés leaves for . . . Iztapalapa, where he encounters towns and cities on the water and a paved roadway [to the right]. Moteuczoma leaves Mexico [Tenochtitlan] to receive him and he presents him [Cortés] with a chain that he was wearing around his neck. Cortés goes to embrace him but he is held back because this is not the custom among them. Four kings [use?] the throne platform, which they carry on their shoulders.

Cortés–1
Moteuczoma–2
Marina–3
Pedro de Alvarado–4
Cristóbal de Olid–5
The throne of Moteuczoma–6

The Spaniards now had a clear destination in mind: Moteuczoma's capital, the rich island city of Tenochtitlan. Getting there from Veracruz, however, would not prove easy: inclement weather, inhospitable geography, and hostile indigenous populations were the primary problems. This part of their journey did, however, provide Cortés and his men with their most significant group of allies: the Tlaxcalans, who were both independent of and hostile to the Aztec Empire. An alliance, however, was only reached following a series of ferocious battles between Spaniards and Tlaxcalans. Shortly thereafter, these new allies helped Cortés and his men carry out a large-scale massacre at Cholula, a city that was part of Moteuczoma's empire. Given the triumphal tenor of these works of art, it is not surprising that this event from the history of the Conquest was not included in the series. The Spanish expedition traveled with their new allies through the high and rugged terrain surrounding the volcano Popocatepetl ("the mountain that smokes") to reach the Valley of Mexico in November 1519.

After spending the night in the city of Iztapalapa, Cortés and his men marched across one of three broad causeways that connected the island city of Tenochtitlan to the mainland. The meeting between Cortés and Moteuczoma, which occurred outside the city on the shores of Lake Texcoco, was peaceful, if socially awkward. Contemporary accounts state that Moteuczoma wore rich clothing and sandals. His lords, or *caciques,* carried a canopy for him to stand under; it was decorated with green feathers, gold and silver embroidery, and precious stones. Chieftains swept the ground before him, while other dignitaries held out royal mats so Moteuczoma's golden sandals would not touch the earth. Keeping their heads lowered in reverence, the members of his court did not dare look Moteuczoma in the face.

The painting depicts Cortés's arrival at this scene of refined theatrical spectacle. Cortés has dismounted from his horse, and he approaches Moteuczoma with his arms opened in a gesture of embrace, which the Mexica leader respectfully rejects by raising his left hand. Moteuczoma's idealized body, dignified stance, full beard, aristocratic nose, and the golden sword he holds in his right hand owe more to European ideas about the appropriate appearance of a king than to ethnographic accuracy. Describing him, Solís stated that "his nose was aquiline . . . his look majestick [sic] and thoughtful" (Bk. 3:57). In addition, the feather skirts worn by Moteuczoma and his court were part of the standard iconography for depicting Indians, although this article of clothing was not worn in Mexico or anywhere else in the Americas. Comparison with a contemporary illustration of the same event from the 1724 English translation of Solís demonstrates the care the artists of the Kislak paintings lavished on details of dress and ornamentation, much of which is highly convincing. Great attention has also been paid to the clothing of Malinche, who stands besides Cortés as one of the primary figures in this composition. Although Solís described Moteuczoma as having "a fairer Complexion than the generality of the Indians" (Bk. 3:57), here it is not the king but Malinche who has been granted pale, European skin, which further links her to Cortés (Cortez, Chapter 4, this volume).[5] A small yellow dot in the sky to the left of the volcano may represent a comet that appeared in the sky over Tenochtitlan at this time. According to some sources, its appearance contributed to Moteuczoma's inability to address the Spanish threat effectively because it was interpreted as an omen of disaster (see Gillespie, Chapter 2, this volume).

Painting 4 (Plate 4)

The Death of Moteuczoma at the Hands of His Own People / Moteuczoma lapidado por su pueblo

Second half of the seventeenth century
Mexico
Oil on canvas, 48" × 78"
Kislak Collection, Library of Congress No. N8214.5.A45 C65 1750. 0004

Nº 4

Viendose cercados los españoles de[n]tro de las casas de Mexico, [h]acen asomar a Moctezuma a un terrado y desde alli los apasiguaba, pero un indio le tiro una pedrada y los demas indios lan[z]an unes flechasos de q[ue] m[urió?]. pones fuego a los apesentos.

Montesuma–1
El indio q[ue] rivo–2
Frar Bartolome de olmedo–3
Bernal dias del Castillo–4
Cristoual de Oli[d]–5
gonçalo de Sandoual–6
Casas de Montesuma–7

No. 4

The Spanish, finding themselves trapped in the palace in Mexico [Tenochtitlan], make Moteuczoma appear on a roof terrace and from there he quieted them, but an Indian threw a stone and the rest launched arrows from which he died. They burn the rooms [perhaps of the temple in the background].

Moteuczoma–1
The Indian who wounded [him]–2
Friar Bartolome de Olmedo–3
Bernal Díaz de Castillo–4
Cristóbal de Olid–5
Gonzalo de Sandoval–6
House of Moteuczoma–7

After the Spanish and their allies entered Tenochtitlan, Moteuczoma put the palace of Axayácatl at their disposal. The new arrivals were entertained and given tours of the city, which by all accounts was a beautiful, well-ordered place. According to Cortés's Second Letter (Carta de Relación, published in 1522), soon thereafter Moteuczoma offered himself and his people as vassals to the king of Spain; whether Moteuczoma ever made such a statement and what he might have understood it to mean is still a highly contentious subject for historians of Mexico. There is no doubt, however, that the Spanish and Tlaxcalan presence in Tenochtitlan produced a deep sense of disquiet within the Mexica population, especially when Cortés began to preach Christianity. After learning of an attack on his men left behind in Veracruz, Cortés made his boldest move by taking Moteuczoma hostage. In their palace, the Spanish discovered a treasure room of gold and precious objects, supplemented by additional "gifts" from Moteuczoma, and it seems clear that tension also began to build among the Spanish about how they could retain this hoard of gold in an environment that seemed increasingly unfriendly.

In May 1520, Cortés left Tenochtitlan with a group of men to address a challenge to his authority in the form of a ship sent from Cuba. During his absence, his remaining men and their Tlaxcalan allies, under the leadership of Pedro de Alvarado, massacred a large number of Mexica elite during an important religious festival and destroyed major cult figures in the Templo Mayor, the largest and most important building of Tenochtitlan's ceremonial complex. Both Spanish and indigenous sources make it clear that this was a horrific, unprovoked attack. When Cortés returned to Tenochtitlan, the city and its inhabitants were in an uproar: the city erupted into violent struggles between the Spaniards and their allies and the Mexica. Although the exact date of his death is unclear, at some point during this time sources indicate that Moteuczoma appeared in public on the upper level of the palace Axayácatl in an attempt to ease his people's hostility. What followed is a matter of some uncertainty; rocks were thrown and Moteuczoma was hit, but the severity of the wound is unknown. Spanish accounts blame his death on a rock-throwing Mexica warrior, while Nahuatl accounts suggest that the injury was minor and that the Spanish instead killed Moteuczoma in secret.

In the painting, Moteuczoma stands in a precarious position on the edge of the wall on the roof of the palace, here depicted as a large, fortress-like structure. The Mexica leader, dressed in his traditional crown and finery, has not yet received his fatal blow, and his facial expression suggests empathy for the Spanish as well as concern for his people. This is close to how the scene is described by Solís, who stated that Moteuczoma "shew'd himself to the expecting multitude, with a contenance of severity mix'd with lenity, which at once express'd both his Anger and Fear" (Bk. 4:210) In the painting, one gets a clear sense that suicide is not out of the question.

In the foreground, Mexica warriors swarm angrily below on the street in front of the palace. Great attention has been paid to these figures' costumes, especially those of the jaguar and eagle warriors, the highest-ranking soldiers in the Mexica military. A Mexica man wearing long red feathers in his hair and holding the fatal stone is depicted in the foreground, standing almost on the bottom edge of the canvas. The stone he clutches is about to be launched, adding tension to the scene. The billowing clouds of smoke in the background also create drama and may represent Spaniards setting fire to the idols from the Templo Mayor. The prominence of the priest standing next to Moteuczoma is both a foreshadowing of the latter's death and a reminder of the importance of Christianity and conversion in New Spain. One recent scholar has pointed out the formal similarities between this composition and images of Jesus as "Ecco Homo" (Behold the Man) (García Saíz 1999a:132–134). Based on the Gospel of John, images of this subject show Jesus standing on a balcony, looking sorrowfully down at a jeering crowd below. As in the biblical story, in this painting Moteuczoma is denied and even struck down by his own people. Moteuczoma, with his compassionate expression and inevitable death, becomes a Christ-like figure.

Painting 5 (Plate 5)

The Sad Night / Noche triste

Second half of the seventeenth century
Mexico
Oil on canvas, 48" × 78"
Kislak Collection, Library of Congress No. N8214.5.A45 C65 1750. 0005

N° 5

Sale Cortes de Mexico con los suyo[s] a las 11 de la noche que habia oscuro y llobisnava . . . los indi[os] iban sobre ellos y quitan la puente que llevaban, llenose el foso de Alvarado de hombres, caballos y tlaxcaltecos muertos van a los rremedios donde se hazen fuertes en el Cu. N° –6

Fernan Cortes–1
Cristobal de Oli[d]–2
Gonzalo de Sandoval–3
Pedro de Alvarado–4
Indios tlascaliscos–5

No. 5

Cortés and his men leave Mexico at 11 on a dark and rainy night. . . . [T]he Indians follow them and they remove the bridge they [the Spanish] took with them. Alvarado's hole [a hole in the causeway] was filled with dead men, horses and Tlaxcalans. They go to the fortifications on the pyramid, where they regain their strength. No. – 6.

Hernán Cortés–1
Cristóbal de Olid–2
Gonzalo de Sandoval–3
Pedro de Alvarado–4
Tlaxcalan Indians–5

Following the death of Moteuczoma and given the increasingly difficult situation of the Spanish, who remained trapped in the palace of Axayácatl in the center of Tenochtitlan, Cortés determined that the time had come to leave the Mexica capital. Midnight on July 1, 1520, was the time chosen for retreat. It was a rainy, misty, and inhospitable night, according to eyewitness observer Bernal Díaz. Spotted soon after leaving their stronghold, the Spanish and their allies were the victims of fierce attacks by the Mexica. Although Cortés and most of the leaders of the Spanish contingent managed to escape to the mainland on makeshift bridges, hundreds of Spanish soldiers and thousands of Tlaxcalans died, either drowned in the lake or pierced by arrows shot by the Mexica from their canoes. According to various accounts, the water was clogged with corpses of men and horses. Made under the cover of darkness, this disastrous retreat is known as the *Noche triste* because of the heavy casualties inflicted upon Cortés and his followers. In addition to the loss of life, the loss of much of the huge hoard of looted gold undoubtedly made this a "sad night" indeed for the Spanish.

This spectacular nocturnal image highlights the Spanish participants in the battle, who are portrayed as noble men on horseback, imparting a curious sense of heroism to what was in fact a disastrous retreat. The foreground is dominated by three large figures on horseback, Cortés's armor-clad captains, who ride off in opposite directions, providing a sense of drama and movement to the work but also framing and drawing the viewer's eye to the center of the painting. There, the much smaller figure of Cortés is shown seated on a rearing horse, brandishing his sword triumphantly over the chaos that surrounds him. In the deep background, Tenochtitlan is represented as a ghostly, abandoned city, rendered in a palette of grays and pale, smoky browns, distant and oddly disconnected from the furious battle that rages in front of it. In contrast, banners of red and lightning-like flashes of light and color give a spooky, almost sinister quality to the battle scene, which dominates the work. As seen in other paintings from the series, a hierarchy of scale is established in which the Spanish are both the largest and the most prominent figures. Evidence of the treasure lost or left behind can be seen scattered on the ground in the form of small rectangular bars of yellow gold. It was never recovered.

Painting 6 (Plate 6)

The Battle of Otumba / La batalla de Otumba

Second half of the seventeenth century

Mexico

Oil on canvas, 48" × 78"

Kislak Collection, Library of Congress No. N8214.5.A45 C65 1750.0006

Nº 6

Gananles el estandarte R[eal] con que tuvieron una [calida?] batalla de que se [vieron?] los espanoles muy apretados, suceden este dia casos memorables en que se mostro al animo de Cortes y sus capitanes.

Fernan Cortes–1

Capitan de los mexi[canos] en Otumba–2

Cristobal de Oli[d]–3

Gonzalo de Sandoval–4

Pedro de Alvarado–5

Otros capp[itanes]–6

No. 6
The Spanish capture the royal standard from them, with whom they had a [fierce] battle, in which the Spaniards found themselves in dire straits. This day, memorable events occurred in which Cortés and his men showed their bravery.
Hernán Cortés–1
Captain of the Mexicans in Otumba–2
Cristóbal de Olid–3
Gonzalo de Sandoval–4
Pedro de Alvardo–5
Other captains–6

After the defeat of the Spaniards during the *Noche triste*, Cortés marched the survivors away from the city in the direction of Tlaxcala. During this flight from Tenochtitlan, Cortés took his men through the Valley of Otumba. There Cuitlahuac, the new Mexica leader of the Aztec Empire and a brother of Moteuczoma II, mounted a major battle against the invaders. The Europeans and their allies were both outnumbered and in a weakened condition, and at the beginning of the battle the outcome did not look promising for them. With a small group of men, however, Cortés attacked the main leaders of the Mexica army. By capturing most of these men, who were easily distinguishable because of their banners and elaborate costumes, the Spanish were able to take control and win the battle. Spanish histories of the Conquest emphasize the significance of this battle as a key turning point in the fortunes of the Spanish in Mexico, who then continued their journey to Tlaxcala—the home of Cortés's most important allies—from whence they were able to recover, regroup, enlist new men, and return to Tenochtitlan in December to continue the battle. In Solís's version of this battle, Cortés is the great commander who rallies his men with the strong but stern words "our Case is now such . . . that we must either die or conquer" (Bk. 4:249).

The left foreground of the painting focuses on the key capture of the Mexica leaders. Like most of the other indigenous soldiers in this painting, these five men are dressed in elaborate costumes. The leader on the left is clearly recognizable as a jaguar warrior. Surrounded by Spanish soldiers in armor on the left, the men face Cortés, whose wildly rearing horse threatens to trample them. Cortés holds a rapier to the chest of the man closest to him, who also clutches a rapier in his hand, presumably captured from the Spanish. The background of the painting gives way to furious fighting between the Spanish and the Mexica.

Painting 7 (Plate 7)

The Conquest of Tenochtitlan / La caída de Tenochtitlan

Second half of the seventeenth century

Mexico

Oil on canvas, 48" × 78"

Kislak Collection, Library of Congress No. N8214.5.A45 C65 1750. 0007

CONQUISTA DE MEXICO POR CORTES. No. 7

Vltimo conbate de mexico por Cortes y los suyos por las tres calça[das] que van a mexico, y por la Laguna los vergantines a quien davan cruda g[u]erra los indios. Gana Pedro de Alvarado el alto cu de guichilobos, y pone las banderas de Su Majestad.

Fernan Cortes–1
Calçada de Sn. Anton–2
Cristoval de Oli[d]–3
Pedro de Alvarado–4
Calçada de Tacuba–5
Gonsalo de Sandoval–6
Calçada de Guadalupe–7
Sacerdot[e] del idolo–8
Guichilobos q[ue] va rodado–9

CONQUEST OF MEXICO BY CORTÉS. No. 7

The final battle for Mexico [Tenochtitlan] by Cortés and his men by way of the three roadways that lead to Mexico and with the brigantines through the lagoon, which the Indians fought savagely. Pedro de Alvarado wins the pyramid of Guichilobos [Templo Mayor] and raises His Majesty's flag.

Hernán Cortés–1
Road of San Antón–2
Cristóbal de Olid–3
Pedro de Alvarado–4
Road of Tacuba–5
Gonzalo de Sandoval–6
Road of Guadalupe–7
Priest of the idols–8
Guichilobos [Huitzilopochtli] that is surrounded–9

The battle for Tenochtitlan between the Spanish under Cortés and the Mexica under the last Aztec leader, Cuauhtemoc, is more properly called a siege. Beginning in May 1521, it lasted well into August of that year. During this period its inhabitants experienced biological warfare in the form of a smallpox epidemic that decimated much of the population, including the new emperor (see Chávez Balderas, Chapter 9; Few, Chapter 8, this volume). Indeed, it is now clear that the successful Conquest of the Aztec Empire by Cortés, his men, and their indigenous allies can only be understood as resulting from a highly complex mix of biological, technological, and social factors. As part of their battle preparation, the Spanish constructed a fleet of small, maneuverable ships called brigantines, which would play a central role in their eventual victory. The brigantines, which could hold up to forty men, were outfitted with cannon, and they allowed the Spanish to control the lake and blockade the city. In addition to cutting the Mexica off from their sources of food, the Spaniards were also able to disrupt their water supply.

Cortés separated his men, the vast majority of whom were indigenous allies such as the Tlaxcala, into three armed groups led by his most highly trusted officers: Pedro de Alvarado, Cristóbal de Olid, and Gonzalo de Sandoval. During the siege Cortés ordered the complete destruction of Tenochtitlan, formerly praised by many—including Cortés—for its beauty (see Díaz Balsera, Chapter 3, this volume). The Mexica put up a spirited and skilled resistance against the invaders, but months of diminished food and inadequate water, in addition to an epidemic of smallpox, meant that by August they could no longer defend the city. The surrender of the survivors, the destruction of the main temple, and the capture of Cuauhtemoc, Cuitlahauc's successor, depicted in the last painting of this series, marked the end of both the battle for Tenochtitlan and the Aztec Empire.

The painting attempts to distill all the excitement, bloodshed, and drama of the siege into a series of key moments. The background is dominated by the main pyramid of Tenochtitlan; the swirling forms of the three causeways and the aqueduct extending out from it almost give it the appearance of a starfish-like creature, curling up its legs in defense. The most prominent figure in the foreground is Cortés, who leads his Spanish armies on horseback across one of broadest causeways, which creates a dramatic diagonal into the city. He is shown in a confident manner, seated on a rearing horse with the baton of command held firmly in his left hand and a rapier held high in his right. A number of fallen Mexica are pictured on the causeway under the rearing hooves of the Spaniards' horses. In other parts of the canvas, Cortés's most trusted captains also lead their troops toward the center of the city and the main temple compound with the pyramid in its center. Only five brigantines are visible on the lake, defending the Spaniards from the Mexica in canoes.

This dramatic, panoramic landscape with its large groups of fighting figures brings to mind the German Renaissance painter Albrecht Altdorfer's impressive *Battle of Alexander and Darius at Issus* (Munich, 1529). Both paintings display epic, mythic battles in which the very survival of civilization appears to be at stake. In the Kislak image, large numbers of Mexica, distinguished by their brown skin, engage equally large numbers of Spanish troops, easily recognizable in their silver helmets and armor. The Indian allies of the Spanish, pictured at the distant ends of the causeways, are not given a central role in the battle as depicted, although their contribution was vital to the success of the siege and they far outnumbered the European participants.

Despite the ferocity of the battle, the success of Cortés and his armies has already been assured. Flames emerge from the main pyramid, and the Spanish flag has been mounted on the roof of the shrine to Huitzilopochtli.

Painting 8 (Plate 8)

The Capture of Cuauhtemoc / La prisión de Cuauhtemoc
Second half of the seventeenth century
Mexico
Oil on canvas, 48" × 78"
Kislak Collection, Library of Congress No. N8214.5.A45 C65 1750. 0008

Salen huyendo Guatemoc ultimo Rey de mexico, con los suyos en canoas en que llevavan oro y plata y demas joyas. danles alcanse los vergantines. Y prendenlo a [h]ora de visperas de S. Hipolito, con que se concluyo el cerco de Mexico en nombre de Su Majes[tad].
Guatemoc, Rey de Mex[ico]–1
Bergantín que le alcaço–2
Canoas de oro y plata–3
Carrisales–4
Indios que iban huyendo–5
Muger de Guatemoc–6

Guatemoc [Cuauhtemoc], last king of Mexico [Tenochtitlan], flees with his men in canoes, in which they carry their gold and silver and other jewels. The brigantines reach them and arrest him at the hour of the vespers of S. Hipolitus, after which the siege of Mexico was concluded in the name of his majesty.
Guautemoc [Cuauhtemoc], King of Mexico–1
Brigantines catching up to them–2
Canoes with gold and silver–3
Reeds–4
Fleeing Indians–5
Wife of Guautemoc [Cuauhtemoc]–6

The Mexica noble Cuauhtemoc, whose name roughly translates to swooping or falling eagle, was the eleventh and last *tlatoani* of the Aztec Empire. He ruled from December 1520, following the death of Cuitlahuac from smallpox, to August 1521, when the city fell to the Spanish. Although Cuauhtemoc was apparently quite young, he was already known as a great warrior.

In preparation for the battle with Cortés and his allies, Cuauhtemoc had attempted to strengthen and renew alliances with various peoples in the empire. His inability to find reliable allies isolated the Mexica in their final battle with the Spanish. During the siege, the Mexica fought bravely and impressed the invaders with their tenacity and skill in fighting. Given the resistance they encountered, Cortés and his men were unable to defeat the Mexica except by completely destroying Tenochtitlan. Thus, they set about systematically razing the capital city. In August, after much of Tenochtitlan had been destroyed, Cuauhtemoc was captured as he fled the city in a canoe. At this time Cuauhtemoc was delivered to Cortés, who received him with great honor. In 1525 Cuauhtemoc was executed because of reports that he was planning a rebellion against Spanish rule.

The painting is dominated by a watery, boggy landscape filled with canoes and brigantines, which proudly fly red and white imperial flags. According to some accounts, Cuauhtemoc fled with fifty canoes, carrying his relatives, other Mexica nobles, and especially his riches, and this is the version depicted in this painting. In the foreground Cuauhtemoc, recognizable because of his feathered and jeweled finery and impressive headpiece, stands in his canoe among three Spaniards—one of whom looks like Cortés (on the left), although he was not in fact present for the capture. This mustached Spaniard—identified in written accounts as García de Holgúin, the commander of a brigantine—stretches out his left arm to embrace the nobleman, although he also holds a rapier in his right hand. Although the artist certainly never saw the individuals depicted in this work, a surprising degree of attention is paid to the individual features of both Cuauhtemoc and his captors.

As Cuauhtemoc appears here, it is not impossible to imagine him delivering to de Holgúin the sensitive and elegant speech Solís wrote for him: "I am your Prisoner, and ready to go whithersoever you think fit to conduct me: all I desire of you is, that some regard may be had to the Honour of the Empress my Consort, and to that of the Women who accompany her" (Bk. 5:146). Cuauhtemoc maintains his dignified composure despite the difficult circumstances, and his noble bearing is comparable to that of Mocteuzuma as pictured in the third painting of the series, when he met Cortés for the first time.

NOTES

1. Some of the material in this chapter was originally published in Jackson and Brienen(2003). It is reproduced here by permission of the Kislak Foundation and the Lowe Art Museum. Among the publications consulted for this chapter, we would like to single out *Los princeles de la historia el origen del reino de la Nueva España, 1680–1750* (1999), especially the important work of Jamie Cuadriello and María Concepción García Sáiz. For the historical narrative, in addition to the letters of Cortés and the accounts by Díaz, Gomera, and Solís, we consulted Schwartz (2000), Lockhart (1993), and modern works such as Thomas (1993).

2. In the exhibition catalog, *Imagenes de los Naturales* (2005), it is suggested that the paintings were made in Spain, not Mexico. We think this is highly unlikely.

3. Evidence regarding when and where the paintings were acquired by the Chomley family is unfortunately limited to an account written in 1852 by Hennrietta Strickland, which is entirely anecdotal. She notes the family tradition that the paintings were acquired by Sir Hugh Cholmley, 4th Baronet (1632–1688), while he served in Tangier, which was

abandoned by the British in 1683. In his 1935 *Country Life* article "Howsham Hall—II," A. Oswald suggested that the paintings could alternatively have been acquired in 1669, when Sir Chomley traveled in Spain and France. Nonetheless, most of the extant screens made in New Spain showing images from the Conquest date to the 1690s. See also see the exhibition catalog, *Imagenes de los Naturales* (2005), ed. Elisa Vargas Lugo. The writers of the catalog argue that the paintings must have been made between 1660 and 1680 and were certainly in England before 1683, basing their arguments on the previously mentioned sources.

4. For example, in the fourth painting, *Moteuczoma lapidado por su pueblo / The Death of Moteuczoma at the Hands of his Own People,* the caption includes a possibly unintentional slur against the Spanish. As noted by Dr. Schreffler, "cercados" was originally spelled "cerdos" (pigs).

5. It was quite common in European travel accounts and literature from the eighteenth century to describe non-European royalty as having Caucasian features or skin color.

Works Cited

ABBREVIATIONS

CONACULTA	Consejo Nacional para Cultura y las Arts
ENAH	Escuela Nacional de Antropolía e Historia
FCE	Fondo de Cultura Económica
INAH	Instituto Nacional de Antropologia e Historia
SEP	Secretaría de Educación Publica
UNAM	Universidad Nacional Autónoma de México

ARCHIVES AND LIBRARIES

JCBL. John Carter Brown Library, Brown University, Providence, RI.

BOOKS, ARTICLES, AND MANUSCRIPTS

Acosta, Fr. José de. 2002 [1590]. *Natural and Moral History of the Indies,* ed. Jane E. Mangan, trans. Frances M. López-Morillas. Durham, NC: Duke University Press.

Aguilar, Fr. Francisco de. 1993 [ca. 1559]. The Chronicle of Fray Francisco de Aguilar. In *The Conquistadors: First-Person Accounts of the Conquest of Mexico*, ed. and trans. Patricia de Fuentes, 134–164. Norman: University of Oklahoma Press.

Alcalá, Jerónimo. 1980. *La Relación de Michoacán*. Estudio preliminar de Francisco Miranda, Colección de Estudios Michoacanos. Morelia, Mexico: FIMAX publicistas.

Alva Ixtlilxóchitl, Fernando. 1952 [ca. 1600–1640]. *Obras Históricas*. Notes by Alfredo Chavero. 2 vols. México: Editora Nacional.

———. 1977 [ca. 1600–1640]. *Obras históricas*, ed. Edmundo O'Gorman. 2 vols. México: UNAM.

———. 1997. Relación de la venida de los españoles y principio de la ley evangélica. In Fray Bernardino Sahagún, *Historia General de las Cosas de la Nueva España*, Apéndices de Ángel María Garibay. México: Editorial Porrúa 300.

Alvarado, Pedro de. 1924 [1525]. *An Account of the Conquest of Guatemala in 1524*, ed. Sedley J. Mackie. New York: Cortés Society.

Alvarado Tezozómoc, Fernando. 1944. *Crónica Mexicana: escrita hacia el año de 1598*. Notes by Manuel Orozco y Berra. México: Editorial Leyenda.

———. 1980 [ca. 1598]. *Crónica Mexicana* (preceded by the *Códice Ramirez*), ed. Manuel Orozco y Berra. 3rd ed. México: Editorial Porrúa.

Ángeles Jiménez, Pedro. 2005. Ocho grandes lienzos de la conquista. In *Imágenes de los naturales en el arte de la Nueva España, siglos XVI al XVIII*, 42–61. México: Fomento Cultural Banamex.

Armella de Aspe, Virginia. 1990. La influencia asiatica. In *La concha nácar en México*, ed. Teresa Castelló Yturbide, 74–80. México: Grupo Gutsa.

Artiñano y de Galdácano, Gervasio de, and José Gabriel Navarro. 1930. *Aportación al estudio de la cultura española en las Indias*. Madrid: Espasa Calpe.

Avellaneda, José Ignacio. 1995. *The Conquerors of the New Kingdom of Granada*. Albuquerque: University of New Mexico Press.

Aveni, Anthony. 2001. *Skywatchers*. Austin: University of Texas Press.

Ávila Hernández, Julieta. 1997. El influjo de la pintura china en los enconchados de Nueva España. México: INAH.

Baldick, Chris. 1990. *The Concise Oxford Dictionary of Literary Terms*. Oxford: Oxford University Press.

Barley, Nigel. 1995. *Bailando sobre la tumba*. Barcelona: Crónicas Anagrama.

Basave, Agustín. 1983. *Metafísica de la muerte*. México: Editorial Limusa.

Beidelman, T. O. 1966. Swazi Royal Ritual. *Africa* 36:373–405.

Benavente, Toribio (Motolinía). 1971 [ca. 1536–1543]. *Memoriales*, ed. Edmundo O'Gorman. México: UNAM.

Bennett, Clinton. 1996. *In Search of the Sacred: Anthropology and the Study of Religions*. London: Cassell.

Berdan, Frances F. 1982. *The Aztecs of Central Mexico: An Imperial Society*. New York: Holt, Rinehart and Winston.

Berlin-Neubart, Heinrich, ed. 1948. *Fuentes para la Historia de Mexico*. Mexico: Antigua Librería Robredo.

Berlin-Neubart, Heinrich, and R. H. Barlow. 1948. *Anales de Tlatelolco. Uunos anales históricos de la nación mexicana) y Códice de Tlatelolco,* ed. H. Berlin. Fuentes para la Historia de Mexico, Mexico: Antigua Librería Robredo.

Boone, Elizabeth Hill. 2000. *Stories in Red and Black: Pictorial Histories of the Aztecs and Mixtecs.* Austin: University of Texas Press.

Borah, Woodrow. 1964. America as Model: The Demographic Impact of European Expansion upon the Non-European World. *Actas y Memorias del XXXV Congresso Internacional de Americanistas* 3:379–387.

Brading, David A. 1991. *The First America: The Spanish Monarchy, Creole Patriots and the Liberal State, 1492–1867.* Cambridge: Cambridge University Press.

Bricker, Victoria. 1989. *El Cristo Indígena el Rey Nativo*. México: FCE.

Brienen, Rebecca P. 2003. The Image of the "Indian" in Early Modern Europe and Colonial Mexico. In *Visions of Empire: Picturing the Conquest in Colonial Mexico,* ed. Margaret A. Jackson and Rebecca P. Brienen, 29–36. Coral Gables, FL: University of Miami and Jay I. Kislak Foundation.

Broda, Johanna. 2003. La fiesta azteca del Fuego Nuevo y el culto a las Pléyades. In *Huizachtepetl. Geografía sagrada de Iztapalapa,* ed. Ismael Arturo Montero, 147–154. México: Gobierno de la Ciudad de México.

Brooks, Francis J. 1995. Motecuzoma Xocoyotl, Hernán Cortés and Bernal Díaz del Castillo: The Construction of an Arrest. *Hispanic American Historical Review* 75(2): 149–183.

Brothertson, Gordon. 1992. *The Book of the Fourth World.* Cambridge: Cambridge University Press.

Brown, Jonathan. 1986. *Velázquez, Painter and Courier.* New Haven: Yale University Press.

———. 1988. Enemies of Flattery: Velázquez' Portraits of Philip IV. In *Art and History: Images and Their Meaning,* ed. Robert I. Rotberg and Theodore K. Rabb, 137–154. Cambridge: Cambridge University Press.

———. 1995. *Kings and Connoisseurs: Collecting Art in Seventeenth-Century Europe.* Princeton: Princeton University Press.

Burke, Marcus. 1992. Pintura y escultura en Nueva España: El barroco. México: Grupo Azabache.

Burke, Peter. 1990. Historians, Anthropologists and Symbols. In *Culture through Time: Anthropological Approaches,* ed. Emiko Ohnuki-Tierney, 268–283. Stanford: Stanford University Press.

Burkhart, Louise M. 1988. The Solar Christ in Nahuatl Doctrinal Texts of Early Colonial Mexico. *Ethnohistory* 35:234–256.

———. 1992. The Amanuenses Have Appropriated the Text: Interpreting a Nahuatl Song of Santiago. In *On the Translation of Native American Literatures,* ed. Brian Swann, 339–355. Washington, DC: Smithsonian Institution Press.

———. 1996. *Holy Wednesday: A Nahua Drama from Early Colonial Mexico.* Philadelphia: University of Pennsylvania Press.

———. 2000. The Narrative Translator as Critic: A Nahua Playwright's Interpretive Practice. In *Possible Pasts: Becoming Colonial in Early America,* ed. Robert Blair St. George, 73–87. Ithaca: Cornell University Press.

Cabrera Torres, José, and María de los Ángeles García Martínez Mayo. 1998. Utilización, modificación y reuso de los espacios del edificio sede del Hospital Real de San José de los Naturales. Tesis de Licenciatura. México: ENAH.

Calvo Pérez, José Luís, and Luís Grávalos Conzález. 1983. *Banderas de España*. Madrid: Silex.

Carrasco, Davíd. 1982. *Quetzalcoatl and the Irony of Empire: Myths and Prophecies in the Aztec Tradition*. Chicago: University of Chicago Press.

Carrasco, Pedro. 1979. Las fiestas de los meses mexicanos. In *Mesoamérica, Homenaje a Pual Kirchhoff*, ed. Jiménez Moreno Wigberto, 50–59. México: INAH, SEP.

Careño Velázquez, Elvia. 2000. *Catálogo de Incunables*. México: INAH.

Carrera, Magali M. 2003. *Imagining Identity in New Spain: Race, Lineage, and the Colonial Body in Portraiture and Casta Paintings*. Austin: University of Texas Press.

Caso, Alfonso. 1956. Los barrios antiguos de Tenochtitlán y Tlatelolco. *Memorias de la Academia Mexicana de la Historia* 15:7–63.

———. 1958. *The Aztecs: People of the Sun*, trans. Lowell Dunham. Norman: University of Oklahoma Press.

Castelló Yturbide, Teresa, and Marita Martínez del Río de Redo. 1970. *Biombos mexicanos*. México: UNAM.

Cervantes, Fernando. 1994. *The Devil in New Spain*. New Haven: Yale University Press.

Cervantes de Salazar, Francisco. 1985 [1566]. *Crónica de la Nueva España*. Prologue by Juan Miralles Ostos. México: Editorial Porrúa.

Chavero, Alfredo. 1892. El Lienzo de Tlaxcala. In *Antigüedades mexicanas publicadas por la junta colombina de México en el cuarto centenario del descubrimiento de América*. 2 vols. México: Oficina Tipográfica de la Secretaría de Fomento.

Chávez, Ximena. 2002. Los rituales funerarios en el Templo Mayor de Tenochtitlan, Tesis inédita. México: ENAH.

———. In press. *Rituales funerarios en el Templo Mayor de Tenochtitlan. Colección Premios*. México: INAH.

Checa, Jorge. 1986. Cortés y el espacio de la Conquista: la Segunda carta-relación. *Modern Language Notes* 111:187–217.

Chimalpahin Cuauhtlehuanitzin, Domingo Francisco de San Antón Muñón. 1965 [ca. 1606–1631]. *Relaciones originales de Chalco Amaquemeca*, trans. Silvia Rendón. México: FCE.

Clendinnen, Inga. 1991. "Fierce and Unnatural Cruelty": Cortés and the Conquest of Mexico. *Representations* 33:65–100.

Cline, S. L. 1988. Revisionist Conquest History: Sahagún's Revised Book XII. In *The Work of Bernardino de Sahagún: Pioneer Ethnographer of Sixteenth-Century Aztec Mexico*, ed. J. Jorge Klor de Alva, H. B. Nicholson, and Eloise Quiñones Keber, 93–106. New York: Institute for Mesoamerican Studies, University at Albany, State University of New York.

———, ed. 1989. Introduction. In *Conquest of New Spain, 1585 Revision, by Bernardino de Sahagún*, trans. Howard F. Cline, 1–21. Salt Lake City: University of Utah Press.

Codex Aubin. 1963 [1576–1596]. *Historia de la nación mexicana: Reproducción del Códice de 1576 (Códice Aubin),* ed. and trans. Charles E. Dibble. Madrid: José Porrúa Turanzas.

Codex Ramirez. 1980 [attributed to Juan de Tovar, 1583–1587]. *Códice Ramirez. Relación del origen de los indios que habitan esta Nueva España, según sus historias,* 3rd ed., ed. Manuel Orozco y Berra. México: Editorial Porrua.

Codex Ríos. 1996 [ca. 1566–1589]. *Códice Vaticano A (Codex Vatic. Lat. 3738 de la Biblioteca Apostólica Vaticana.* Graz, Austria: Akademische Druck- und Verlagsanstalt.

Codex Telleriano-Remensis. 1995 [ca. 1562–1563]. *Ritual, Divination and History in a Pictorial Aztec Manuscript,* ed. Eloise Quiñones Keber. Austin: University of Texas Press.

Códice Borgia. 1993. Ed. Anders Ferdinand, Jansen Maarten, and Luis Reyes. México: Akademische Druk- und Verlagsanstalt y F.C.E; Spain: Sociedad Estatal Quinto Centanario.

Códice Chimalpopoca, Leyenda de los Soles. 1992. Trans. Primo Feliciano Velázquez. México: UNAM.

Códice Florentino. 1979. 3 vols. México: Secretaria de Gobernación–Archivo General de la Nación.

Códice Magliabechi. 1996. Ed. Ferdinand Anders, Maarten Jansen, and Luis Reyes Garcia. México: Akademische Druk- und Verlagsanstalt y F.C.E.

Códice Ramírez. 1975 [1583–1587]. Relación del origen de los indios que habitan la Nueva España según sus historias, attributed to Juan de Tovar. México: SEP.

Códice Ramírez. 1980 [attributed to Juan de Tovar, 1583–1587]. *Relación del origen de los indios que habitan esta Nueva España, según sus historias,* ed. Manuel Orozco y Berra. 3rd ed. México: Editorial Porrua.

Códice Vaticano A. 1996. 2 vols. Ed. Ferdinand Anders et al. Graz, Austria: Akademische Druck- und Verlagsanstalt.

Collis, Maurice. 1954. *Cortés and Montezuma.* London: Robin Clark.

Colston, Stephen A. 1985. "No Longer Will There Be a Mexico": Omens, Prophecies and the Conquest of the Aztec Empire. *American Indian Quarterly* 9:239–258.

Comaroff, John, and Joan Comaroff. 1992. *Ethnography and the Historical Imagination.* Boulder: Westview.

Comas, Juan. 1954. Influencia indígena en la medicina hipócratica en la Nueva España del siglo XVI. *América Indígena* 14:327–361.

Cook, Noble David. 1998. *Born to Die: Disease and New World Conquest, 1492–1650.* New York: Cambridge University Press.

Cook, Sherburne F., and Woodrow Borah. 1960. *The Indian Population of Central Mexico 1531–1610.* Berkeley: University of California Press.

———. 1963. *The Aboriginal Population of Central Mexico on the Eve of the Spanish Conquest.* Berkeley: University of California Press.

Coronado, Nicolás. 1946. Introducción. In *Hernán Cortés,* ed. Carolos Pereyra, xii–xxv. Buenos Aires: Emecé.

Cortés, Hernán. 1971. *Letters from Mexico,* trans. A. R. Pagden. New York: Orion. [Second Letter 1520; Third Letter 1522].

———. 1983 [1519–1526]. *Cartas de Relación*. México: Editorial Porrúa.

———. 1986. *Letters from Mexico* [1519–1526], trans. Anthony Pagden. New Haven: Yale University Press.

———. 1994. *Cartas de Relación*. México: Editorial Porrua, Sepan Cuantos.

Costumbres, Fiestas, Enterramientos y diversas formas de proceder de los indios de la Nueva España. 1945? In *Tlalocan, a Journal of Source Materials on the Native Cultures of México,* vol. 2, 37–63. México: Federico Gómez de Orozco.

Crosby, Alfred. 1972. *The Columbian Exchange: Biological and Cultural Consequences of 1492.* Westport, CT: Greenwood.

———. 1986. *Ecological Imperialism: The Biological Expansion of Europe, 900–1900.* Cambridge: Cambridge University Press.

Cuadriello, Jaime. 1999. El origen del reino y la configuración de su empresa: Episodios y alegorías de triunfo y fundación. In *Los pinceles de la historia: El Origen del Reino de la Nueva España 1680–1750,* 50–107. México: Instituto Nacional de Bellas Artes.

Curiel, Gustavo. 1999. Los biombos novohispanos: Escenografías de poder y transculturación en el ámbito doméstico. In *Viento detenido: Mitologias e historias en el arte del biombo,* ed. Gustavo Curiel, 9–32. México: Asociación Carso, A.C.

De la Maza, Francisco. 1968. *La ciudad de México en el siglo XVII.* México: FCE.

Denevan, William M. 1992. *Native Populations of the Americas in 1492.* Madison: University of Wisconsin Press.

De' Olwer and H. F. Cline. 1973. Sahagún and His Works. In *Handbook of Middle American Indians, Guide to Ethnohistorical Sources,* pt. 2, ed. Howard F. Cline, 186–207. Austin: University of Texas Press.

Díaz, Juan. 1993. The Chronicle of Juan Díaz. In *The Conquistadors: First-Person Accounts of the Conquest of Mexico,* ed. and trans. Patricia de Fuentes, 3–16. Norman: University of Oklahoma Press.

Díaz Balsera, Viviana. 1989. Estrategias metatextuales de Hernán Cortés, autor de la Conquista de México. *Neophilologus* 73:218–229.

Díaz del Castillo, Bernal. 1632. *Historia verdadera de la conquista de la Nueva España.* Madrid: Impr. del Reino.

———. 1956. *The Discovery and Conquest of Mexico,* ed. Genaro García, trans. A. P. Maudslay, introduction by Irving A. Leonard. New York: Farrar, Straus and Giroux.

———. 1963. *The Conquest of New Spain,* ed. J. M. Cohen. London: Penguin.

———. 1979. *Historia verdadera de la conquista de la Nueva España.* 2 vols. México: Promesa editores.

———. 1994 [ca. 1568]. *Historia verdadera de la conquista de la Nueva España.* 16th ed. México: Editorial Porrúa.

Dibble, Charles E., ed. 1963 [1576–1596]. *Historia de la nación mexicana: Reproducción del Códice de 1576 (Códice Aubin),* ed. and trans. Charles E. Dibble. Madrid: José Porrúa Turanzas.

Dujovne, Marta. 1972. *La conquista de México por Miguel González.* Buenos Aires: Museo Nacional de Bellas Artes.

———. 1984. *Las pinturas con incrustaciones de nácar.* México: UNAM, Instituto de Investigaciones Estéticas.

———. 1998. Los enconchados de la Conquista de México. In *Los enconchados de la Conquista de México*, ed. Miguel González, n.p. Buenos Aires: Museo Nacional de Bellas Artes.

Durán, Diego. 1967 [1579–1581]. *Historia de las indias de Nueva España e islas de la tierra firme,* ed. Ángel Ma. Garibay K. 2 vols. México: Editorial Porrúa.

———. 1971. *Book of the Gods and Rites and the Ancient Calendar*, trans. Fernando Horcasitas and Doris Heyden. Norman: University of Oklahoma Press.

———. 1984. *Historia de las Indias de la Nueva España.* 2 vols. México: Porrúa.

———. 1994. *The History of the Indies of New Spain*, trans. Doris Heyden. Norman: University of Oklahoma Press.

———. 1995. *Historia de las Indias de la Nueva España e Islas de tierra firme*, estudio preliminar de Rosa Camelo and José Rubén Romero. 2 vols. México: CONACULTA, Cien de México.

Edgerton, Samuel Y. 2001. *Theatres of Conversion: Religious Architecture and Indian Artisans in Colonial Mexico.* Albuquerque: University of New Mexico Press.

Elliott, J. H. 1963. *Imperial Spain, 1469–1716.* New York: St. Martin's.

———. 1967. The Mental World of Hernán Cortés. *Transactions of the Royal Historical Society*, 5th ser., 17:41–58.

———. 1986 [1976]. Cortés, Velázquez and Charles V. In *Hernán Cortés: Letters from Mexico,* xi–xxxvii, trans. Anthony Pagden. New Haven: Yale University Press.

Evans-Pritchard, E. E. 1948. *The Divine Kingship of the Shilluk of the Nilotic Sudan.* Cambridge: Cambridge University Press.

Farmer, Paul. 1999. *Infections and Inequalities: The Modern Plagues.* Updated ed. Berkeley: University of California Press.

Feeley-Harnik, Gillian. 1985. Issues in Divine Kingship. *Annual Review of Anthropology* 14:273–313.

Fernández-Armesto, Felipe. 1992. "Aztec" Auguries and Memories of the Conquest of Mexico. *Renaissance Studies* 6:287–305.

Fernández Bayton, V., ed. 1975. *Inventarios Reales. Testamentaria del Rey Carlos II, 1701–1703.* 3 vols. Madrid: Museo del Prado.

Fernández de Calderón, Cándida. 2005. *Imagenes de los naturales en el arte de la Nueva España.* México: Banamex.

Fernández del Castillo, Francisco. 1936. *La cirugía mexicana en los siglos XVI y XVII.* México: R. E. Squibb and Sons.

Few, Martha. 2002. *Women Who Live Evil Lives: Gender, Religion, and the Politics of Power in Colonial Guatemala.* Austin: University of Texas Press.

———. 2003. Invasion and Conquest in Mexico. In *Visions of Empire: Picturing the Conquest in Colonial Mexico*, ed. Margaret A. Jackson and Rebecca P. Brienen, 19–27. Coral Gables, FL: Lowe Art Museum, University of Miami.

———. 2005. "That Monster of Nature": Gender, Sexuality, and the Medicalization of a "Hermaphrodite" in Late Colonial Guatemala. *Ethnohistory* 54(1) (Winter): 159–176.

———. Forthcoming. *Colonial Medicine and Atlantic World Healing Cultures in Guatemala, 1680–1830.*

Fogelson, Raymond D. 1989. The Ethnohistory of Events and Nonevents. *Ethnohistory* 36:133–147.

Frazer, James George. 1940. *The Golden Bough: A Study in Magic and Religion.* 1 vol., abridged. New York: Macmillan.

Freidel, David, Linda Schele, and Joy Parker. 1993. *Maya Cosmos.* New York: William Morrow.

Furst, Jill Leslie McKeever. 1995. *The Natural History of the Soul in Ancient Mexico.* New Haven: Yale University Press.

Gallego, Julián. 1984. *Visión y símbolos en la pintura española del siglo de oro.* Madrid: Cátedra.

García Saíz, María Concepción. 1980. *La pintura colonial en el Museo de América* (II): *Los enconchados.* Madrid: Museo de América.

———. 1992. Precisiones al estudio de la obra de Miguel González. In *Manuel Toussaint: Su proyección en la historia del arte mexicano,* 105–116. México: Instituto de Investigaciones Estéticas.

———. 1994. La conquista de México por Hernán Cortés: Una iconografía a los intereses encontrados de criollos y peninsulares. In *Actas del Congreso Internacional: Llerena, Extremadura, y América,* 213–222. Llerena: Ayuntamiento de Llerena.

———. 1999a. La conquista militar y los enconchados: Las peculiaridades de un patrocinio indiano. In *Los pinceles de la historia: El Origen del Reino de la Nueva España 1680–1750,* 108–141. México: Instituto Nacional de Bellas Artes.

———.1999b. Nuevos materiales para nuevas expresiones. In *Los siglos de oro en los virreinatos de América,* 127–139. Madrid: Sociedad estatal para la conmemoración de los centenarios de Felipe II y Carlos V.

Garza, Mercedes. 1997. El perro como símbolo religioso entre los mayas y los nahuas. *Estudios de cultura Náhuatl* 27:111–133. México: UNAM.

Gerhard, Peter. 1972. *A Guide to the Historical Geography of New Spain.* Cambridge: Cambridge University Press.

Gibson, Charles. 1964. *The Aztecs under Spanish Rule: A History of the Indians of the Valley of Mexico, 1519–1810.* Stanford: Stanford University Press.

———, ed. 1971. *The Black Legend: Anti-Spanish Attitudes in the Old World and the New.* New York: Knopf.

Gillespie, Susan D. 1989. *The Aztec Kings: The Construction of Rulership in Mexica History.* Tucson: University of Arizona Press.

———. 1998. The Aztec Triple Alliance: A Postconquest Tradition. In *Native Traditions in the Postconquest World,* ed. Elizabeth Hill Boone and Tom Cummins, 233–263. Washington, DC: Dumbarton Oaks.

———. 1999. A Clash of Temporalities: The Aztec Conquest as a Matter of Time. Paper presented at the 98th Annual Meeting of the American Anthropological Association, Chicago, IL.

Gillespie, Susan D., and Scott O'Mack. 1991. Cortés and Alvarado: Recasting Aztec Dual Sovereignty. Paper presented at the 47th International Congress of Americanists, New Orleans, LA.

Gómara, Francisco López de. 1964. *Cortés: The Life of the Conqueror by His Secretary,* ed. and trans. Lesley Byrd Simpson. From the *Istoria de la Conquista de Mexico* [1552]. Berkeley: University of California Press.

Gomez de Orozco, Federico. 1945 [ca. 1553]. Costumbres, fiestas, enterramientos y diversas formas de proceder de los indios de Nueva España. *Tlalocan* 2:37–63.

González-Echevarría, Roberto. 1988. *Myth and Archive: A Theory of Latin American Narrative.* Durham, NC: Duke University Press.

Graulich, Michel. 1994. *Montezuma ou l'apogé et la mort de l'empire aztèque.* Paris: Fayard.

———. 1997. *Myths of Ancient Mexico,* trans. Bernard R. Ortiz de Montellano and Thelma Ortiz de Montellano. Norman: University of Oklahoma Press.

Grilli, Elise. 1970. *The Art of the Japanese Screen.* New York: Weatherhill.

Gruzinski, Serge. 1982. *Painting the Conquest: The Mexican Indians and the European Renaissance.* Paris: Unesco-Flammarion.

———. 1989. *Man-Gods in the Mexican Highlands: Indian Power and Colonial Society 1520–1800,* trans. Eileen Corrigan. Stanford: Stanford University Press.

Halbwachs, Maurice. 1992. *On Collective Memory.* Chicago: University of Chicago Press.

Harris, Max. 1993. *The Dialogical Theatre: Dramatizations of the Conquest of Mexico and the Question of the Other.* New York: St. Martin's.

Hassig, Ross. 1988. *Aztec Warfare: Imperial Expansion and Political Control.* Norman: University of Oklahoma Press.

Herren, Angela Marie. 2000. Representing and Reinventing Doña Marina: Images from the *Florentine Codex* and the *Lienzo de Tlaxcala. Latin American Indian Literatures Journal* 16 (2) (Fall):158–180.

Herrera y Tordesillas, Antonio. 1601–1615. *Historia general de los hechos de los castellanos en las Islas I Tierra Firme del Mar Oceano.* Madrid: Emprenta Real.

Hill, Jane H., and Kenneth C. Hill. 1986. *Speaking Mexicano: Dynamics of Syncretic Language in Central Mexico.* Tucson: University of Arizona Press.

Histoire Mexicaine. 1998 [1573]. *Histoire mexicaine depuis 1221 jusqu'en 1594,* trans. Xóchitl Medina González. Manuscript 40, Bibliothèque Nationale, Paris. México: INAH, Serie Etnohistoria.

Horcasitas, Fernando. 1974. *El teatro náhuatl: Épocas novohispana y moderna.* México. UNAM.

Huntington, Richard, and Peter Metcalf. 1979. *Celebrations of Death: The Anthropology of Mortuary Ritual.* Cambridge: Cambridge University Press.

Jackson, Margaret A., and Rebecca P. Brienen, eds. 2003. *Visions of Empire: Picturing the Conquest in Colonial Mexico.* Coral Gables, FL: University of Miami and Jay I. Kislak Foundation.

Kagan, Richard. 2000. *Urban Images of the Hispanic World, 1493–1793.* New Haven: Yale University Press.

Kamen, Henry. 1980. *Spain in the Later-Seventeenth Century.* London: Longman.

Karttunen, Frances. 1983. *An Analytical Dictionary of Nahuatal.* Austin: University of Texas Press.

———. 1997. Rethinking Malinche. In *Indian Women of Early Mexico,* ed. Susan Schroeder, Stephanie Wood, and Robert Haskett, 291–312. Norman: University of Oklahoma Press.

Katzew, Ilona. 2004. *Casta Painting: Images of Race in Eighteenth-Century Mexico.* New Haven: Yale University Press.

Keen, Benjamin. 1990 [1971]. *The Aztec Image in Western Thought.* New Brunswick, NJ: Rutgers University Press.

Klein, Cecelia F. 1993. The Shield Women: Resolution of an Aztec Gender Paradox. In *Current Topics in Aztec Studies: A Symposium in Honor of H. B. Nicholson,* ed. Alana Cordy-Collins and Douglas Sharon, 39–64. San Diego: San Diego Museum of Man.

———. 1994. Fighting with Femininity: Gender and War in Aztec Mexico. In *Gender Rhetorics: Postures of Dominance and Submission in Human History,* ed. Richard C. Trexler, 107–146. Center for Medieval and Early Renaissance Studies, vol. 113. Binghamton: State University of New York at Binghamton.

Kleinman, Arthur. 1980. *Patients and Healers in the Context of Culture: An Exploration of the Borderland between Anthropology, Medicine and Psychiatry.* Berkeley: University of California Press.

Kleinman, Arthur, Veena Das, and Margaret M. Lock, eds. 1997. *Social Suffering.* Berkeley: University of California Press.

Klor de Alva, J. Jorge. 1992. El discurso nahua y la apropriación de lo europeo. In *De palabra y obra en el nuevo mundo. Vol. 1: Imágenes interétnicas,* ed. Miguel León-Portilla, Manuel Gutiérrez Estévez, Gary H. Gossen, and J. Jorge Klor de Alva, 339–368. México: Siglo Veintiuno.

Lafaye, Jacques. 1976. *Quetzalcóatl and Guadalupe: The Formation of Mexican National Consciousness, 1531–1813,* trans. Benjamin Keen. Chicago: University of Chicago Press.

Landa, Diego de. 1938. *Relación de las Cosas de Yucatán.* Notes by Héctor Pérez. México: Editorial Pedro Robredo.

———. 1982 [1566]. *Relación de las cosas de Yucatán.* México: Editorial Porrúa.

Lanyon, Anna. 1999. *Malinche's Conquest.* Crow's Nest, New South Wales: Allen & Unwin.

Lara, Jaime. 1999. Cristo-helios americano: la inculturación del culto al sol en el arte y arquitectura de los virreinatos de la Nueva España y del Perú. *Anales del Instituto de Investigaciones Estéticas* 74/75:29–50.

Las Casas, Fray Bartolomé. 1995. *Brevísima relación de la destrucción de las Indias,* ed. André Saint-Lu. Madrid: Cátedra.

León-Portilla, Miguel. 1962. *The Broken Spears: The Aztec Account of the Conquest of Mexico,* trans. Lysander Kemp; Náhuatl translations, Angel María Garibay K. Boston: Beacon.

———. 1964. *El Reverso de la Conquista.* México: Joaquin Mortiz.

———. 1974. Quetzalcóatl-Cortés en la conquista de México. *Historia Mexicana* 24:13–35.

———. 1979. *Filosofía Náhuatl.* México: UNAM.

———. 1991. The Codex Fejérváry-Mayer. In *Circa 1492*, ed. Jay A. Levinson, 540–541. Washington, DC: National Gallery of Art, and New Haven: Yale University Press.

———. 2001. Cuauhtémoc. In *The Oxford Encyclopedia of Mesoamerican Cultures*, ed. Davíd Carrasco, vol. 1, 289. Oxford: Oxford University Press.

Leonard, Irving A. 1959. *Baroque Times in Old Mexico*. Ann Arbor: University of Michigan Press.

El Lienzo de Tlaxcala. 1979 [ca. 1550]. Ed. Alfredo Chavero. México: Editorial Innovación.

Lindemann, Mary. 1999. *Medicine and Society in Early Modern Europe*. New York: Cambridge University Press.

Lockhart, James. 1972. *The Men of Cajamarca*. Austin: University of Texas Press.

———. 1991. *Nahuas and Spaniards: Postconquest Central Mexican History and Philology*. Stanford: Stanford University Press.

———. 1992. *The Nahuas after the Conquest: A Social and Cultural History of the Indians of Central Mexico, Sixteenth through Eighteenth Centuries*. Stanford: Stanford University Press.

———. 1993. *We People Here: Nahuatl Accounts of the Conquest of Mexico*. Berkeley: University of California Press.

Lockhart, James, and Enrique Otte, eds. 1976. *Letters and People of the Spanish Indies*. Cambridge: Cambridge University Press.

López Austin, Alfredo. 1969. *Augurios y abusiones*. México: Instituto de Investigaciones Históricas.

———. 1973. *Hombre-Díos: Religión y política en el mundo náhuatl*. México: UNAM.

———. 1989. *Cuerpo humano e ideología*. 2 vols. México: UNAM.

———. 1990. *Los mitos del tlacuache*. México: Alianza Editorial.

López de Gómara, Francisco. 1941 [1552]. *Historia de la conquista de México*. 2 vols. Madrid: Editorial Espalsa Calpe.

———. 1964 [1552]. *Cortés: The Life of the Conqueror by His Secretary, Francisco López de Gómara*, ed. and trans. Lesley Byrd Simpson. Berkeley: University of California Press.

López de Hinojosos, Alonso. 1977 [1578]. *Suma y recopilación de cirugía con un arte para sangrar muy útil y provechosa*. México: Academic Nacional de Medicina.

López Luján, Leonardo. 1993. *Las ofrendas del Templo Mayor de Tenochtitlan*. México: INAH.

Lovell, W. George. 1991. Disease and Depopulation in Early Colonial Guatemala. In *Secret Judgments of God: Old World Disease in New World Contexts*, ed. Noble David Cook and W. George Lovell, 51–85. Norman: University of Oklahoma Press.

MacLeod, Murdo. 1973. *Spanish Central America: A Socioeconomic History*. Berkeley: University of California Press.

Magaloni-Kerpel, Diana. 2003. Visualizing the Nahua/Christian Dialogue: Images of the Conquest and Their Sources in Sahagún's *Florentine Codex*. In *Sahagún at 500: Essays on the Quincentennary of the Birth of Fr. Bernardino de Sahagún O.F.M.*, ed. John Frederick Schwaller, 193–222. Berkeley: Academy of American Franciscan History.

———. 2004a. Imágenes de la Conquista de México en los códices del siglo XVI, una lectura de su contenido simbólico. *Anales del Instituto de Investigaciones Estéticas* 82:5–46.

———. 2004b. "Images of the Beginning: The Painted Story of the Conquest of Mexico in Book XII of the *Florentine Codex*." PhD dissertation, Department of Art History, Yale University.

Malvido, Elsa. 1999. Ritos funerarios en el México Colonial. *Revista de Arqueología Mexicana* 7(40):46–51. México: Editorial Raíces.

Malvido, Elsa, and Carlos Viesca. 1985. La epidemia de cocoliztli de 1576. *Historia* 11: 27–33.

Marks, Richard Lee. 1993. *Cortés: The Great Adventurer and the Fate of Aztec Mexico.* New York: A. A. Knopf.

Márquez, Lourdes. 1984. *Sociedad colonial y enfermedad: un ensayo de osteopatología diferencial.* Colección Científica 136. México: INAH.

Martínez, José Luis. 1986. Los dos mundos que se encontraron en el México antiguo. In *Actas del primer congreso internacional sobre Hernán Cortés,* ed. Alberto Navarro González, 386–402. Salamanca: Ediciones Universidad de Salamanca.

———. 1990. *Hernán Cortés.* México: UNAM, FCE.

Martínez Baracs, Rodrigo. 1998. Contactos y Presagios. *Historias* 40:29–34.

Martínez–San Miguel, Yolanda. 2000. Poder y narración: representación y mediación de undeseo americano en la Segunda carta-relación. In *Agencias criollas. La ambiguedad "colonial" en las letras hispanoamericanas,* ed. José Antonio Mazzotti, 99–130. Pittsburgh: Biblioteca de América, Instituto Internacional de Literatura Iberoamericana.

Matos, Eduardo. 1986. *Muerte a filo de obsidiana.* México: SEP.

Maturo, Carol L. 1994. "Malinche and Cortés, 1519–1521: An Iconographic Study." PhD dissertation, Department of History, University of Connecticut.

Mauss, Marcel. 1990. *The Gift: The Form and Reason for Exchange in Archaic Societies,* trans. W. D. Halls. New York: W. W. Norton.

Mendieta, Gerónimo (de). 1993 [1870]. *Historia eclesiástica indiana.* México: Porrúa.

———. 1945. *Historia Eclesiástica Indiana.* 4 vols. México: Editorial Salvador Chávez Hayhoe.

Merrim, Stephanie. 1986. Ariadne's Thread: Auto-Biography, History and Cortés's *Segunda carta-relación. Dispositio* 11:57–83.

———. 1996. The First Fifty Years of Hispanic New World Historiography: The Caribbean, Mexico and Central America. In *The Cambridge History of Latin American Literature. Discovery to Modernism,* ed. Roberto González-Echevarría and Enrique Pupo-Walker, vol. 1, 58–100. 3 vols. Cambridge: Cambridge University Press.

Metropolitan Museum of Art. 1990. *Mexico: Splendors of Thirty Centuries.* New York: Little, Brown.

Milbrath, Susan. 1989. Seasonal Calendar with Venus Periods in *Codex Borgia* 29–46c. In *The Imagination of Matter: Religion and Ecology in Mesoamerican Traditions,* ed. David Carrasco, 103–127. Oxford: BAR International Series 515.

———. 1999. *Star Gods of the Maya: Astronomy in Art, Folklore and Calendars.* Austin: University of Texas Press.

Moffitt, John F., and Santiago Sebastián. 1996. *O Brave New People: The European Invention of the American Indian.* Albuquerque: University of New Mexico Press.

Molina, Alonso de. 1970. *Vocabulario en lengua castellana y mexicana y mexicana y castellana.* Facsimile of 1571 edition, ed. Miguel León-Portilla. México: Editorial Porrúa.

Morán Turina, José Miguel, and Fernando Checa. 1985. *El coleccionismo en España: De la cámara de maravillas a la galleria de pinturas.* Madrid: Ediciones Cátedra.

Morin, Edgar. 1979. *El hombre y la muerte.* Barcelona: Editorial Kairos.

Motolinia, Fray Toribio de. 1951. *History of the Indians of New Spain,* trans. Francis Borgia Steck. Washington, DC: Academy of American Franciscan History.

———. 1970 [ca. 1536–1543]. Memoriales. In *Memoriales e historia de los indios de la Nueva España,* ed. Fidel de Lejarza. Biblioteca de Autores Españoles, vol. 240. Madrid: Atlas.

———. 1996. *Memoriales,* ed. Nancy Jo Dyer. México: El Colegio de México.

Muñoz Camargo, Diego. 1978 [late sixteenth century]. *Historia de Tlaxcala.* México: Editorial Innovación.

———. 1991. Enterramientos. Funerales. Incineración. Víctimas voluntarias. Estatuas formadas de las cenizas. Inhumación. In *Tlaxcala: Textos de su historia*, ed. Beatriz Paredes Rangel and Angel García Cook, vol. 4, comp. Aguilera, Ríos, and Meyer, 561–566. México: Consejo Nacional para Cultura y las Artes.

Muriel, Josefina. 1956–1960. *Hospitales de la Nueva España.* 2 vols. México: Editorial Justicia.

Nicholson, H. B. 2001. *The "Return of Quetzalcoatl": Did It Play a Role in the Conquest of Mexico?* Lancaster, CA: Labyrinthos.

"Ocho grandes lienzos de la conquista." 2005. From the exhibition catalog *Imagenes de los naturales en el arte de la Nueva España.* México: Banamex.

O'Mack, Scout. 1990. The Sun, the King and el Paso de Cortés. Paper presented at the Annual Meeting of the American Society for Ethnohistory, Toronto, Ontario.

Orellana, Sandra de. 1987. *Indian Medicine in Highland Guatemala: The Prehispanic and Colonial Periods.* Albuquerque: University of New Mexico Press.

Orso, Steven N. 1986. *Philip IV and the Decoration of the Alcázar of Madrid.* Princeton: Princeton University Press.

Ortiz de Montellano, Bernard. 1990. *Aztec Medicine, Health and Nutrition.* New Brunswick, NJ: Rutgers University Press.

Oswald, A. 1935. Howsham Hall II. *Country Life,* 221–223.

Oudijk, Michel, and Matthew Restall. N.d. Mesoamerican Conquistadors in the Sixteenth Century. In *Indian Conquistadors: Native Militaries in the Conquest of Mesoamerica,* ed. Laura Matthew and Michel Oudijk. Unpublished manuscript.

Padden, R. C. 1967. *The Hummingbird and the Hawk: Conquest and Sovereignty in the Valley of Mexico, 1503–1541.* New York: Harper & Row.

Padrón, Ricardo. 2004. *The Spacious Word.* Chicago: University of Chicago Press.

Pagden, Anthony, trans. and ed. 1986. *Hernán Cortés: Letters from Mexico.* Introduction by J. H. Elliott. New Haven: Yale University Press.

Park, Katharine. 1995. The Life of the Human Corpse: Division and Dissection in Late Medieval Europe. *Journal of the History of Medicine and Allied Sciences* 50:111–132.

Parker, Geoffrey. 1996. *The Military Revolution: Military Innovation and the Rise of the West, 1500–1800.* 2nd ed. Cambridge: Cambridge University Press.

Paso y Troncoso, Francisco del. 1900. *Adoración de los reyes: Auto en lengua mexicana (anónimo).* Florence: Tipografía de Salvador Landi.

Pastor, Beatriz. 1992. *The Armature of Conquest: Spanish Accounts of the Discovery of America, 1492–1589,* trans. Lydia Longstreth Hunt. Stanford: Stanford University Press.

Paz, Octavio. 1985. *The Labyrinth of Solitude; and the Other Mexico; Return to the Labyrinth of Solitude; Mexico and the United States; the Philanthropic Ogre,* trans. Lysander Kemp, Yara Milos, and Rachel Phillips Belash. New York: Grove.

Peterson, Jeanette Favrot. 1988. Florentine Codex Imagery and the Tlacuilo. In *The Work of Bernardino de Sahagún: Pioneer Ethnographer of Sixteenth-Century Aztec Mexico,* ed. J. Jorge Klor de Alva, H. B. Nicholson, and Eloise Quiñones Keber, 273–294. New York: Institute for Mesoamerican Studies,University of Albany, State University of New York.

———. 1993. *The Paradise Garden Murals of Malinalco: Utopia and Empire in Sixteenth-Century Mexico.* Austin: University of Texas Press.

———. 1994. Lengua o Diosa? *In Chipping Away on Earth, Studies in Prehispanic and Colonial Mexico in Honor of Arthur J.O. Anderson and Charles E. Dibble,* ed. Eloise Quiñones Keber, 187–202. Lancaster, CA: Labyrinthos.

Phelan, John Leddy. 1956. *The Millennial Kingdom of the Franciscans in the New World.* Los Angeles: University of California Press.

———. 1970. *The Millennial Kingdom of the Franciscans in the New World: A Study in the Writing of Gerónimo de Mendieta, 1525–1604.* 2nd ed. Berkeley: University of California Press.

Prem, Hanns J. 1992. Disease Outbreaks in Central Mexico during the Sixteenth Century. In *Secret Judgments of God: Old World Disease in New World Contexts,* ed. Noble David Cook and W. George Lovell, 20–48. Norman: University of Oklahoma Press.

Prescott, William H. 1873 [1843]. *History of the Conquest of Mexico,* ed. John Foster Kirk. 3 vols. Philadelphia: J. B. Lippincott.

———. 1994 [1843]. *History of the Conquest of Mexico.* Introduction by Felipe Fernández-Armesto. London: Folio Society.

Quezada, Noemí. 1976. La herbolaria en el Mexico Colonial. In *Estado actual del conocimiento en plantas medicinales mexicanas,* ed. Xavier Lozoya, 51–69. México: Instituto Mexicano para el Estudio de las Plantas Medicinales.

Race, William H. 1993. Ekphrasis. In *The New Princeton Encyclopedia of Poetry and Poetics: The Most Comprehensive Guide to World Poetry,* ed. Alex Preminger and T.V.F. Brogan, 320–321. New York: MJF Books.

Ranke, Leopold von. 1981. *The Secret of World History: Selected Writings on the Art and Science of History,* ed. and trans. Roger Wines. New York: Fordham University Press.

Restall, Matthew. 2003. *Seven Myths of the Spanish Conquest*. Oxford: Oxford University Press.

———, and Florine G.L. Asselbergs. 2007. *Invading Guatemala: Spanish, Nahua, and Maya Accounts of Conquest Wars.* University Park: Pennsylvania State University Press.

Richards, Audrey I. 1969. *Keeping the King Divine. Proceedings of the Royal Anthropological Institute* 1968, 23–35. London: Anthropological Institute of Great Britain and Ireland.

Risse, Guenter B. 1987. Medicine in New Spain. In *Medicine in the New World: New Spain, New France and New England*, ed. Ronald L. Numbers, 12–63. Knoxville: University of Tennessee Press.

Rivero Lake, Rodrigo. 1994. Sincretismo Mexicano Japonés. *Artes de México* 23:115.

Robertson, Donald. 1994. *Mexican Manuscript Painting of the Early Colonial Period.* Norman: University of Oklahoma Press.

Rozat, Guy. 1993. *Indios imaginiarios e indios reales en los relatos de la Conquista de México.* México: Tava Editorial.

Rubio Mañé, Jorge Ignacio. 1983. *El virreinato*. 3 vols. México: Universidad Autónoma de Mexico and FCE.

Sahagún, Fray Bernardino de. 1950–1982 [ca. 1578–1580]. *General History of the Things of New Spain. Florentine Codex*. 12 vols., ed. and trans. Charles E. Dibble and Arthur J.O. Anderson (order of names varies by volume). Santa Fe: School of American Research, and Salt Lake City: University of Utah.

———. 1979. *Historia General de las Cosas de la Nueva España*. Facsimilie edition. 12 vols. México: Gobierno de la República and Archivo General de la Nación.

———. 1981. *Historia general de las cosas de Nueva España,* ed. Angel María Garibay K. 4th ed. 4 vols. México: Editorial Porrúa.

———. 1989a. *Conquest of New Spain: 1585 Revision,* ed. S. L. Cline, trans. Howard F. Cline. Salt Lake City: University of Utah Press.

———. 1989b. *Historia general de las cosas la Nueva España,* ed. Alfredo López Austin and Josefina García Quintana. 2 vols. México: Alianza Editorial Mexicana.

———. 1997 [ca. 1578–1580]. *Historia General de las Cosas de la Nueva España,* no. 300. México: Editorial Porrúa.

Sahlins, Marshall. 1982. The Apotheosis of Captain Cook. In *Between Belief and Transgression. Structuralist Essays in Religion, History and Myth*, ed. Michel Izard and Pierre Smith, trans. John Leavitt, 73–102. Chicago: University of Chicago Press.

———. 1985. *Islands of History*. Chicago: University of Chicago Press.

Schedel, Hartmann. 1930. *The Nuremberg Chronicle, or the Book of the Chronicles from the Beginning of the World, the Most Famous of German Picture Books of the Fifteenth Century, Printed in the City of Nuremberg in the Year 1493,* ed. L. Henry Bullen. Jersey City: Library Museum in Jersey City, and San Francisco: The Book Club of California.

———. 2001 [1493]. *Chronicle of the World, the Complete and Annotated Nuremberg Chronicle of 1493.* Facsimile edition. Köln: Taschen.

Scholes, France V., and Ralph L. Roys. 1968. *The Maya Chontal Indians of Acalan-Tixchel: A Contribution to the History and Ethnography of the Yucatan Peninsula.* Norman: University of Oklahoma Press.

Schreffler, Michael J. 2004. "No Lord without Vassals nor Vassals without a Lord": The Royal Palace and the Shape of Power in Seventeenth-Century Mexico City. *Oxford Art Journal* 27(2):155–171.

———. 2007. *The Art of Allegiance: Visual Culture and Imperial Power in Baroque New Spain*. University Park: Pennsylvania State University Press.

Schwartz, Stuart. 2000. *Victors and Vanquished: Spanish and Nahua Views of the Conquest of Mexico.* Boston: Bedford/St. Martin's.

Sell, Barry D. 2004. Nahuatl Plays in Context. In *Nahuatl Theater: Death and Life in Colonial Nahua Mexico*, ed. Barry D. Sell and Louise M. Burkhart, 3–28. Norman: University of Oklahoma Press.

Sell, Barry D., and Louise M. Burkhart, eds. 2004. *Nahuatl Theater: Death and Life in Colonial Nahua Mexico.* Norman: University of Oklahoma Press.

———, eds. and trans. In prep. *Nahuatl Theater Volume Four: Nahua Christianity in Performance.* Norman: University of Oklahoma Press.

Serralta, Frédéric. 1986. Nueva biografía de Antonio de Solís y Rivadeneyra. *Criticón* 34:51–157.

Shattuck, George Cheever. 1938. *A Medical Survey of the Republic of Guatemala*. Washington, DC: Carnegie Institution of Washington.

Shedd, Margaret. 1971. *Malinche and Cortés*. New York: Doubleday.

Sigüenza y Góngora, Carlos de. 1992 [1662–1700]. *Relaciones Históricas,* ed. Manuel Romero de Terreros. México: UNAM.

Smith, Whitney. 1975. *Flags through the Ages and Across the World.* New York: McGraw-Hill.

Solís, Antonio de. 1684. *Historia de la conquista de México*. Madrid: Impr. de B. de Villa-Diego.

———. 1724. *The History of the Conquest of Mexico by the Spaniards,* trans. Thomas Townsend. London: T. Woodward, J. Hooke, and J. Peele.

———. 1968. *Historia de la conquista de México*. México: Editorial Porrúa.

Somolinos D'Ardois, Germán. 1956. Hallazgo del manuscrito sobre el cocoliztli, original del Dr. Francisco Hernández. *La Prensa Medica Mexicana* 21:115–123.

Soustelle, Jacques. 1996. *El universo de los aztecas.* México: FCE.

Stenzel, Werner. 1980. Quetzalcoatl von Tula: Die Mythogenese einer Postkortesischen Legende. *Zeitschrift fur Lateinamerika-Wien* 18:7–91.

Tedlock, Dennis, ed. 1985. *Popol Vuh: The Mayan Book of the Dawn of Life*. New York: Simon and Schuster.

Thielicke, Helmut. 1984. *Vivir con la Muerte.* Barcelona: Editorial Herder.

Thomas, Hugh. 1993. Conquest: Montezuma, Cortés and the Fall of Old Mexico. New York: Simon and Schuster.

———. 2000. *Who's Who of the Conquistadors*. London: Cassell.

Thomas, Louis-Vincent. 1983. *Antropología de la muerte.* México: FCE.

———. 1995. Lo sagrado y la muerte. In *Tratado de Antropología de lo Sagrado,* ed. Julien Ries, vol. 1, 214–232. Madrid: Trotta.

Tira de Tepechpan. 1978 [1596]. *Tira de Tepechpan: Códice colonial procedente del Valle de México,* ed. Xavier Noguez. México: Enciclopédica del Estado de México.

Todorov, Tzvetan. 1985. *The Conquest of America: The Question of the Other,* trans. Richard Howard. New York: Harper & Row.

Tomicki, Ryzard. 1986. Las profeciías de los aztecas de principios del siglo XVI y los contactos maya-españoles. Una hipótesis. *Xochipilli* 1:19–30.

Torquemada, Fray Juan de. 1723. *Monarquía indiana.* Madrid: Rodríguez Franco.

———. 1975 [1615]. *Monarquía indiana.* 5th ed. 3 vols. México City: Editorial Porrúa.

———. 1977 [1615]. *Monarquía Indiana,* ed. Miguel León-Portilla, vol. 4. México: UNAM.

Toussaint, Manuel. 1948. *Arte colonial en México.* México: UNAM, Instituto de Investigaciones Estéticas.

———. 1952. La pintura con incrustaciones de concha nácar en Nueva España. *Anales del Instituto de Investigaciones Estéticas* 20(5).5–20.

Townsend, Thomas, trans. 1724. *The History of the Conquest of Mexico by the Spaniards.* London: T. Woodward, J. Hooke, and J. Peele.

Tovar, Juan de. 2001 [1583–1587]. *Historia y creencias de los indios de México.* [*Historia de la benida de los yndios apoblar a Mexico*], ed. José J. Fuente del Pilar, transcrip. Susana Urraca Uribe. Madrid: Miraguano Ediciones.

Tovar de Teresa, Guillermo. 1990. Los artistas y las pinturas de incrustaciones de concha nácar en México. In *La concha nácar en México,* ed. Virginia Armella de Aspe, 106–134. México: Grupo Gutsa.

Townsend, Camilla. 2003. Burying the White Gods: New Perspectives on the Conquest of Mexico. *The American Historical Review* 108:659–687.

Townsend, Richard F. 1992. *The Aztecs.* London: Thames and Hudson.

Turner, Terence. 1988. Ethno-Ethnohistory: Myth and History in Native South American Representations of Contact with Western Society. In *Rethinking History and Myth: Indigenous South American Perspectives on the Past,* ed. Jonathan D. Hill, 235–281. Urbana: University of Illinois Press.

Uchmany, Eva Alexandra. 1980. Cambios religiosos en la conquista de México. *Revista Mexicana de Estudios Antropológicos* 26:1–57.

Umberger, Emily. 1987. Events Commemorated by Date Plaques at the Templo Mayor: Further Thoughts on the Solar Metaphor. In *The Aztec Templo Mayor,* ed. Elizabeth Hill Boone, 418–436. Washington, DC: Dumbarton Oaks Research Library and Collection.

———. 1996. The Monarchia Indiana in Seventeenth-Century New Spain. In *Converging Cultures: Art and Identity in Spanish America,* ed. Diana Fane, 46–58. New York: Brooklyn Museum in association with Harry N. Abrams.

Valeri, Valerio. 1985. *Kingship and Sacrifice: Ritual and Society in Ancient Hawaii,* trans. Paula Wissing. Chicago: University of Chicago Press.

Varey, Simon, ed. 2000. *The Mexican Treasury: The Writings of Dr. Francisco Hernández*, trans. Rafael Chabrán, Cynthia L. Chamberlin, and Simon Varey. Stanford: Stanford University Press.

Vargas Lugo, Elisa. 1993. Imágenes de la conquista en el arte novohispano. In *Sentido y proyección de la conquista*, ed. Zea Leopoldo, 127–155. México: Instituto Panamericano de Geografia e Historia, FCE.

———. 1994. La pintura de enconchados. In *México en el mundo de las colecciones de arte, Nueva España 1*, 119–123. 7 vols. México: El Gobierno de la República.

———. 2005. Imágenes de la conquista en el arte des siglo XVII: dos visions. In *Imágenes de los naturales en el arte de la Nueva España, siglos XVI al XVIII*, 94–123. México: Fomento Cultural Banamex.

Widdifield, Stacie G. 1996. *The Embodiment of the National in Late Nineteenth-Century Mexican Painting.* Tucson: University of Arizona Press.

Wood, Stephanie. 1991. Adopted Saints: Christian Images in Nahua Testaments of Late Colonial Toluca. *The Americas* 47:259–294.

———. 2003. *Transcending Conquest: Nahua Views of Spanish Colonial Mexico.* Norman: University of Oklahoma Press.

Yates, Frances A. 1966. *The Art of Memory*. Chicago: University of Chicago Press.

Index

Page numbers in italics indicate illustrations.